Adventures with Ari

Adventures with Ari

a puppy, a leash & our year outdoors

KATHRYN MILES

Skyhorse Publishing

Skyhorse Publishing books may be purchased in bulk at special discounts for sales promotion, corporate gifts, fund-raising, or educational purposes. Special editions can also be created to specifications. For details, contact the Special Sales Department, Skyhorse Publishing, 307 West 36th Street, 11th Floor, New York, NY 10018 or info@skyhorsepublishing.com.

Visit our website at www.skyhorsepublishing.com.

10 9 8 7 6 5 4 3 2 1

Library of Congress Cataloging-in-Publication Data

Miles, Kathryn.
Adventures with Ari : a puppy, a leash, and our year in the great outdoors / Kathryn Miles.
p. cm.
ISBN 978-1-60239-638-8
1. Puppies--Maine--Anecdotes. 2. Dogs--Behavior. 3. Human-animal relationships. 4. Women dog owners--Attitudes. 5. Miles, Kathryn—Homes and haunts. 6. Nature studies--Maine. 7. Year. I. Title.
SF426.2.M54 2009
636.7--dc22
2008056060

Cover design by Adam Bozarth and LeAnna Weller Smith

Paperback ISBN: 978-1-63450-257-3
Ebook ISBN: 978-1-62636-767-8

Printed in the United States of America

The lasting pleasures of contact with the natural world are not reserved for scientists but are available to anyone who will place himself under the influence of earth, sea, and sky and their amazing life.

—Rachel Carson

Contents

Introduction

When my husband and I adopted a timid puppy from the local shelter, I expected lots of changes: stains on the rug, chew toys scattered throughout the house, walks through rain and sleet, and more. I never considered, though, that with Ari would also come an entirely new way of seeing—a novel way of being in the world. But that, I am quickly learning, is the thing about dogs. Most of the ones I've met possess an admirable willingness to give themselves over to any experience, particularly if that experience involves sand dunes or musty forest floors or hidden nooks in a rock wall. Dogs understand the value of such places, and they remind us that we ought to as well. To paraphrase Walt Whitman, they offer us a ready invitation to loaf with them on the grass and loosen the collar from our throat.

That is precisely what I have spent the past year trying to do.

I didn't set out to become a canine naturalist, and I certainly never planned on devoting twelve months of my life to the pursuit of a dog's-eye view. Instead, I began as a reluctant dog owner who wasn't even certain how to be around dogs. Growing up, I never once pressed my parents for a pet dog. At the homes of friends, I would give the family pooch a begrudging pat and then quickly wash my hands. Dogs just never had the appeal other creatures did. In fact, before Ari, there was just one other dog in my life: Kinch, a blue-tick-hound-

and-beagle mix whose indomitable will was eclipsed only by his olfactory motivation. Kinch belonged to Greg, my boyfriend-turned-husband. As far as the hound was concerned, I was a third wheel. In turn, I always considered Kinch my step-beagle: He was about seven when we met, and he had long-since established what he thought was a perfectly satisfactory—and somewhat exclusive—relationship with Greg.

The three of us lived in a tiny Pennsylvania apartment while the two humans finished writing doctoral dissertations. These were tight quarters, and not always compatible ones. Kinch seemed to keep a list of grievances about me: I didn't like him in our bed; I took over the passenger seat in Greg's car; I adjusted the morning walk schedule because I had to be up early. As for me, I had a list of complaints as well. I didn't like his snoring or bad habit of wandering off when we were about to entertain guests or catch transcontinental flights. I thought he smelled funny.

At best, ours was a relationship of mutual tolerance—a kind of begrudging stasis. And it might have continued as such almost indefinitely, had the end of graduate school and the start of our careers not taken center stage for me and Greg. In the summer of 2001, we packed up Kinch and our cat Cam, then moved to Maine to start college teaching jobs. There, the four of us settled into a house in the woods, where everyone had the space and time they needed. Things looked rosy for all four of us. Until, suddenly, they weren't. A few summers later, Kinch contracted a cancerous tumor in his throat. Greg and I had hoped he was just too stubborn to be beaten by a mere disease, so when we heard the diagnosis, we scheduled an operation to remove the tumor and made plans to spend our fall with the beagle. Fate had different plans. The morning of the operation, Greg called from the vet's office, sobbing. The tumor had so aggressively infiltrated Kinch's trachea, there was nothing they could do. He was euthanized on the operating table, and none of us got to say good-bye.

It took us the rest of the day to dig a proper grave, since neither Greg nor I could go for more than a few minutes without breaking down in tears. Once the hole was dug, we unfolded a corner of the blanket in which the veterinarian had swaddled Kinch's body. We stroked his paws and spotted forearms, and tried too late to say our farewells. Neither of us could bear to unwrap him any further—we didn't want to see the emptiness of his face in death. And once we finally managed to lower his body into that newly dug hole, we sat by the grave for most of the afternoon, both of us inconsolable.

For the rest of the week, Greg and I stayed close to home, feeling the weight of loss. And through it all, I couldn't escape the unfortunate irony: In Kinch's death, I had found a love for his life.

In time, of course, our grief lightened. But even with our cat Cam, the cozy house continued to feel cavernous and lonely without a dog in it. As autumn came and went, I missed arriving home to the familiar face poking out of his house under the apple tree. With no excuse to take a stroll, I stopped making a daily walk part of my routine. I even began to pine for the snoring. Before I knew what I was doing, I was pressing Greg for another dog. I couldn't really explain why—I was just certain that our house needed one.

Greg said he wasn't ready. Kinch had been more than a pet to Greg—Kinch had been his very best friend for ten years. Greg worried that he couldn't love another dog like he had loved Kinch—or worse, that he might resent the dog for not *being* Kinch. And the thought of raising another pet and devoting the kind of emotional and physical time that a puppy would need wearied him. Greg didn't think he could do it—not yet, anyway.

I told him he wouldn't have to. I would be the primary caregiver. I would take the walks and clean up the messes; all he would have to do was love this creature. Besides, I said, I felt safer with a dog in the house, especially when he was gone. We had to have another dog: of that I was certain.

As I made my case, Greg looked at me with quiet skepticism—and rightfully so. I was notorious for truncating Kinch's walks whenever possible; I knew precious little about canine behavior or how to care for one. I was simply not a natural dog owner. Still, I persisted. And the more I thought about it, the more resolute I became. I wanted a companion. More than that, I *needed* a dog in my life. I upped the intensity of my campaign, reciting interesting dog facts at dinner or sighing melodramatically whenever we passed a dog on the street. I brought home pictures of homeless dogs in our area, knowing perfectly well they would weaken Greg's resolve. Finally, I tried my trump card: Should we decide to adopt a new friend, Greg could even pick it out. I could tell he liked that idea.

And so, on a cold Saturday in early February, we drove to a nearby shelter. We didn't stop to pick up all the normal pet things like food and water dishes and collars and leashes. We were just looking—just dipping our big toes into the notion of a new canine friend, right?

Wrong.

The shelter was a shabby, narrow building made of corrugated metal and located behind its operator's house. Inside, a dozen or so inmates—mostly huskies and malamutes along with some classically indeterminate shelter dogs—barked from their ramshackle pens. The noise echoed off the metal siding. So did the smell of partially cleaned kennels. It was overwhelming. Neither Greg nor I said a word, but it was clear we agreed: We *would* free an animal from this place—it was the least we could do. But which one? We looked in each of the small kennels, surveying the ranks, hoping one would speak to us.

Noticing that we seemed particularly taken with the huskies, the shelter proprietor suggested we consider one of her purebred pups. But even if we hadn't seen the five-hundred-dollar price tag, we would have said no. We were not purebred *anything* owners. We just wanted a healthy, active pup, we explained. Besides, we wanted to help a dog who really needed a home. Kinch had been a shelter dog, as had most of the other pets Greg and I had owned throughout our lives.

With this explanation, the shelter owner's eyes lit up. She had just the dogs for us, she said, leading us to the end of the narrow corridor. As she did, she told the torrid story of a canine love affair gone awry. Several months earlier, an unneutered rescue husky—tall, intense, wolfish—had been placed in the same outdoor pen with an unspayed female jindo—a Korean dog described as robust, agile, and pleasant. The result was a short-lived romance and five puppies—pound love-children, really—in need of a home. Two of the males, who favored their father in size and temperament, had been adopted. The third was on hold for a potential customer. He paraded around the cinder-block cell with a look of entitlement that seemed to say, *I'm tough and I'm claimed.* I had to appreciate his bravado, though I was fairly certain I didn't want it taking over my home.

Sharing his living quarters were the puppy's two sisters: tawny and dangerously thin little creatures scrunched into a pile against the chain link. Despite their lineage, they seemed neither robust nor agile, and they were far too frightened to be considered pleasant. Even so, Greg and I were enchanted. We entered the dirty kennel, sending all three remaining puppies fleeing into the farthest corner, where they wriggled under and over one another. We stood by patiently, looking for glimpses of personality from the pile. After about ten minutes, Greg felt confident enough to pick out ours: the pup with one white paw, a matching blaze running down her nose, and a mischievous habit of chewing on clothing tags and zippers whenever we got close. As we concluded our deliberation, the puppy summited the pile of her siblings and wobbled precariously with a tentative grin.

Forget enchanted; we were smitten.

The shelter insisted on a rigorous application process, with far more bite to it than our marriage license, tax forms, and job applications put together. We provided character references and pay stubs; we agreed to home visits and a juried examination of Kinch's vet records. We even answered essay questions about living arrangements and preferred training techniques. In return, the manager explained that, normally, the shelter required a waiting period of at least a week so that the board of directors could consider an application. But—because (1) she was making up this policy, (2) she really liked us, or (3) she thought we'd back out of the deal—she waived the review process and sent us home that day with a tiny light brown dog who had eyes so blue, they seemed to embody all of the winter sky.

Our first weeks with the pup were hard. She was a leaky vessel with no sense of housebreaking during the day. At night, she howled with the strength of forty dogs. Worst of all, she was so terrified by her new living arrangements she would drop into a submissive role any time we even looked at her.

Meanwhile, my productivity at the college where I teach came to a screeching halt: I no longer had time to grade essays or prepare for class, not with the bathroom breaks every two hours and the constant policing of a puppy who had never before set foot in a house. I was grouchy and late for meetings. And when I returned home from an exhausting day, there were countless messes to clean. In addition to developing an early resistance to the concept of housebreaking, the puppy soon cultivated a penchant for shredding paper and relished every opportunity to gnaw on books or mangle important documents.

I tried telling my students that the dog ate their homework, but they were not amused. Frankly, neither was I.

Sometime during the second week of our new living arrangements, I began to rethink the adoption altogether. Our living room smelled like urine. No one had gotten a good night's sleep in days. Most significantly, I began to doubt my ability to provide appropriate care for this little animal. I blamed myself for her constant messes and speculated that she might be better off with someone else: someone who had more time and knowledge and skill.

On one particularly bad night, the puppy managed to eat two books and pee in three different rooms—all over the course of about fifteen minutes. As she did, Greg gave me a meaningful look: half empathy, half *I told you so.* I gently coaxed the puppy into her crate, put on my winter jacket, and went outside. There, underneath the sharp night sky, I considered our options. I could, tail between my legs, return the puppy to the shelter. That would also mean returning her to a dingy place I distrusted. I could advertise her at school, where there were bound to be students who wanted to adopt dogs. I could take her to another shelter, plead my stupidity, and hope they'd find her a better home.

Looking up into the stars, I tried to imagine the details of these options. I summoned a picture of me packing up this little dog and driving her to a new home or another crowded shelter, of boxing her newly acquired dishes and toys and returning to the quietude of a house inhabited only by two humans and a cat.

There was a certain appeal to this vision—a slim one. All in all, though, I hated the prospect and what it would mean. I paced up and down the driveway, trying unsuccessfully to stay warm. My heart felt heavy; my gut felt hollow. I had pledged to raise this creature, for better or worse, until death do us part. It wasn't her fault I was exhausted. It wasn't her fault she didn't know the rules. Giving up on her now felt like a betrayal. Still, raising her—and raising her well—seemed impossible.

We were stuck.

Many hours later, I fell asleep—so deeply, in fact, that I didn't hear the pup's whine for her 4 AM bathroom break. Greg rose silently, slipping outside with the little dog. When they returned, both clambered into bed. I awoke two hours later to find myself curled up with a soft, subdued puppy. I felt her warm breath on my cheek. I opened my eyes and met hers. We stayed that way for some time, just watching each other. *Can you do this?* she seemed to ask. *Can you raise me? Are you sure you want to?* I reached over and felt her downy fur. She licked my hand, then nestled deeper into my chest. For the first time, I felt the heaviness in my heart lighten. We would find a way to make this work. This little dog would become a real part of our family.

That meant she needed a name. And not just any moniker, but one that really fit. We considered the puppy's heritage. We knew she was half Siberian husky. Maybe we could name her after a dog sledding term or the snowy terrain of the Arctic. But other than her big blue eyes, there was little that seemed reminiscent of her robust Nordic ancestors. That left the jindo—a dog about which, in America at least, there is shockingly little information. A search on the World Wide Web revealed only basic facts. The dog is medium-sized with coyote-like ears and tail. Jindos are fiercely loyal, amazingly athletic, and an official Korean national monument. The last of these attributes intrigued us. This roly-poly, leaky vessel of a creature maintained important cultural status across the Pacific? Unbelievable.

We looked up from the computer screen and studied our new friend closely—*does she know her breed's significance?* She grinned goofily and snapped at our noses with her sharp puppy teeth, then tumbled onto her back. *Doubtful,* we concluded.

Nevertheless, Greg and I both loved this fact about the pup. We decided that, in the interest of international relations and the preservation of global culture, we owed it to this little dog to honor her monumental status. A student from Korea was in one of Greg's writing courses, and he brought her several words and phrases to translate. It was still mid-February, so most of them dealt with the epic coldness of a Maine winter: words like *snow, mitten, storm,* and *ice.* Could any of these words become a name for our half Korean dog?

Hyun-Ju raised an eyebrow. "I don't know if any of these will really work," she warned. But she was polite enough to indulge us nevertheless.

Greg called home during lunch that day. I had returned for the second of four daily bathroom breaks, and the pup and I took the phone outside where I could talk and she could pee. Greg read off the Korean phrases, struggling with the phonetic spelling. As he did, I watched the puppy carefully—looking for a sign that we had stumbled upon the right name. Hyun-Ju was right: Most of them were a stretch. Except for one: *Bung Ari Jang Gab,* which means "mitten." Or more exactly, it means "glove without fingers." Somehow, it just seemed right.

Making this name manageable, however, was a different story entirely.

Over the next few days, we tried out several colloquial variations: Rijang, Fungari, Jangab. Our neighbor gave up and just began calling her Red Dog. My mother asked what was wrong with names like Spot or Rex. They both had a point—the dog's full name was ungainly, and didn't seem to have an obvious truncated form. Each time we called her, Greg and I stumbled over our own tongues, trying to make it work. Then early one sleepy morning as I rose to take the pup outside for yet another bathroom break, the name slipped out: Ari. Simple. Pronounceable. And somehow fitting, I thought.

Greg disagreed. "Ari means 'without,'" he objected. "You can't name a dog 'without.' That's absurd."

He had a point. It did seem silly. *Without what?*

But it was too late: By then, the name had already stuck, and even he was calling the puppy Ari. Besides, in a way, that's exactly what this shy little dog had been. *Without* her littermates. *Without* a name. *Without* a place.

Over the next few weeks, Ari gained all of those things. She had a new family, albeit a human one; she learned her name, at least in its shortened form; she came to think of our house as her home, though she continued to pee in it.

In return, we gained quite a bit too. Every morning, we were greeted as if we were the most interesting, delightful people she had ever met. *Without fear.* Each day, she forgave our foibles as we startled her in the kitchen or tripped over her in the dark. *Without judgment.* And when the sun slowly brought the temperature up above zero, she compelled us to run and romp in the backyard as if we were ten-year-olds. *Without restraint.*

We were still sleep-deprived; I wasn't getting any more work done; and the household casualties—more chewed books, more ruined rugs—continued to mount. But despite these problems, I was driven. I was even happy. I found myself looking forward to those little breaks in the day when I could put on my winter boots and race around the yard. I discovered the joy of burying my face in puppy fur. I watched in wonder as she explored a single patch of ground for hours, curious to know what she was finding to catalog.

Clearly, I had a lot to learn from this puppy. Far more, I suspected, than she had to learn from me.

I reconsidered the puppy's aptitudes. For her, everything outside was new and positively fascinating, even in the lunar landscape of deep winter. She wanted to roll in snow and lick icicles and all of the other things I had forgotten that I once loved to do. She could see in the dark or hear a passing car long before I did. She smelled the frozen earth under two feet of icy, sterile snow and divined where all the treats lay dormant on the cold ground.

Amazing.

Now I realized it was I who was without. Without her excitement, without her clarity of vision, without the strength of her sensations. I wanted to know the world as she was learning it—as a place of wonder and new encounters, as an experience so flush and intense that it fills the eyes and ears and nose and, eventually, the heart. Gradually, I found myself practicing this new art of seeing, whether in the woods around our house or even just in our living room. I'd crouch down and look up at trees from her vantage, or stretch out on the floor where we could lie, shoulder-to-shoulder, and watch the flames in the woodstove. It felt delightful.

What would happen, I began to wonder, *if I really did let Ari be my teacher? What could I learn about the world? How would my life be different?*

This book details my year-long commitment to answer each of these questions. And as soon as I hatched the project, I knew it would be a worthwhile one. I just needed a plan.

We began with the basics. I would dedicate myself to twelve months of canine naturalism, whatever that might mean. For starters, at least, Ari and I would take long walks and play in the woods, stopping to explore and ask questions about the ecology surrounding us. These were already things we loved to do together. The difference, though, is that we would now do so deliberately: We would pause to reflect, slowing down long enough not only to let sensations wash over us, but to record and meditate on them as well. We'd create classifications and deepen our knowledge of the environment along the way. These were tasks the puppy had already mastered; she'd have to be patient while I struggled to catch up.

It would, I knew, take a full year for me to do so. And that's fitting, I think. Too often, we lose sight of the cyclic nature of our lives—of the tremendous sense of reward available to those who mark a full revolution and return to home. I'm a firm believer in the anchoring effect of seasons and their ability to complete one another. Hot and cold; feast and famine. Yin and yang. In some very real ways, that's what life is all about.

We planned our year, then, not based on calendar dates, but rather on seasonal ebbs and flows. *Adventures with Ari* is also organized based on the four seasons, beginning with the rebirth of spring and continuing through the annual growing cycle. That seems an apt metaphor for an infant dog and a human committed to change. I also appreciate the historical precedent behind such an organization. From *The Farmer's Almanac* to Thoreau's *Walden* and Aldo Leopold's *Sand County Almanac,* so much of our written relationship with the natural world is based on seasonal cycles. This book—our record of these cycles—would do the same.

I didn't know it at the time, but by its completion, our project would include far more than local ecology. We would learn plenty of that, but we'd also devote at least as much time to larger issues such as the impact of domestic animals on nature and culture as well as the ways in which those relationships can—and often do—dictate the ones we form within our own species. In fact, through our project, just about every connection in my life—from my love-hate relationship with my garden to my very definition of family—would evolve and grow.

Even in the early stages, I knew this would be a life-changing experience. I just didn't know how much so. Still, I suspected we were on to something, and so I began to define the project for real. As February drew to a close, I sketched out a schedule of weekly forays to our town forest. Once we arrived, Ari would dictate our agenda; I was along for the ride, wherever it might take us. To make sense of our experiences, I could turn to a few basic field guides and the knowledge of my scientifically minded colleagues at the college—but only insofar as they could confirm newly identified objects or provide the biological background I need to make sense of what I saw. When necessary, I could explore beyond these sources, calling on experts to help explain our experiences. A fair compromise, I thought, considering that I lacked Ari's strength in sensory observation.

She agreed to this concession. Or rather, she agreed to spend time curled up beside me back at the house, where I would leaf through books, search through databases for taxonomies and explanations, or make phone calls to scientists and scholars. This seemed fair to her: provided, of course, that we returned each day to the seat of knowledge—the natural world. And that, of course, seemed more than fair to me.

Finally, we had a plan we both agreed upon. We shook on it, but didn't linger over such formalities. After all, we needed to get outside.

Getting Started

[march]

Spring. In ancient Greece, this was the time when Persephone would rise out of Hades to decorate fields with wildflowers and new wheat. It's when members of the Bear Tribe in Washington State say good-bye to the white buffalo of winter and greet what they call "the season of clarity and illumination" by burning tobacco and blessing gardens with cornmeal. In Celtic mythology, the start of spring is called *Imbolc*, or "in milk." The season ushers out *Faoilleach*—the wolf month—and the world is reborn as a young bride brimming with her own fertility. I can think of no better time for me and Ari to embrace our new project than this, when the whole world seems filled with hope.

Even the stars are aligned for us. The Chinese New Year began recently, ushering in with it the year of the dog. Dog years (which occur one in every twelve) are ruled by compassion and attention to family; these years are further divided by the four elements. This year—the first in sixty—the element will be fire. According to Chinese astrologers, this means that compassion and kin will be flavored with a particular vivacity and emphasis on intense activity. I take this to be a positive omen for me and my fiery little dog.

Closer to home, we are beginning to see the usual commercial signs of the new season. Cartoonish Easter bunnies and daffodils grace bakery packaging and school windows. The local classical music station seems to play nothing but Vivaldi's "Spring" over and over again. That's okay—we're ready for it. Eager, even.

These visual and cultural markers exist for a reason, and they tap into a primitive, almost instinctual response to the natural world. As the Northern Hemisphere again tilts toward the sun and the ground begins to warm, our energy returns. So, too, does our food. Both mean that chances for reproduction improve as well. It's a great time to have—or be—a kid, whether that kid has two legs or four or a hundred. It's also a perfect opportunity to act like one. Pop-culture motifs like egg-bearing rabbits are a good reminder of that fact. So are the lengthening days and shrinking snow piles.

Bolstered by ages of tradition and a newly balanced planet, Ari and I determine to begin our experiment this week, and we couldn't be more excited. The pup has been a part of our family for nearly two months now. For the most part, we're starting to get adjusted. Greg and I have given ourselves over to sleepless nights and a constant process of washing towels and blankets. We have learned the sound of the puppy's different cries and what they might mean. We understand, at least in part, the trials of new parents. We also feel some of their joy.

Perhaps most importantly, we are establishing something that almost looks like a daily routine. Each day, Ari wakes us up around three or four in the morning by yowling like a creature ten times her size; we take her outside to pee, then she gets to nestle at the foot of the bed for an hour or two until we wake up for real. After that, it's a walk, breakfast, nap, walk, lunch, nap, walk, dinner, walk, and (some) sleep.

At least, that's what it is on paper. Like any good artist, though, Ari understands the virtues of improvisation. Sometimes lunch needs to come right after breakfast, especially if I've left an English muffin unattended on the coffee table. Sometimes getting outside for walks just isn't part of her plan, especially if there is any paper to chew. Earlier this week, she decided to change our protocol when I raced home in between meetings to let her outside. We romped in the yard for fifteen minutes without a bathroom break. Nothing. I hooked her to her leash and took her to her favorite places for peeing. Nothing. Finally, late for my next appointment and wondering if she really even *had* to pee, I brought her back inside. The minute she was off her leash, she raced into the living room and squatted. I swore she was smirking as she did.

It's easy to write about these little acts of creativity with bemused detachment, but when they happen, they can really be frustrating. I keep trying to remind myself that they contain a lesson—a kind of Taoist gift of reflection that I ought to appreciate. Here is an opportunity to learn patience and to be reminded what it is to be a child. It's difficult, though. Especially since, in truth, I'm no more formally Taoist than Ari is. Still, I continue to believe it's a valuable lesson when I can remember to view it as such. Most importantly, it's a reminder that I'm supposed to be restructuring my life to make time for such moments.

Spring, then, represents the opportunity for a new existential approach. And why not? We have literary and cultural antecedent for such a choice. Plus, we have all this new sunlight and temperatures in the upper twenties—downright balmy by our standards.

I tell Ari that it's time: to turn over a new leaf, to become real canine naturalists.

Time, also, to get down to the brass tacks of our project.

I am beginning with a basic hypothesis: Like most dogs, Ari maintains an enviable relationship with the natural world. She is closer to the ground, to the uncivilized world, to the genetic makeup of the critters leaving tracks in my snowy yard. Her species has evolved with eyesight capable of spotting prey in a heartbeat—particularly at dawn or dusk—or making sense of smells as if they were a Zagat's guide to nature. She can find routes in the forest I would otherwise miss. She knows what animals have walked a path before us, along with details like their sex, health, and age. With such skills, she can be my ambassador to the natural world and reveal more than any printed page. I've already seen this happen a hundred times in our yard. I firmly believe it will happen a thousand more, particularly if we commit to a year of this kind of inquiry. But how to go about it?

I begin with location. Our house—a small log cabin—is located at an appealing crossroads where nature meets culture. It is abutted by a long dirt road called Stagecoach that, despite its humble appearance, is far from your average gravel thoroughfare. A hundred years ago, Stagecoach Road was one of the major routes in the state of Maine. It once carried Henry David Thoreau up north, where he would gather the research needed for his book *The Maine Woods*. John James Audubon was said to wander this way with his canine companion—a giant Newfoundland—by his side. When they and countless others passed this way, they were traveling through a real hub. At that time, our town served as an important hinterland for the mid-coast ports, and it was filled with dozens of farms, creameries, schools, and taverns. As the years progressed, industries changed, taking the dairy boom farther south. Then the Great Depression struck, taking many residents farther west. Houses were abandoned and eventually crumbled in on themselves, leaving only errant cellar holes and cultivated fields that were slowly reclaimed by the forest.

In response to the Depression and its diaspora, the town leaders organized their own version of the Civilian Conservation Corps and planted thousands of pine trees where the dairy farms once stood. Lumber, swore the town elders, was much more reliable than money in the bank. Foster it, and you'll foster economic stability for the town.

The plan worked—at least in part. Pine telephone and electrical poles, once part of our forest, now stretch from here to Turkey. And the hundreds of acres that were once the town center persist as thick coniferous groves. As for the once famous dirt road, it's currently more recreational than functional, providing routes for snowmobiles and hikers instead of cream trucks and transcendentalists. In short, nature has returned, reclaiming much of the land and leaving only hidden clues about what had come before.

That's good news and bad for the people of this small inland community. Population numbers here have never recovered from their peak in the early twentieth century, and it shows. We have little infrastructure and not much more than a handful of persistent hardscrabble farms alongside smaller residential plots like mine. Ours is a modest village, both in terms of appearance and resource. But it is also one in possession of what few American towns can claim: a wide expanse of publicly held forest accessible by anyone who cares to. Does that help our community pay its tax bills? Not really. But it certainly offers metaphysical perks for its residents.

The town forest will serve as the official classroom for our project. There, Ari will eventually be able to run off leash if we choose, and we will have plenty of uninterrupted space for play and exploration and even contemplation. You couldn't ask for a better location really.

Of course, the real success of this project depends less on the forested landscape and more on my willingness to hand over control. I have resolved that this tiny toddler of a puppy will make most major decisions for us. She will dictate the pace of our walks, the amount of time spent outside, the daily topics with which we might concern ourselves. For my part, I will not feel pressed for time; I will not impart my sense of getting and spending. William Wordsworth is right: The world is too much with us.

Ari doesn't know about my personal revelation or the centuries of vernal myth and local history backing my decisions. Still, she has learned that the appearance of my hiking boots signals a trip outside, and that's exciting enough for a three-month-old dog. So, too, are the new promises I've made. Already they've meant extra long walks and fewer baths. Both appeal greatly to the pup, as does the increased time we play outside.

And why not? This is a dog who desperately wants to be outside. More than that, she needs to be out. A member of the Canidae family, she shares her DNA with wolves, coyotes, foxes, dingoes, and jackals. All are omnivores, capable of wearing down their prey over long distances or undertaking protracted scavenging missions. All are also digitigrades, meaning they walk on their digits (fingers and toes) but not on the soles of their hands and feet. This physiology allows them to lengthen their strides while remaining efficient movers. Meanwhile, their brains are programmed to spend the better part of their day seeking food—a mental challenge that keeps them from getting bored or restless, so long as they are moving. Ari's ancestors thought nothing of traveling up to fifty miles a day, and then waking up and doing it all over again.

They are not alone. Regardless of breed or species, all Canidae were built for physical work, and their bodies expect to get it. The irony, of course, is that few dogs do. In the United States alone, there are fifty-two million domestic dogs; the overwhelming majority of them are pets or "companion" animals who have their food handed to them pre-killed and processed. At best, many of them get a quick walk or two a day. That's a real problem for any animal with the pent-up energy of a coyote or jackal, neither of whom we want lounging around our living rooms while we're gone at work. Still, we love our domesticated canines, and so we try to accommodate them in our busy schedules with varying degrees of success. This is often not an adequate substitute for a wild existence—at least by the dog's way of thinking.

Life in my house is no exception. Ari has the boundless energy of others in her family and genus—and then some. Half of her genetic pool—the husky—is legendary for unfathomable endurance. Sled dogs run upward of a hundred miles a day, and the elite of their breed tackle the annual eleven-hundred-mile Iditarod race, continuously running at speeds of fourteen miles an hour for ten days straight. The other half of her gene pool is no less active. An article in the *Los Angeles Times*—one of the only published pieces on jindos in all of North America—warns that this primitive breed is known for an ability to hunt independently over a range that can include hundreds of miles, sometimes running at speeds as fast as thirty-five miles per hour. Jindos possess a cat-like agility that allows them to leap six feet in the air, and if an obstacle (like a fence or a wall) is too high to jump over, they scale it.

In other words, this puppy is definitely not a stay-inside dog.

As if to prove her lineage, on this bright Sunday morning Ari dances crazily around my feet, stopping only to chew on my fingers when I try to lace up my hiking boots. Today is the first official day of our project, and my plan is to commence it with a short expedition in the town forest: just an hour or so out in the sun and snow, then we can return to the warmth of the house and the work I must complete before my classes tomorrow. I mistakenly assumed that the hour would mostly be spent somewhere other than the foyer of our house. My canine teacher obviously has other ideas.

Just shy of four months old, Ari is small—about fifteen pounds—and her proportions remain infant-round. One of her ears stands up wolfishly; the other flops over like the RCA dog's. None of this, however, makes her any less of an opponent when it comes to getting things done. Ari's teeth are still the temporary ones allotted to baby animals—jagged little numbers that pierce the skin with little effort. They hurt. A lot. As she bites at my hands, I pick her up and set her on the floor near the kitchen table, wrongly thinking that she will stay seated there. She doesn't, of course. Instead, she springs up again and beats me back to where my other boot rests, eager to continue complicating my attempts at getting dressed and tumbling over our other shoes in the process.

I try reasoning with her and am rewarded with a play-growl and more pouncing. I suggest that this is not helpful. She gives an even bigger, goofier gurgle: *Come on, silly! We're having a ton of fun, right?*

"You may be, but I'm not," I correct aloud, as if to cure the puppy of her naïveté. My response rouses Greg in his office upstairs. His voice wafts down, asking playfully if everything is okay. I assure him that it is—I am in perfect control. My voice belies this assertion. It also prompts Ari to offer an even bigger play-growl, then to topple over onto her back like a clumsy bug. She looks first alarmed and then pleased with this inadvertent floor show, and soon tries it again for the amusement of us both before ducking for cover under a chair.

Like just about any mammalian toddler, this baby dog is nothing short of a rolling ball of contradictions. She vacillates between fierce and terrified with a speed that would dizzy an Olympic ping-pong player. Also like other kids her age, she clowns and tests limits and seeks maternal security all in a single instant. Her attention span is limited to a few bursting seconds; her confidence is as much predicated on mine as it is anything else. I suppose I shouldn't be surprised, then, that biting shoelaces, clamoring to go outside, and flopping onto the foyer tile are all equally interesting to her right now.

Further complicating her child-like tendencies is Ari's life before moving into our house. Animal behaviorists tell us that a puppy's cognition begins in the womb and reaches its first crucial peak at around twelve weeks. What happens along the way has a lot to do with how that dog views—and responds to—the world. Puppies birthed by mothers under a fair amount of stress can exhibit more timidity and emotionality. Those who spend their first weeks without a lot of human contact can grow to be fearful or at least unsure of humans and what they want. Both factors can affect things like trainability, ease of entering domestic life, and ability to bond with a caregiver.

From what we know of Ari's life at the shelter, her early days were far from a doggy Head Start program. Prior to our arrival, she had never left the four-foot-by-four-foot enclosure that was home to her litter. Once they were weaned from their mom, the only contact they had with other creatures was their time together as siblings and the occasional attention of an overworked shelter employee. They had never been inside a house or on any surface other than concrete, nor had they been given the space to distinguish between where they slept and where they pooped. Factor in the DNA of her two primitive-breed parents (both of whom were under plenty of shelter-induced stress during conception and pregnancy), and what we have is something a whole lot like a feral dog on our hands.

Does this affect our feelings about Ari? Only insofar as it makes us want to love her all the more. We want to give Ari the kind of affection and security she should have had from the moment she was born. We would probably want this for any animal who had endured such an experience, but it doesn't hurt that this particular one is beyond adorable in just about everything she does. Like other infant dogs, Ari is a perfect example of Mother Nature's warranty program: She is just too cute in her boxiness, her floppy ear, her curious blue eyes to elicit a reaction other than love, particularly at times like this, when she wags a little puppy tail from under the nearby chair. Momentarily suspending my project to get my hiking boots laced, I reach down and stroke her tawny coat—more fleece than fur—and am rewarded with a warm lick of my palm. Sheer bliss.

It's also sheer biology. We are genetically programmed to adore and coddle baby animals, to serve as willing foster parents should the need ever arise—as it has in this case. One of the first scientists to write about this care impulse was Konrad Lorenz, an Austrian-born researcher generally considered the father of ethology (or the study of animal behavior). Lorenz is my kind of scholar: He received the Nobel Prize in 1973 for his study of animal behavior and, in his official Nobel autobiography, he admits that, for much of his childhood, his greatest goal was to become a wild goose. After failing repeatedly at this metamorphosis, he accepted his parents' consolation prize of pet ducks and their insistence that he become a doctor—a *people* doctor. But Lorenz wasn't easily dissuaded. While in medical school, he began to study physiology and its emotional responses, particularly as both related to human-animal interactions. This study would become the basis of his life's work.

In the 1940s, Lorenz published his *Kindchenschema*, or schema for determining human responses to animal cuteness. Based on this system, Ari's attractability quotient is off the chart. According to Lorenz, certain key features—boxy bodies, big doe eyes, rounded features, and general clumsiness—incite a particularly affected response in adult humans. Lorenz identifies this response as an Internal Releasing Mechanism (IRM), a powerful instinctual motivation intensified by our own cultural values.

In other words, our species rewards itself for puppy love, so we continue to do it as part of our biological imperative. Socially, we get brownie points for being nurturing and considerate. That affirmation makes the impulse an even stronger, nearly involuntary response. We can't help ourselves. Show us a baby anything and we coo, we pet and stroke, we want to snuggle and nurture. It's why even the most austere of us can't help but resort to baby talk when around kittens, infants, or other baby creatures.

Knowing that my response to this very adorable puppy is nothing more than genetic wiring and social practice does nothing to quell the bubble of enthusiastic maternalism I'm beginning to feel around Ari. There can be no doubt about it: I am in love.[1] It's not the first time I've felt this kind of affection, of course. But that only means it's that much easier for me to recognize the signs.

Take my marriage, for instance: a relationship that I, at least, see as a great example of what it is to feel real affection for another being. In the days just after our wedding, Greg and I both experienced an unexpected sense of collusion. There was nothing at all secret about our wedding: no disapproving parents or impetuous decision to elope. Instead, it was a planned, joy-filled affair shared with all the people we hold most dear. Together, we hiked up a small mountain overlooking the sea. We exchanged vows; we pledged to stay true to each other;

[1] Of course, Konrad Lorenz would probably tell me that this is part of the biological process, too. After falling in love with his first pet duck, Lorenz codified notions of imprinting—the process by which an infant learns to adopt the behaviors of mature creatures. Scholars tend to talk about this process in terms of what it offers the young: They learn life-sustaining behaviors, they identify kin, they become socialized. But imprinting benefits mature creatures as well. Most of us like to be needed and to care for something. We want to feel loved.

we offered our unending friendship to those who joined us. In return, they promised their love and support. Afterward, we danced and ate and toasted this community under a late summer's night sky. We did this because we believe in the power of ritual: of speech acts and collective affirmation and any other symbol signifying the outward building of relationships. Such public moments, we insisted, were crucial to the success of any new union.

Nevertheless, Greg and I were both struck by the overwhelming sense of privacy this little wedding created in both of us. We spent the next several days sequestered, hunkering down in quiet, giggling whispers. We had a secret—an inside joke no one else could possibly understand. And why would we want them to anyway? This wasn't about them; it was about us being madly in love and unified together.

Suddenly, we understood the reasons why honeymoons persist as a convention of new marriages. Couples need that private time to get used to the emotional power of their kinship and the way it changes their interaction with the rest of the world. Eventually, they become familiar enough with this new bond to accommodate their other relationships and commitments. The foreign weight of wearing a new ring lessens, as does this strangeness of beginning sentences with *my husband* or *my wife*. The couple learns to function out in the world as a unified entity; they even remember to bicker once in a while about whose night it is to do the dishes. The world rushes back in, and they are there to greet it. Together.

To a lesser degree, our first two months with Ari have felt surprisingly similar to this emotional process. Initially (and even with the continued destruction of carpets and papers), all I wanted to do was get home to the warm, wriggly little creature waiting for me in her crate. I spoke in expectant, hushed tones when I entered the house and was driven to distraction when I couldn't be there. I had a new secret: An utterly vibrant, foreign little creature had joined our house. She brought with her new smells and sounds and an admirable desire to feel a part of our tiny family. We couldn't get enough. We found excuses to be home with her, to watch the house—so lonely after Kinch's death—become filled with a new kind of life.

Of course, our desire to withdraw soon lessened. Ari grew stronger, more confident in herself, more exuberant in her actions. She no longer needed a nursery; she needed an adventure. Greg and I learned to love her all the more for that. And now, a month or so later, I remain utterly unequivocal in my affection. I feel my heart leap up when we are reunited; I experience benevolent concern for her well-being and disapproving censure when I think her development needs it.

But what does this affection mean to Ari?

As best as scientists can tell, the puppy probably doesn't think in terms of love—at least not in a human sense. In fact, for centuries scientists swore animals like her don't think or feel at all. In the past few decades, however, that line of thinking has changed. Most ethologists now agree that Ari and other dogs can, in fact, experience their own brand of joy and affection. Their social natures predispose them to friendly interaction, and they demonstrate real delight while engaged in such moments. They also form lasting relationships with human families, adopting us as family members and those who meet their social needs. This willingness to bond with humans is a large reason why dog population numbers are so high: We want to be around animals who want us, too.

In our house, dog love takes a few different forms. Ari is clearly pleased when I return from work or we set out to play; other times, she likes to stick close, either leaning against me or sleeping with one paw on my foot. She seems to sleep better in that repose—that is, if her little content dog sighs are any indication. And as it turns out, Konrad Lorenz was right: This really is mutually rewarding interaction. Ari gets to feel safe and nurtured, while I get to cuddle with a happy, furry creature. The Centers for Disease Control say that our relationship will lower my blood pressure and cholesterol levels. I'll also become more social, which, in turn will decrease my likelihood of depression. As for our time as canine naturalists, ecopsychologists have proven that the same benefits exist for those who venture outside and experience nature. Put all of this together, and you get one pretty healthy human and a very happy dog.

At least in theory.

The truth of the matter is that neither cuddling nor naturalist inquiry is happening in our house right now. And I doubt my blood pressure is very low, either. In the space of twelve minutes, I've managed to don exactly one hiking boot. One of its long laces rests limply on the slate floor of our entryway. The other extends tautly, a fishing line that has caught a robust dog fish. She backs slowly, pulling tight the slack, then gives a few impatient jerks when she cannot extend the lace any farther. Each time I reach down to free it from her eel-like jaw, she shakes the lace harder, dropping it only to notarize my palm with tiny fang marks. As soon as I pull my wounded hand away, she's back to the lace. As soon as I try to put on the other boot, she launches a similar assault on it.

This process of biting and its seemingly infinite permutations—lace-hand-boot, boot-lace-hand, boot-hand-tail (*ouch!*)—clearly delights the puppy. My mild disapproval only sweetens the moment for her. As far as she is concerned, we couldn't spend our time in a better way if we tried. I respectfully disagree. If I don't put an end to this game, we'll never get outside.

Looking on with horror from atop the kitchen table, our cat Cam gives me an expression that says she thinks getting this dog out of the house is a fabulous idea. No fan of irrepressible puppies, the grouchy tabby's face clearly states, *This canine depravity is unbelievable. Please take this thing outside—before I figure out how to do it myself. Permanently.*

Fair enough. I just need to figure out how to do that.

As Ari continues her work on my boot, I check my watch. We are almost twenty minutes into the hour I have allotted for our walk. I sigh and repeat my new mantra: *I am learning to give up control.* It's a challenge, though, especially since canines don't wear watches or worry about deadlines. This is the first of many lessons I will commit to memory during our project: Dog time and puppy priorities are not at all the same as mine.

Ari is a very thorough teacher. To make sure I fully understand my first lesson, she shifts our focus from my boots to her own wily uncatchability, darting around the house while I don my winter coat, hat, and mittens. Pretending to ignore her, I grab the long, fifteen-foot retractable leash Greg and I purchased the week before and approach her with it. This is her cue to initiate yet another game—and it's a big one. "Catch the Puppy" is not only Ari's favorite sport, but one she plays with astounding skill. Each time I get close, she bobs and weaves, eluding capture. When I reach for her, she scurries just out of reach under a kitchen chair, grinning at the power she has to keep my energies focused on her. When I look like I might give up, she bounds toward me, only to reel away at the last minute, chortling wildly: *Ha! Hahahahahaha. Oh, what fun we are having today!*

Regardless of how distracted she may appear, the pup has already become a master at reading my body language. Doing so is one of her species' most impressive—and well-developed—talents. It's also another reason why they've had such tremendous success ingratiating themselves into our worlds: Oftentimes, they know how we feel before we do.

In this case, Ari is studying my gestures and looking for permission to play. An inch shift left or right, a slight change in my facial expression is evidence enough that I'm willing to participate—at least in her lexicon. As I lean forward to attach her leash, she begins the newest game of tag. And so, we're off—whether or not I actually want anything to do with the chase.

Ari races around the table as quickly as her round little legs will take her. Most of her movement is vertical and lateral, so she isn't actually going all that fast, but she's impossible to catch. She darts this way and that, occasionally knocking into chairs or slipping on the floor. In spite of myself, I make a few halfhearted laps around the kitchen table in pursuit, feeling the temperature quickly rise to an uncomfortable level in my coat. In the human world, I'm telling her, *Come back here!* In hers, I'm saying, *Isn't this game the best ever?*

After three circles, I'm done. I stop chasing and cross my arms—a universal sign for *I quit*. Ari, on the other hand, continues to prance and bounce another loop around the chairs. After some time, she notices I have ceased to follow. Scampering is only fun when you are actually being chased, and so she makes her way on oversized paws once again to lure me back in the game. I pretend to ignore her. She rests on her front forearms, extending out her rump and fiercely wagging her tail. I turn my back. She responds with her toughest puppy playgrowl. I can't help but look, and the eye contact is all she needs to reinstitute the game, knowing perfectly well that I will forget my resolve and join her. Which, of course, is exactly what happens.

Another three loops, and now I'm sweating. I can feel the blush in my cheeks, and I remove my hat. The temperature in my coat continues to rise, so I unzip it and slip off one sleeve. As I do, Ari stops and tilts her head to one side. I can't tell if she is confused about humans' ability to add and remove clothing at will, or if she knows the jacket is a crucial step in our journey outside.

Either way, she has become instantly contemplative, studying my actions with clear-eyed interest. I seize the opportunity and swoop up the little dog in my arms, attaching the leash to her collar as I do. *Victory!* I whisper smugly. She pretends not to notice and wiggles onto her back, trying to chew the arms that now cradle her.

In an awkward dance of coat-and-puppy juggling, we get re-dressed and head out the door. I carry her down the front-porch steps and set her on the dingy snow that surrounds my car. *This is it,* I tell her, *we're finally off to the town forest. Trust me: This is an even better kind of game. You're going to love it!*

But the pup looks like she's not so sure. She stands by the side of my car, again cocking her head and studying my movements. She loves being outside, but we normally content ourselves with the backyard and surrounding woods. What's this car thing all about?

To be honest, I have a few questions of my own. Because we haven't really made it off our property yet, I wonder if this outing is too big a leap—even if it is in the name of noble new beginnings. To make matters worse, Ari has only ridden in an automobile a few times, and each trip resulted in unceremonious vomiting. I assure her we'll be fine but wonder if she can tell I'm not entirely certain.

As I start the car, the puppy looks nervous and clambers back and forth between the front seat and back, knotting herself up in the leash as she does. She begins to pant. I decide we are going too fast at twenty-five miles an hour and turn on my hazard lights as we slow to a crawl. We probably won't run into any other cars on this quiet road, but I don't want to take any chances—an accident now certainly won't make Ari any more roadworthy. The reduced speed seems to calm her, and she puts her one white paw on the steering wheel to get better leverage. This is a hopeful sign. I smile and kiss the top of her head, liking the smell of her baby fur.

Once at the terminus of Stagecoach Road, I open the car door and lower the wriggling dog onto the snow. The white stuff is thicker here, and Ari sinks down to her elbows. She looks up, taking in the scenery and offering a few trial sniffs of the air. *Fascinating.* These are not the smells of our house, nor are they those of our yard. I watch her closely to see how she responds to this realization, but learn little from her expression. She seems tentatively interested—no more, no less.

I try to lead us forward, but Ari isn't sure. *Come on,* I say to the pup by way of encouragement. *Let's see what this big forest has to offer.* She responds by sitting down and flattening her ears. Even I know what this means: passive resistance. *No way, no how.* I sigh. Loudly.

We are now seventy-eight minutes into our hour-long walk. Not counting the race around the kitchen table, we have taken three steps. As it so often does, my mind returns to quotidian pressures: *Will my students believe me if I tell them I didn't grade their papers because I didn't get my boots laced in time? Could I lose my job because I couldn't leash my dog?* This list could go on and on and on some more. I tell myself we have no time to consider such things—it'll only delay us further. I coo at the pup, and she reluctantly agrees to rise. We set off down the well-worn path into the forest, following the route already established by snowmobiles and cross-country skiers. As we do, Ari surges ahead, extending her telescoping leash to its full fifteen feet and kicking up loose snow. She pulls harder, taking short raspy breaths and struggling against the pressure of her collar. I stumble behind, feeling my boots slip on the icy tracks.

In this awkward cadence lies the second lesson of the day: Keeping up with an anxious puppy while taking inventory of one's surroundings is harder than it seems. In fact, I feel like I'm losing track of both. I try to slow our pace, but the pup pulls on, as if channeling all of her mushing forebears into this one glorious moment of movement and ice and camaraderie. She certainly seems to be heading somewhere, although I can't for the life of me determine where. Furthermore, I can't tell if this excitement has any shred of pleasure in it, or if she's just convinced we're about to be eaten by predators.

I try again to slow our pace, telling the pup that we are supposed to be playing naturalists, a role she assumes with aplomb in our own yard. She pretends not to hear. I say—louder this time—that she needs to start sniffing at plants and introducing me to the animals who are waking from their winter hibernation.

"Show me a squirrel," I say. "A fox. A snow flea. A pterodactyl. Anything!"

She looks as if she would laugh at my parochialism. But ever charitable, she instead softens her expression as if to say, *Come on—isn't this what you wanted? Aren't we—at your insistence, I might add—a whole two miles from home and around all these new and unbelievable things? Is it not already overwhelming enough?!*

I can't argue with such logic. I wanted a sense of wonder, and here I have it. I try to be in the moment, to experience the simple gladness of a romp.

It doesn't work. I'm still thinking too much. I try distracting myself, counting trees and mentally recording a few hackneyed adjectives about their thick green foliage—the only color in an otherwise white and gray world.

This seems to help. I expand my vision, scanning the trees for birds, looking up into the web of branches and needles. Ari, meanwhile, continues to cast her gaze down on the ground. In a single moment I understand why.

Without my knowing it, we have begun to descend a small hill. This causes us to accelerate into an involuntary and uncontrolled shuffle. And because I am still foolishly looking for fauna real and imagined, I do not see the patch of ice awaiting my right boot. As soon as we make contact, both feet fly out from under me, and for one brief, shining second, I am airborne. It's too good to last, and soon doesn't. I fall to the ground with a long, dull thud. As I do, the leash leaps from my hand, its thick plastic retractor hitting the ground in a loud aftershock.

Ari hears both and whirls around, panicked. She takes a look at the sprawling human and races off, bolting her way back to the car and trawling the clunky leash case behind her. I catch one last glimpse of her—a bear cub of a dog racing with all of her might to get away from the oafish human and the now-frightening environment.

As her form grows smaller and smaller on the wooded horizon, I fetch my hat, shake out the ice crystals, and rub my hamstring. I stand, trying first to get my bearings and then to locate my dog. The forest is nearly silent, save for the *rat-a-tat-a-tat* of plastic bouncing off frozen snow as Ari continues to flee. I follow the sound, eventually making my way back the half mile to the car. There, a very timid puppy cowers, tail between her legs, hoping against hope that this big metal box with wheels will take her not back into the woods but, instead, back home—where at least she will be safe.

She avoids my gaze as I get closer. Her feelings are hurt, and I get the distinct sense she no longer trusts me. With more crooning sweet nothings, I manage to lure her back inside the car. I try not to wince as I sit down on my bruised behind. Meanwhile, Ari works to put a safe distance between us. The ride home is eventful only because her scorn appears to outweigh her car sickness, and she doesn't seem to notice the increased speed of our return trip. As we pull into our driveway back home, I realize that I've left my field guide out in the woods, along with my notebook and just about all of my pride.

At this rate, we could have a very long year ahead.

On Whelps and Wolves

[april]

Given our failed outing last month, Ari and I decide we need some serious guidance for our project to succeed. I contact Don Hanson, owner of Green Acres Kennel Shop and regional expert on canine behavior. On the phone, I tell him quickly about our caninaturalism, afraid that he will either laugh or think me crazy. But he does neither and, instead, invites me and Ari to visit him at Green Acres.

That, of course, means another car ride.

We make it a full ten miles before the vomiting commences. It's a terrible, viscous cycle whereby Ari throws up her breakfast, eats it, and then vomits again. Each time, the ratio of stomach enzyme to dog food becomes more repugnant, as does the puddle in my backseat. We're driving down a country highway wedged in by a logging truck behind us and a farm tractor in front of us, so there's little I can do other than avert my eyes while I make mental notes about covering my car seats with old bedsheets and several layers of thick plastic wrap.

As soon as we arrive at Green Acres, however, Ari bounds from the car as if utterly unaffected by the traumatic ride. The kennel's day boarders—a collie, a few black labs, and various microscopic terriers—bark at Ari's arrival. She hangs close to me, prepared to duck into her submissive roll if the dogs so much as take a step toward her. Still, her tail wags and her one floppy ear arches up with hopeful amicability. After spending her first two months with only dogs such as these for friends and family, this must seem like a kind of reunion for her.

Once inside, we are greeted by Don, a friendly-looking man in his early fifties with a round face, thinning hair, and a thick black beard. Hanson has a veritable alphabet soup of credentials after his name: CPDT (Certified Pet Dog Trainer), BFRP (Bach Foundation Registered Practitioner and Animal Specialist), CDBC (Certified Dog Behavior Consultant), APDT (past president of the Association of Pet Dog Trainers), and TDI (Therapy Dogs International). Perhaps even more impressive, though, is the fact that he and his entire staff clearly love dogs—*all* dogs. Several employees stop by to say hello to Ari or chat with the canine clients and the resident English setter, all with the comfortable familiarity of people who know exactly what to do around dogs. Don smiles, looking on with approval at the comfortable chaos. He wears a pair of expedition-weight khaki pants and matching shirt, emblazoned only by an embroidered cartoon dog on the right breast pocket. I decide that he looks like he is on a canine safari. That's fine by me—we're here to do the same.

After a handshake between humans, Don invites us up to the large room used for behavior classes. He offers me a folding chair and Ari the opportunity to explore off leash—further proof he is clearly someone who understands dogs. Once free, Ari heads directly to a dog-proof cabinet and tries unsuccessfully to open it. A wheelchair and pair of crutches rest alongside it.

Don notices my curiosity. "We certify dogs for therapeutic uses here," he explains. "They visit hospitals, nursing homes, and cancer wards. Dogs can be a really big lift for people who are ill."

I ask him how the wheelchairs and crutches figure into the training.

"Dogs are leery of new things. And sick people have a lot of scary-looking things around them. We need to know certified dogs won't be frightened by them."

I tell Don I know all about frightened dogs and then sheepishly explain last month's fiasco in the woods. He smiles patiently and listens to my theory that Ari, like her wolf kin, is much more in tune with the natural world and thus ought to be comfortable there. As I finish, he shakes his head knowingly.

"A lot of people think that," he begins politely. "And dogs are related to wolves, of course, but there's a pretty clear split in the family tree. Unlike wolves, dogs have survived more by staying out of nature than in it."

This surprises me. With her long snout and thick coat, Ari certainly looks like a wolf pup. Why wouldn't she act like one?

Because, Don explains, biologically speaking she's not a wolf. At least not really. Dogs and wolves started out as the same creature, but thousands of years of isolated breeding have resulted in noticeable changes.

So how did we arrive at the rambunctious creature weaving between our legs right now?

According to Don, the answer varies tremendously depending upon whom you ask. "Some think that dogs were self-domesticating," he says. "These people believe that, for whatever reason, a few proto-dogs started relying on human settlement for their existence. As they did, they adapted to domestic life, and self-selected those genes compatible with domesticity. Other people argue that humans domesticated wolves. They think that early man plucked a few wolves out of the pack and domesticated them through selective breeding."

I ask Don which theory he believes.

"The first one," he says emphatically. "Our best guess is that wolves are five million years old. Dogs are only about fifteen to forty thousand years old. That's not much time for human intervention. It stands to reason they took care of the job themselves."

Don's theory is shared by the majority of ethobiologists studying dogs and wolves, all of whom say very much the same thing: Wolves self-selected into two distinct groups. The ones with less fear of humans and more interest in an easy meal started hanging around early settlements. The ones who didn't care for this kind of life stayed away. Eventually, they formed two different breeding pools. That's when you start to see serious differences in appearance and behavior. The self-domesticating wolves looked to settlement dumps for their meals, and the less concerned they were about humans, the bigger the meals they enjoyed. The more food they consumed there, the more energy they had for reproduction. Those wolves showing the most friendly and engaging responses to humans were invited to continue their feasts in our homes and barnyards, where they *really* had energy for more reproduction.

This boost has helped domestic canine populations immensely. For every calorie a dog doesn't have to spend searching for food, that dog can devote one more bit of energy to enhancing reproductive prowess and providing for a new litter of pups. And each time a domesticated dog breeds, he or she passes on a genetic docility and dependence on human civilization. Pups frightened of humans tend to peel off from the existing population, taking their wary genes along with them. Pups without that impulse tend to stay and become part of our culture. Moreover, because of human responses to neoteny, we tend to reward those dogs who seem the most adorable in their infantile appearance and behavior. We encourage them to breed; we give them treats and their own bed; we adopt them out to people like Paris Hilton. As a result, there are currently more Chihuahuas in the United States than there are wolves in the world.

Despite the obvious differences between a starlet's pocket companion and a timber wolf, the basic blueprint for both animals is very much the same. When it comes to wolves and domestic dogs, any genetic difference is best considered in terms of degree—and it is a very small degree. Ed Bangs, wolf recovery coordinator for the US Fish and Wildlife Service, explains it this way: "Basically, if you drop your beagle in a blender and look at the DNA, it's pretty indistinguishable from a wild wolf." Such assertions beg two important questions for me: How closely are wolves and beagles really related and, perhaps more significantly, what kind of ghoulish cocktails are served at USFWS parties? I haven't yet found an answer to the second question. But I do know that DNA analysis of the aforementioned species reveal that wolves and domestic dogs share 99.8 percent of their DNA (a 0.2 percent difference). The next closest relative to the wolf is the coyote, which shares only 96 percent of its DNA with the wolf.

We might, then, be best served by viewing dogs and wolves as something between siblings and kissing cousins: close enough to be a part of the same species and even interbreed, but worlds apart when it comes to a few key attributes—particularly those that come to light in the natural world.

This is the real power of genetics. That tiny 0.2 percent of difference between Ari and her lupine kin is all it takes to mold an eighty-pound timber wolf into any number of AKC toy breeds. And that's just the tip of the genetic iceberg. According to Don Hanson, that same 0.2 percent has caused important differences when it comes to a species' relationship with the natural world. For starters, wolves have stronger bodies and brains than most dogs, as well as longer, stronger teeth and a more sharply honed predatory instinct. Dogs who scavenge don't require these attributes. Instead, they do better with blunter teeth and shorter noses, which allow them to sift through castoffs looking for food. As for their brains, they've dropped in size as well.

"Let's just say that dogs are smart enough to root through trash, and willing to keep doing it," says Don with a smile. "These eco-minded folks practicing survival by scavenging from dumpsters could learn a great deal following a feral dog around."

I ask if that also means a wolf would beat Ari at canine Jeopardy.

"I guess it all depends on the categories and the questions," he says. "The wolf and dog are each uniquely developed to thrive in their specialized environment. The dog's environment is so similar to ours, it's natural that we would choose to hang together."

Through the domestication process, dogs move farther and farther away from their wild counterparts. As they worm their way deeper into our hearts and homes, they discover scientifically formulated food, outstanding hygiene, and a whole host of services from doggy day care to hip replacement, all intended to prolong their lives. Provided we don't spay or neuter them along the way, these concessions lead to increasingly robust litters of more adorable little critters we love to love. Meanwhile, wolves keep to the periphery and content themselves with hunting and the occasional nervous scavenging. These are high-energy behaviors, which lead to reduced litter sizes. They are also more dangerous. The average life expectancy of a wolf is about seven years. Compare this with Ari's father, the Siberian husky (fourteen years), or with Charles Darwin's favorite dog, the Jack Russell terrier (sixteen years). In just about every category, domestic dogs trump their wild kin when it comes to survival.

Even so, warns Hanson, these attributes are what compromise Ari's relationship with the natural world. With the evolutionary success of *Canis lupus familiaris* comes a further distancing of dogs from their wild counterparts, particularly with regard to their places in the natural and cultivated worlds. It all comes down to approach tendencies.

"Wolves do everything to avoid us. And they use the natural environment to do so," Don says. "Dogs seek us out, and when they do it means that they don't necessarily experience a lot of nature. Basically, we have created animals that don't exist on their own very well."

That fact might explain both Ari's original reluctance to do much exploring last week as well as her race back to the car, which she already associates with civilization. When you consider that her ancestors spent thousands of years trying to get out of the woods, you can understand the pup's seeming reluctance to be dropped back in there. And why not? Nature can be a scary place. I've witnessed a pack of coyotes move a 150-pound deer carcass overnight. Our neighbors down the street tell us they've repeatedly seen a black bear near their beehives, and they've lost at least three pets to the fisher cat, a particularly pernicious member of the weasel family known for its ability to kill just about anything—including porcupines. Come to think of it, if I were a wisp of a puppy, I might not want to be thrown into such an environment, either.

I'm embarrassed by my lack of foresight and understanding about dogs and nature. Will this be the second and last installment of our canine naturalism project?

I ask Don about the viability of my experiment in the wilderness. "I had this idea that Ari has a better way of being in the world—that I can learn a lot from tagging along and watching the way she interacts with the environment. But maybe it's silly. Am I unreasonable to assume that Ari has the potential to be a first-rate naturalist?"

"Not at all," he assures me.

Thank goodness.

According to Don, Ari's more than up for the challenge—provided we undertake it together, thereby maintaining that bridge to the domestic world. In general, he says, Ari wants to experience nature with me nearby—or at least with the promise of a return to the civilized world. Even though she's genetically a predator, she's not a very good one. On some level she and her domestic dog kin seem to realize that, and they limit their time in the wilderness accordingly.

I still look disappointed. Don pats my hand and tells me not to worry. "Really. This is a good thing," he says. "If she were *too* skilled in the wilderness, you'd never see her again. You wouldn't learn much that way."

I concede he has a point.

"Besides," he continues. "You have a lot to gain by who she is now."

According to Don, Ari possesses several key attributes for the success of our project—despite her timidity. At this stage in her life, she is extraordinarily inquisitive. Perhaps more importantly, she is quickly becoming a world-class sensory machine. While Ari's eyesight may not be all that superior to mine (at least during the full light of day), her hearing and sense of smell far surpass my mere human ears and nose.

"Dogs have the ability to detect smell at a rate at least a hundred thousand times greater than ours," Don says. "In fact, the latest research suggests it might be as much as a million times greater. Think about it. Take the best smell you've encountered or the worst one, and then magnify that by a hundred thousand or more. It's overwhelming. Everything in nature has a smell, and almost all of it registers in her olfactory senses."

He points outside the small window in the room. There, thin icicles are melting into tiny beads of white light, dripping onto the cars below and turning the whole scene into reflecting and refracting wetness. A few patches of early grass poke out of the large corral where dogs enjoy a midday run. The spring thaw. We both smile.

"You two are in for a treat," Don assures me. "Look at it out there—it's as if nature just turned on a five-hundred-watt lightbulb. All the scents of the season are about to come alive. Be sure to get a good walking harness. You're going to need it."

He looks down again at the puppy, who is now contenting herself by chewing on my notebook and strewing soggy mounds of masticated pages about her.

"You might also think about an introductory class or two," he says. "Something to help the two of you get acquainted and establish some ground rules."

Indeed.

On our way to the car, we enroll Ari in a course called Basic Behaviors. But before the session begins, I want to know more about this division between the wild and the domestic—particularly as it relates to me and my new best friend. Animals from angelfish to zebras have been domesticated by humans. But none enjoys the sacred place in our lives currently occupied by dogs. Why?

One answer to this question might be the similarities in our civilizing processes. Humans are socially cooperative animals. Unlike other animals (say, fish) who group together but still maintain independent roles, we primates assume specific and interdependent roles within a society. The same is true for dogs. Canines not only group themselves in task-oriented communities, but also pass down this information through a sophisticated evolutionary mechanism called biological memory inheritance, which some scholars contend we possess as well. Moreover, our two species are among the only ones that have self-domesticated in the sense that we chose to move into civilization, rather than waiting for civilization to make that decision for us. And we've done it so well that we now depend upon externalities like fire, a good pair of mittens, and more hamburgers than is healthy for either species.

But despite our anchor in this coiffed, fast-food nation, humans and dogs retain some inklings of their wild selves. We like the natural world. Some of us even crave it. But who are we when we're in it? And can we ever reclaim that chthonic self?

To answer these questions, Greg and I leave Ari in the care of my very dependable student Cara while we make the trek across the New Hampshire border. There, Fred Keating runs the Loki Clan Wolf Refuge, an expansive bit of ground abutting the White Mountain National Forest. This refuge is the last stop for semi-domesticated wolves and wolf-dogs who tried unsuccessfully to make a go in the civilized world. More than just about any other animals, these canines offer an appealing study of what happens when nature and culture try to sit down for a cup of twig tea.

We pull up to the small trailer that serves as refuge headquarters and are greeted by their intern, Sarah. As we shake hands, the reverberating din of dozens of wolf howls echoes off the mountain walls. They sound both eerie and exhilarating. Greg and I look at each other with wide eyes and eager smiles—it's as if a supernatural force is at work here.

"Nope," says Sarah matter-of-factly. "It's just vitamin time. We roll the pills in hamburger balls so they'll go down easier."

After introducing us to Fred and giving us a lesson in skull sizes for wolves and dogs, Sarah asks if we are ready to meet the animals.

We are very ready.

She leads us down the gravel road toward the animal enclosures. Up here, in the shadows of the mountains, it's still awfully cold, and the gravel is covered in thick snow and slush. As we walk, Sarah explains the history of the refuge.

"Fred founded Loki Clan fifteen years ago—the hard way. He always liked animal mythology and Native American stories about wolves. Eventually, he became interested in a growing breed of hybrids called wolf-dogs, and he adopted two himself. But the more he looked into it, the more he realized most of them really can't be pets. He started taking in wolf-dogs that families couldn't handle, and before long he had too many animals for his location. So he incorporated as a nonprofit organization and moved here, where the wolves and wolf-dogs can live in pack structures in an environment that mimics their life in the wild."

I ask her how many of each they have.

"We have ninety animals altogether. But who's a wolf and who's a dog? That's hard to tell. I don't think we'd know for certain without genetic testing."

This surprises me. After talking to Don, I have been operating under the impression that there are wolves and dogs and not a lot in between. Surely there must be differences, I say.

"Sort of," Sarah concedes. "In some cases, we can look at physiological differences. Wolves are aerodynamic: their skulls are narrow and streamlined; so are their bodies. Dogs look boxier. They have short snouts and bigger chests, or hulkier frames. Sometimes we can tell if an animal is part German shepherd or malamute just by how wide they are."

I tell her about Don's theory of different approach tendencies for wolves and dogs.

"That's right," she says. "If a wolf sees a human, it'll run away. If a dog sees a human, it'll usually either bark and declare its presence, or it'll approach you and want to be friends. But either way, the dog sticks around. You'll probably never see the wolf."

I ask her about other differences.

"Group interaction is a big one," she says. "Like with vocalization. If a pack member does something to offend a wolf, that wolf will scold the other one, but then it's over. There's a clear order and hierarchy to everything. Dogs, on the other hand, will vocalize continuously or sometimes even get into a fight. They don't seem to have the same structure to their interactions that wolves have."

We continue our walk up the hill. Along the middle of the facility, a row of surveyor medallions sit wedged in tree trunks or fastened to fence posts. I ask Sarah what they mean.

"That's the state border," she says. "Maine pens are on this side." She points to the right. "New Hampshire pens are on that one. Right now, you've got a foot in each place."

I tell her that sounds a lot like the condition of these wolf dogs.

We cross into New Hampshire, where Sarah says the wolfiest of the wolves reside. She opens an imposing twelve foot gate, attached to an equally imposing twelve foot fence. "This is the perimeter fence," she explains. "Each enclosure is fenced as well, so this is just extra protection. We really want to make sure the wolves stay inside the refuge."

The philosophy of Loki Clan necessitates that everyone here walk a delicate line between the wild and the controlled. Rehabilitation wolves are kept in relatively domestic spaces—enclosures with prepared meals and human contact. By comparison, the rescued domestic wolf-dogs have reverted to a wilder state, even though they reside in the same space. In theory, this situation ought to equalize their behaviors and create fewer variables for teasing out the specific attributes of the two subspecies.

The entire refuge is organized around this idea. Each acre-sized pen contains one pack—anywhere between two and six animals who have been placed together based on their social compatibility. As we walk the snow-covered path around the enclosures, Sarah tells us about each pack. The first several are undeniably wild. She advises that we avoid eye contact and stay a safe distance from the fence. In some instances, we never see an animal.

"That's what I mean about wolves," she explains. "They just disappear. They know how to use the landscape to their advantage."

In other cases, a few brave canids pace the perimeter of the fence, keeping careful watch on us. As we approach, they tilt their snouts into the air, taking in our scents. I wonder if they can smell my nervous excitement.

These animals create an imposing presence. It's an intimidating feeling to have a fully grown and very wild-looking wolf stare you down. I tell Sarah that that gaze is all it takes to convince me that humans are as much prey as they are predator. She laughs. "That's what myths and pop culture want you to believe. But I think you're much safer here than you are on most city streets."

We turn a corner at one of the pens and walk about two hundred yards uphill, crossing back into Maine. As we crest the rise and approach another enclosure, a group of about five animals start yipping and barking. Three of them stand on their hind legs, eager to get our attention. All are wagging their tails. They share a physical appearance with the wilder wolves we just saw. Yet these are totally different animals. The sounds coming from the wolf-dogs grow in excitement as we get closer: They whine and yip and bark. Barking is definitely not a wolfie attribute. Neither is the performance they stage for our benefit. They dance little circles and paw at the fence, teasing tree limbs and one another. Without a doubt, these are dogs.

"See what I mean?" Sarah asks, grinning.

She invites us to hold our hands, palms flat, against the chain link. We do nervously. The wolf-dogs give us a quick sniff, then lick every square inch of our hands. Unlike the carefully orchestrated positions held by wolves within the other packs, these animals are more frenetic and have little social order that we can discern. Instead, they seem much more interested in interacting with us. One tips over his water bucket and tosses it in the air, increasing his efforts once he's won our attention. Another cocks her head fetchingly. The rest just hop about, continue to lick our hands, and enjoy their unfocused exuberance. They dance with increasing intensity, spinning and leaping around the pen and bouncing off the trunks of nearby trees as they sing and grin. These are nothing short of furry clowns.

I ask Sarah about their domesticity. "They seem just like pets," I tell her. "How would they do in a home environment?"

"It's hard to say. Some would probably be fine," she says. "They might just be a little bit of a handful."

"So why are they here?"

"Because, legally, an animal that has any wolf at all in it is considered a wolf. And they're considered wild. If any member of this pack accidentally scratched my leg or bit me while we were playing, technically we'd have to put it down. A lot of shelters euthanize these types of animals as soon as they arrive. Their owners decided they couldn't deal with them, so it was either here or death in a lot of cases. The wolf-dogs are safer here. They can live out their lives without fear. People just don't understand what they're getting into when they adopt an animal. And a lot of times, it's the animal that suffers as a result."

She tells us about a woman who contacted the refuge several years ago. The puppy she had adopted was out of control—chewing on furniture, chasing her house cats, that kind of thing. The breeder had been vague about the pup's lineage, and the woman became certain what she had adopted was part wolf. She asked Fred to take the animal. He agreed, and advised her about the protocols for shipping live animals. When the crate arrived from Pennsylvania, he opened it and found himself face-to-face with a six-month-old golden retriever.

"What happened?" I ask with disbelief.

Sarah shrugs again. "The woman just couldn't deal with the puppy, so she made herself believe she had a wolf."

"No, I mean once Fred received it."

"We put him in with this group, and he did just fine. He lived to old age and seemed real happy. But he probably would have done the same in a house."

Sarah turns, letting this story sink in as she leads us back to the trail.

The doggiest of the pens is our last stop on the tour. We walk with Sarah back to the car, thank her for the information, and then set out for home.

Once there, we are greeted with tail wags and lots of licking. As we roll around on the living room floor with our wolfie-looking pup, we understand more than ever: Genetics and early development aside, this is a dog, and we are her family.

The next week, Ari and I throw ourselves into the process of domestication. More than ever, I am certain: We need to be on common ground if our lives are going to be safe and fulfilling. I spend a lot of time reading the brochure given to us by Don Hanson. It promises to help with our own domestication process by teaching us socialization and polite manners—two areas where we can both use some serious instruction. After our trip to Loki Clan, I'm really looking forward to working more with Don and his staff. Plus, I'm ready to admit defeat when it comes to training the rambunctious pup. It shows—particularly in our much-suffering living room. Regardless of her lupine-like DNA and appearance, Ari is a domestic animal. That means she needs to learn to live in a house without destroying it.

Looking ahead to the start of class, I construct wild fantasies about a well-behaved dog who exists in the world with a kind of debonair quality that elevates us all. Greg, on the other hand, does not attempt to hide his skepticism.

"Why not let a dog be a dog?" he says after reading the brochure. "Why would you want to train it to be anything else?"

I point out the general chaos in our house, and the semi-feral animal who is growing in size and strength. Currently, said animal is working hard at turning a piece of firewood into tiny bits of kindling, which she then tosses about the living room. Cam, perched high on a window sill, looks on with disgust: *For the love of God,* the cat seems to say. *Take this creature to school. And fast!*

I point to the disapproving feline and then the oblivious puppy. "Do you really want a house of mangled furniture and lack of rule?" I ask. I am playing on Greg's propensity for tidiness and controlled living, I know.

He shakes his head, not persuaded by my rhetoric. "That's the comfortable unpredictability of having a dog. You have to be prepared for messes and things. Training doesn't really answer that, anyway. Their answers to any behavior problems are in human logic, not dog logic. I just don't think it works all that well. Besides," he says, now clearly on a roll, "it's a control thing. I guess I'm not in the mood to listen to people tell me what I'm doing wrong. I'd rather figure it out myself. Kinch never went to school, and he turned out fine. He figured out how to be a house pet."

I've figured out things, too. Like this response signals Greg's commitment to his position. Case closed. Particularly when Kinch is concerned. Despite what I would take to be some serious character flaws, Kinch is the gold standard of canineness for Greg. I will get nowhere with this argument, so I drop the subject and attend the human-only orientation myself.

There, I am introduced to our two instructors, Joel and Erin. Both are in their mid-to-late twenties: Joel has a tidy ponytail and clunky, cool-guy glasses; Erin has long brown hair and a big smile. They seem delighted to be here. In the room with us are about a dozen other people. Half are here for a class called Puppy Manners; the other half are enrolled in Basic Behaviors. I frankly think we need both, but Ari's advanced age of four months has qualified her for the latter course, so I join a young artsy-looking couple, a family in NASCAR T-shirts, and two middle-aged women on our designated side of the room.

The session is an intense three hours with a lot to keep straight: hierarchies of rewards, types of training, theories of the canine mind. I scribble notes like a harried student and hope there won't be a test later. During the lecture, Joel echoes much of what Don has already told me—that dogs are intensely social, but not necessarily eager to please us (unless doing so allows for even more social time). He also tells us that, while dogs may have an innate sense of direction, they lack any semblance of a moral compass.

"Dogs don't know right from wrong," Joel warns us. "They just know safe and dangerous."

In other words, they will be bad when they think it safe, and will refrain when it is not. Outside in the woods, then, Ari will most likely be motivated by what she can get away with. In other words, if Ari perceives any action as safe and in her best interests, she is likely to do it. We can use this fact, Joel tells us, to shape behavior through repetition.

Like most animals, dogs learn well through operant conditioning. If you can lure a dog into a behavior and then reward him, he'll repeat that behavior over and over again. Not only that, but his very DNA is programmed to make him one of the most trainable of all mammals through this methodology.

However, Joel adds, this training is far more important to the human participants than it is the canine ones. "Everything you teach your dogs is just a silly trick to them. Sitting, rolling over, coming when called—they're all just human requests that result in food rewards," says Joel.

This revelation surprises me. Even knowing that dogs are opportunists and do not subscribe to our moral code, I somehow always believed that they really want to please us. I say as much to the group.

"Maybe," Joel concedes unconvincingly. "Dogs are not inherently programmed to please us. They're much more likely to respond because they get something out of the deal. We tend to romanticize dogs—like Lassie. Really, though, they're about self-preservation before they're about any bond with us. As Don always says, 'If Lassie were a real dog, she would have stolen Timmy's sandwich, pushed him into the well, and, when asked, acted like she had no idea where he was.'"

So much for my fantasies about canine-human relationships.

A few days later, Ari and I report for our first official—and chaotic—day of dog school. Five young dogs bursting with energy and no sense of decorum strain, swirl, and bark in an attempt to get close to one another. In two minutes, we are all a tangled, writhing mess of humans and pets.

"Social animals," Joel reminds us firmly. He is unfazed by the din but instructs the humans to keep their dogs separated. "Play," he tells us, "is for outside time."

While Joel continues to school the humans, Erin smiles and strokes the dogs, endearing herself to each one. The basic premise of positive reinforcement is engagement: You reward your dog for gazing into your eyes and figuring out what you want. When she does, you shower her with treats. This requires a dog to relinquish any last wolfie vestiges she maintains. Luckily, the dogs in the room don't seem to mind. In fact, they are positively smitten with Erin and her treat bag. When she approaches Ari, Erin holds a small snack just above the pup's forehead and slowly moves it backward. As she does, Ari sits. Erin clicks her little metal clicker and gives Ari the treat.

I'm amazed. Greg and I have made multiple—and highly unsuccessful—attempts at home to achieve the same behavior. We've gently pushed her bottom onto the floor, mimicked the sit we want, waited until she sat on her own, and then exclaimed, "Sit!" thinking she would make the connection. All of these approaches, I soon learn, are absolutely wrong. When it comes to training, dogs favor visual cues and what trainers call lured behaviors: Hold a treat over a dog's nose, and he'll have to reposition his tush on the floor if he wants to snatch it. Soon, tush + floor = snack.

I tell Erin I always suffered in math classes.

"Don't worry," she assures me. "You'll get it soon enough."

True to Erin's word, Ari is sitting consistently on cue by the end of the month. We have also built the framework for the most important command we will learn at Green Acres: recall. When mastered, this skill means that Ari will come to me immediately when called. Such a skill has tremendous appeal: Learning it means that I can consistently let Ari off leash in the town forest and count on her to return. But Joel stresses it can take years to establish what he calls "a reliable recall." Until then, I'll never really know for certain if I can trust Ari to stick with me.

And, Joel adds, achieving a solid recall proves much more difficult for the humans than the dogs. This is largely because the command flies in the face of our own instincts. Joel explains to us that under no circumstance—and no matter how frustrated we feel—are we to call angrily, even if the dogs are raiding our refrigerator or burying our shoes or kidnapping a neighborhood child. Instead, we are to be cheerleader-perky and always, always, *always* offer treats. This, explain Joel and Don, is all about probability. Dogs know the odds are so good that they'll be rewarded, they don't even think about not doing it.

We try out our recall a few times in class. Joel tells the humans to jump up and down, to use terms of endearment, to coo and laugh. In other words, to make utter fools of ourselves. Canine naturalist lesson number three: Dog school is all about leaving your social comfort zone. When it is my turn, I find myself suffering from an unexpected case of stage fright and make a halfhearted try. Ari looks at me suspiciously. She turns to Joel as if to ask, *Has this human lost her mind? Why on earth would I run over to this flailing lunatic?* He tells me to jump higher and coo louder. I do, but the pup looks more wary than ever.

"Try holding up a treat," Joel advises.

I do. The pup looks tempted. I hold it out farther and smile more broadly.

"Here's a treat," I say in my best friendly voice. "But you have to come take it from me."

Aha! Ari seems to say. *Now I get it.* She trots—albeit a little warily—over to me. Outstanding.

At the end of class, Joel tells us to practice our recall constantly—but always in a safe place. We take his directions to heart and work in the living room, the backyard, the corral at dog school. I become arrogant about Ari's success as a student. And so, on the last day of the month, we walk through the woods to our neighbor's pasture. I've picked this locale as a compromise: Ari can still roam free, and best as I can tell, there's little that would lure her away. Furthermore, we're bound in by old rock walls and formidable blackberry bushes, so the pup's opportunities to stray are severely limited. As we step into the clearing, I cup my hand and ask Ari to sit. She does. I bend down and unhook her leash, holding my breath as I do. She looks momentarily confused, and then delighted. I inhale deeply, ready to take off in pursuit, but Ari stays put. We begin a walk around the circumference of the field. Every three seconds, I look down to make sure the pup is sticking close. She is—contenting herself with some tight little serpentines around my path and always checking in.

We make it all the way around the pasture without incident. I begin to let down my guard, just enough to take in the scenery. It's a blustery day, and the western wind still holds an arctic chill even though it's nearly May. The gusts kick up last season's leaves and cause them to dance about. Ari is interested in something, but it's not these gyrating leaves. Instead, she casts her gaze far outward, as if no longer content with what's at the end of her nose. I look across the field, and soon spy the cause of her fascination: the other side of the pasture appears to be moving and shifting upon itself, as if it were alive.

We walk closer to investigate. As we do, Ari raises her puppy hackles, looking cartoonish in her attempt at fierceness. She tries an assertive bark, still high and thin with youth. It's enough to startle whatever continues to hop across the pasture, and one of them takes flight. As it does, I see an undeniable rosy patch on its breast. A robin! I look more closely. Sure enough, the pasture is filled with nearly fifty robins hunting for earthworms in the few patches of soft ground.

The puppy has seen birds at our feeders and a few chickadees in the trees outside our house, but these are different. Not only are they strong in number, but they're all around us and showing no signs of straying. Ari flattens her hackles and instead raises her tail in a robust, full-circle wag. Forget about wolfie predation, these birds could be doggy friends! She takes off in pursuit, arcing through the air in what can only be described as pure joy. She stumbles and tumbles in her excitement, looking more like a rubber ball than a puppy. As she does, the robins disperse, rising en masse to the birch and pine trees.

In response, Ari runs harder, hoping they might let her follow. I do the same, following not the birds but rather the racing puppy.

"Ari, come!" I shout, knowing the command futile before I even open my mouth. "Ari! Ari?"

Meanwhile, the birds have ensconced themselves high in the trees, where they sit silently, their soft brown eyes taking in the actions of the pup. Standing below them, Ari appears first confused, then hurt. The robins don't seem to share her enthusiasm, and they've clearly rejected her overture of friendship. She drops her tail and turns to look at me. I feel badly for her. I do my best cheerleader dance, opening wide my arms.

"Come'ere, puppy," I sing at the top of my lungs. "Come on, Ari Jindo! Bung Ari Jan Gab!"

She eyes me and then the robins, as if weighing the appeal of both. I squat down, opening my arms wider.

"Arr-ii," I sing.

She eyes me hopefully. I redouble my efforts. "Aarrrrrrriiiiiiiii. Come back, pup."

Finally, it works. She smiles tentatively, then trots over to accept both a treat and her leash. Time to be a domestic dog again. Time to return home.

The Great Chain

[may]

I've been thinking a lot this month about what it really means to be a canine naturalist. I cannot literally perceive the world as a dog would, so I must rely, instead, on preferences. When Ari finds something interesting, I need to stop and investigate it, too. When she is repelled by something (which, admittedly, happens very rarely), my job is to determine why. An approximation of these value judgments is, I think, the closest I can get to seeing the natural world through a dog's eyes. But even in this mitigated form, my project is a challenge. I'm still not sure I understand the rules of attraction for Ari. And try as I might, I cannot make myself embrace the idea of burying my nose in manure, nor can I relish a good roll on thawing muck.

What it really comes down to, I think, is a divergence in natural values. Whether they are instinctual or learned, canines and humans clearly possess them. Greg's and mine find their antecedent in classic Western hierarchies and notions of the Great Chain of Being. First developed by Plato, this system considers existence a paltry skill, whereas attributes such as animation, desire, and spirit grant an object superior essences. The chain itself was represented in its most literal terms by Didacus Valades, a sixteenth-century artist. In his famous work, *Rhetorica Christiana,* Valades depicts the Great Chain of Being as a series of ascending platforms strung together by a long, thin line. The illustration looks like a tea cake stand—layers of little animal sandwiches and petits fours on elegantly elevated plates.

On the top level of this stand, angels kneel in orderly prayer; one level below sits a consort of men in considerably less order. The rest of the mammals—which are situated below the relatively tidy birds and slightly more mobbish fish—are nothing less than a cacophony of badly ordered beasts. Horses, manes and tails swirling about, gallivant around what appear to be bats, their wings extended in irritation. Goats prepare to butt the butts of dogs, who look on at antelope and camels in bemused wonder. There's a fair amount of chaos here, and I can only imagine the disdain felt by those creatures higher up the tea cake stand. Still, the disorder of these creatures is clearly better than the tree stumps and rocks, which rest dumbly below.

What interests me most about the schema is the subgrouping of animals based on domesticity. Within the charismatic fauna, those animals not considered domesticable—like eagles and wolves—were considered more perfect and, thus, more godly. Indeed, when it came to early human values, wild was definitely in: Offer a group of ancient Greeks a wolf and a pharaoh hound, and they'll congratulate the wolf for its greater degree of perfection every time, whether or not they're at war with Egypt.

Not so today. Although traces of the Great Chain of Being continue to dictate our natural aesthetics and ethics, the overwhelming majority of our culture would think those Greeks absurd in their judgment. As we learned last month at the Loki Clan Refuge, few people in America see anything perfect about the wolf. In fact, *Canis lupus* has endured incredible persecution, ranging from literary portrayals as the Big Bad Wolf to extermination methods including mass poisonings and trappings. Currently, the state of Alaska encourages individuals to hunt down wolves with single-engine planes, redefining the rules of "fair chase" to include a hundred years of aviation advances and 160-horsepower engines.

Where I live in the Northeast, few people are willing to even say the "W" word, preferring to believe that our political border with Canada has been sufficient to keep wolves securely under the maple leaf. Most locals get a steely look in their eyes when the subject of wolves comes up. Its brethren the coyote certainly isn't welcome. As Tim, our county's game warden, recently told me: "Coyotes are pretty much blamed for everything around here. You find something you don't like, I'll bet dollars to doughnuts coyotes did it: high property taxes, poor test scores in schools, your mom's cholesterol level, your golf swing—you name it, it's a coyote's fault."

In fact, locals are so convinced of the coyote's perniciousness that the state recently decided its open season on coyote hunting isn't enough: It has added a special nighttime season to increase the total kill each year. Radio telemetry, baiting, and packs of dogs are all encouraged. For a while, the state gave away cash prizes for the largest coyotes killed each year, but it was soon decided that bounty hunting wasn't the best way to diversify tax dollars. Even so, *Canis latrans* are no friends of the state. Or the rest of the country, for that matter. They're just too wild, too undomesticated to elicit any sympathy.

As much as we adore them now, domestic dogs have had their own wild ride on the likability scale. The reason lies, at least in part, with their complicated relationship to wild kin. This is particularly true in terms of the dietary practices of domestic dogs, which closely resemble those of the coyote. Whether or not they're hungry, domestic dogs love to scavenge in the wild. And their affinity for unmentionables made them outcasts in many ancient (and not-so-ancient) cultures. In ancient Egypt, for instance, feral dogs were deemed pariahs because of their affinity for excrement and human corpses. A similar version of this belief existed in medieval Europe, where, once again, dogs' predilection for taboo substances landed them in all sorts of perils. For nearly a thousand years, dogs were believed to be consorting with all brands of demons and devils—why else would they be so interested in graveyards and corpse carts? As a result, many a scavenging dog was hanged, drawn, and quartered. Their sympathetic human friends were burned at the stake.

A lesser version of this ostracization still occurs in some cultures. Many Muslims, for instance, maintain a strict belief that dog saliva is *najis* (impure). Those who encounter it must purify the body and clothes that came in contact with the dog. Some practitioners of Islam interpret the Koran as prohibiting dogs from living within the home for any reason. Others allow for dogs, provided they are only used to hunt or guard property. And plenty of non-Muslim people I know would prefer not to pet a dog, for fear they might pick up a parasite or germ.

At the root of these prohibitions seems to be a dog's reluctance to locate itself within a single link of the Great Chain. For many people, dogs are useful—and even pleasurable to be around; however, they never really exist under our control or submit to our cultural mores. That presents a problem when it comes to our moral codes.

This much is certainly true in my house, where three species work with varying degrees of success to find a compatible way of being. Cam, for instance, is consistently outraged that Ari does not acknowledge the feline's supremacy or even her sense of property. The puppy thinks nothing of sipping from Cam's water dish or borrowing a little foam ball without asking—and these are grave offenses in the feline world. Ancient philosophers and Renaissance artists seem to agree. Less domesticated than the dog, the cat lives higher on Valades's Chain of Being. That ought to endow her with more rights. For the life of her, Cam can't understand why Ari doesn't see that.

Personally, I'm not so worried with positions on a tea cake stand as I am household harmony. And in my clearly flawed notion of how to achieve this harmony, I believe the other species in my house should follow my moral code. Minimally, I believe these rules for conduct ought to include an agreement not to pee on any rug or chew on anything that isn't food. They ought to also mean that no one swipes at me—claws extended—as I pass the kitchen table on the way to the bathroom in the middle of the night, or wakes me at four o'clock in the morning by placing a warm puppy tongue in my mouth.

Admittedly, these rules are not overly sophisticated. Human value systems are created based on needs: If an object meets a need, we value it. Those things that fulfill basic needs like food and shelter maintain essential worth within our culture. But humans also have more individualized needs for emotional stimulation, particularly for feelings such as pleasure. We *want* to feel pleased and satisfied—so much so that actualizing these emotions becomes a seriously motivating desire in us. Anything that can please us—from a sunset over the ocean to a double scoop of mocha chocolate chip in a waffle cone—assumes significant personal value for us as well.

Contemporary ethobiologists now theorize that dogs create values in similar ways—at least insofar as achieving pleasure is concerned. This impulse is not based on any sort of philosophical principle, but rather something much closer to hedonism: If it feels good, do it; if it feels really good, do it some more. Some of these pleasures are related to basic breed considerations: Retrievers are delighted, not surprisingly, by retrieving, while a hound might consider the pastime absurd. Dachshunds or corgis, on the other hand, can think of nothing more lovely than a day poking their snouts into places where rats or foxes might live.

Humans take these impulse affinities and use them to our advantage. We select out those dogs who show an interest and skill in certain arenas and breed only those dogs, hoping to enhance this natural preference. The rest of the dogs in a litter or group tend to be cut loose. That's how Kinch entered Greg's life: The beagle had a first-rate nose, but he was terrified of guns. That's a serious flaw where most Southern hunters are concerned. When Greg met Kinch at a North Carolina animal shelter, the beagle had all but spent the two-week grace period allotted to dogs before they are euthanized. There were just too many abandoned hunting dogs and not enough non-hunting hound lovers to go around. Greg's chance arrival undoubtedly saved Kinch's life. And as it turned out, Kinch and Greg were also a perfect match: Both loved slow, meandering walks and lazy Sunday afternoons on the couch. It was a match made in heaven—and they both clearly found pleasure in their time together.

The fact that all dogs are motivated by pleasure has been a boon to the human-canine relationship, provided the humans are willing to tap into this motivation. Canine hedonism is why operant conditioning and positive reinforcement work so well in dog training. Dogs *really* like rewards. Most humans aren't so different, of course. I know I'm easily wooed by a promise of that sunset or ice cream cone. And Ari has already figured out that a tilt of her head and a winsome blue-eyed expression will undoubtedly gain her a reward from this smitten human. The question for me, then, is this: Why do some things provide great pleasure for Ari and not for me?

May is a good month to ask this question. At no time will Ari and I be so divided in our sense of what makes for naturalized recreation. This month is the height of mud season in New England: several weeks of a rapid thaw that turns the entire landscape into brown ooze and makes simple tasks like walking to the mailbox harrowing adventures. It's no fun—at least for humans.

Hating mud season has been a time-honored tradition here for centuries. And everything about it really is an epic event. Over time, the region's human inhabitants have developed different coping strategies for this six-week period of gunk. Grocery stores run specials on wet vac rentals and cleaning supplies; travel agents offer cut-rate deals on vacations to more arid environments. For those intrepid enough to hang around this time of year, there are plenty of mud banquets, chocolate mousse fundraisers, and other diversions—provided, of course, you can manage to get your car out of the driveway. This year, a local pottery collective launched its own response to mud season: an art exhibit of mugs made entirely from local clay. They even began scooping out buckets of the stuff so that local schoolchildren could learn to make art out of aggravation.

And *aggravation* is putting it mildly. The bulk of the humans I know really do detest this season: the constant cleaning, sinking up to your knees in your own yard, finding familiar roads suddenly impassable thanks to both the ooze and the newly hatching potholes.

Dogs, on the other hand, seem to find infinite possibility in this mucky landscape. When Nathaniel Hawthorne—a New Englander well acquainted with mud—visited the Erie Canal, he was overwhelmed by its omnipresent gunk. He described the canal as nothing more than an "interminable mud-puddle—for a mud-puddle it seemed, and as dark and turbid as if every kennel in the land paid contribution to it." I can't say precisely to what degree kennels have contributed to our current mud (though judging by the enormous amount of dog poop uncovered by receding snow, I'd say it's significant). However, after a week of investigation, I feel confident in stating that contemporary kennel occupants are unreasonably ecstatic about mud in general.

Stir-crazy from the limits of a snowy winter, local dogs are eager to get outside and experience the thawing world firsthand. Once there, they seek out mud with tremendous enthusiasm, wallowing and wading their way from coiffed pets to indeterminate swamp things. So prevalent is this behavior that a columnist for a local paper has created a blog dedicated to dogs in mud season—a sort of support group for people enduring the effects of very messy pets. Readers respond by sending in their dirtiest, muckiest, stinkiest pictures of canine mud baths. There is no shortage of photos on this site: Awards are given to a "dirty doodle" submerged up to its nose in clay-colored gunk as well as a chocolate Lab wearing matching ooze. Dozens of honorable mentions follow shortly behind. They are so unsightly in their muck that I can't help but wonder how in the world these dogs decided this kind of thing constitutes a fine day out.

I suppose I ought not be surprised. After all, there's plenty of canine revelry at our house as well. Born and reared in the frozen landscape of winter, Ari has had no experience with wet, other than her water bowl and the much-feared hose at the shelter. Now, however, liquid is everywhere—and she can't get enough. On our first long walk of the month, the pup stops at a large puddle and cocks her head quizzically. This was a snowbank a few weeks ago, and she looks as if she's not sure what to make of the transformation. Deciding it requires further investigation, she puts a tentative paw into the water. Unlike ice, it neither supports her weight nor cracks from the pressure. Instead it gently yields, engulfing her paw until she hits the soft bottom below. This confuses her. She tries again, more cautiously this time. After a few tentative pokes, she begins to splash, pawing at both her reflection and whatever lies underneath the surface. As she does, she churns up decayed matter and sediment. She wades in a few more steps, eventually letting the water lap at her knees as she puts her snout into the puddle itself. She surfaces, clearing her airways in a hearty snort of slime and smiling proudly. *This month is going to be great fun,* she seems to say.

As the weeks progress, Ari becomes more bold around liquid—she zigzags across the trail, seeking out puddles of all ilk. When the caninaturalist finds one, she pounces madly upon it, sending up a plume of water and sediment, and then turning to give me an open-mouth grin: *Yup, just as I suspected. This stuff is fantastic. If I had known about it earlier, we could have started having a good time out here MONTHS ago!* I can only grimace in response.

By the middle of the month, my timid puppy has become a veritable daredevil when it comes to water and mud. No longer content with the tame depressions on our path, she leaps from the trail, tripping over her hind legs and belly flopping into any liquid body she can find. When she returns, she brings decaying leaves, soil, and all sorts of microbes embedded in her drenched coat. She also brings with her the newest lesson in caninaturalism: Woodland exploration stinks. A lot.

Ari's fur usually smells of cut hay—a little bit sweet, a little bit dusty. Now, however, she moves about in a cloud of noxious sulfur, which soon insinuates itself into my car, our carpets—even my clothes. She has discovered the joys of a thaw and all the aroma that comes with it. Forget about Don Hanson's five-hundred-watt lightbulb, we're now dealing with a floodlight stronger than those that illuminate a major-league game. The woods are teeming with odors, and my little dog wants to become intimate with every single one of them. Horse manure? *Don't mind if I take a dip.* Slug slime? *Why thank you, I'd love some.*

The warming days only enhance this earthy bouquet. On an unexpectedly balmy afternoon, Ari discovers a rotting water snake carcass and flops upon it with pure hedonism. She moans with pleasure as she wriggles across the carcass until it is mashed deeply into her fur. For the rest of the walk, she prances, clearly thrilled with the find. The snake routine becomes a regular part of subsequent walks, and my moans of disgust do little to dissuade her. If anything, she looks at me with disappointment and maybe even a little pity. *Don't you humans understand how great rotting snakes smell? And more to the point, how great I smell wearing rotten snake?* No, I try to explain. Really no. And no some more.

Not that my preferences in situations like this really matter that much. Much to the chagrin and confusion of their human companions, dogs have been rolling in unmentionables since time immemorial, which is probably one more reason for their pariah status. People used to believe dogs roll in the stinkiest thing they can find to camouflage themselves for a hunt. But that theory has been debunked in recent years. After all, a lumbering, crashing cloud of decayed stink is not going to pacify any prey or woo it into sticking around. Deer and squirrels may not watch zombie movies, but surely they have no desire to come face-to-face with moving death.

Fellow dogs, on the other hand, find the aroma delightful. That's why the current thought is that dogs roll in stink as a way of reporting on the sights and sounds out in the world. By matting a particularly ripe smell into their coats, dogs can bring back more of it to the pack as evidence of their great exploits. Just like juicy gossip probably upped your value in a high school cafeteria, bits of rotten stuff elicit positive attention from other housemates. Unless, of course, your family is two annoyed humans and an incensed tabby cat.

It doesn't seem to matter to Ari that none of us is impressed by the bits of decaying snake and mud in her fur. She believes in the worth of these new fragrances, even if we refuse to. For my part, all I can do is make excuses for the residual odors in my car and on my person. I beg off carpooling and traveling with friends. At work, I make constant apologies for the condition of my shoes and pants. And through it all I try to find some contentment in the notion that Ari is happier than I have ever seen her outdoors.

Which, of course, is absolutely true. The thawing landscape has become an oasis for my otherwise overwhelmed pup. This is particularly so in areas where vernal pools are exposed. While around them, Ari loses sight of her anxiety and reluctance; in their place, I see pure carpe diem. Luckily for her, these mysterious pools are appearing everywhere. Nearly every step of our path is now flanked by a discrete body of water, and it appears as if our forest has assumed a distinctly Venetian quality. In the midst of it all, a gondola of a dog steers her way from pool to pool, her tail making a most peculiar *ricciolo*.

We adjust our daily schedule to accommodate this new routine and begin leaving for our walks earlier each day. I am learning that puddle exploration cannot be rushed, and I become accustomed to waiting patiently on the trail, silently cringing as a soggy dog drops herself into the muck. Once home, we make time for baths, towel drying, and clean clothes.

As for our naturalism, I cannot deny that the muck has provided the kick-start we need. On a late-morning walk before my creative writing class, Ari hones in on movement in one of the smaller mud puddles—a frog! Enchanted, the pup pounces into the thick mire, sinking softly. The frog makes one last leap before burrowing into what looks like stagnant brownie batter. *No problem, buddy,* Ari seems to say. *I'll come along, too!* She buries her snout deeper and deeper into the mud, plunging up to her ears and not caring that the gunk is oozing into her nose, her tear ducts, and beyond. When she surfaces for a breath, she is completely covered—an unknowing canine minstrel.

So entire is this carnival transformation that when Ari spies herself in a mirror at home she barks furiously at the dark-faced puppy who has invaded our house. Hackles raised and teeth bared, she threatens the reflected pup. *Get out,* she snarls. *This is my place.* Her behavior strikes me as existentially astute. The new woodland Ari is a different dog—chthonically bold, even Dionysian at times. Perhaps in the domestic light of our home, that seems offensive or inappropriate to her. She barks fiercely, snarling and snapping at the reflection. I crouch down next to her, pointing first to myself and then to her mirror image. We make eye contact in the glass. *Do you see?* I ask her. *This is me, and that is you.* She raises her downfolded ear thoughtfully. I believe she is considering my point. But before I can make any further philosophical leaps, she's back to the furious barking—even louder this time—and not even a piece of leftover chicken can lure her away from this reflected intruder. It's only after the mud dries, becoming translucent and revealing a scrap of her white blaze, that Ari concedes she may be barking at her own self. And by then, I'm more than late for class.

Despite Ari's great love of mud season, I'm still not persuaded other creatures are as enthralled. Or maybe I'm just projecting? To find out, we stop by to see Dave Potter, my favorite resident naturalist. A biology and fisheries professor by day, Potter is a local legend for his off-the-clock naturalism and enigmatic charisma. He's also easy to pick out of a crowd. Opposed to winter clothes of any sort, he prefers to layer shirt upon shirt until it is warm enough to step outside. By January or February, he is a garish wash of colors and plaid patterns—sometimes sporting as many as seven or eight shirts of various sizes and prints. By spring, he begins peeling them away in symphony with the warming temperatures.

This is a well-tested and sophisticated meteorological response. Our students have learned to predict the daily weather based on how many flannel shirts Potter has on when he steps out of his car in the morning, and they plan their own wardrobes accordingly (though with considerably less color and panache).

Eccentric fashion aside, Potter repeatedly earns the respect of all those interested in the natural world. He's a whiz at identification and makes a point of knowing just about everything that lives within a ten-mile radius of campus. The students love this. Among other terms of endearment, they often refer to him as the Chickadee Whisperer: Many mornings he can be seen, dressed in four or five flannel shirts, gurgling at a stand of pine trees. Wait a few minutes, and you'll see birds appear by the dozens—arriving in anticipation of a morning meal provided out of his own pocket.

When we stop by to see Dave in his office late on this particular afternoon, he is wearing only two shirts, though he has complemented them with a fluorescent orange stocking cap and what look like wading boots. Somehow, the ensemble seems to work.

Fit and always mischievous, Potter looks and acts considerably younger than his rumored age, often teasing me like a schoolboy. Today is no different; he takes a few shots at my mud-caked shoes and harried expression. But when I mention I'm here for a lesson in naturalism, he becomes mostly business-like. I tell him I need some answers to mud season—how does it affect the way animals get around this time of year? Do they have the same difficulties we do? Do they also dislike it?

Dave smiles wryly and shakes his head. "If you can write the story of the geology of mud season, permafrost, melting, hydrology, and automobile navigation, you'll have a powerful essay that will pay far more than any manuscript about canines or naturalists or canine naturalists."

I tell him I'm prepared to start small and explain my new interest in the Great Chain of Being and animal values. *What about undomesticated animals in the area?* I ask. *Does mud season present a problem for them? And if so—and given their proximity to us on the Great Chain—doesn't that somehow justify my thinking about the season?*

These questions amuse Potter as much as the first. He tells me that my worry over languishing moose and chipmunks might be exaggerated. Still, he concedes, it's certainly not easy going this time of year.

"Mud on feet is heavy," he says, pointing to the caninaturalist's paws. "And mud on hairy feet sticks more than mud on keratinized hooves. Animals like big canines probably get stuck in mud just as much as animals like moose might."

And smaller animals?

"Probably small mammals run on top of mud and jump from rut rim to rut rim on muddy roads, so it's not much of a hindrance in that way," Potter speculates. "Their tunnels and dens might get flooded. That'd make them easy targets for assorted predators when they leave for drier sites. Salamanders in particular have difficulty with rutted mud. They're often diverted from their normal path and end up in new breeding pools along the rutted roads."

I ask him about the implication of these detours. He shrugs, playing the skeptic. "Maybe a mechanism for gene flow? Could be if salamanders migrate to a different pool for breeding. If so, they might appreciate the season—at least in terms of evolution."

As Potter reflects silently on this likelihood, I look around his chaotic office. Student papers from decades ago are stacked in piles around his desk. A few stuffed (but still stinky) alewives sit staring at me, perched atop a pile of flannel. The rest of the cramped space is filled with indeterminate fishery supplies—stun guns, nets, and other aquatic tools.

Potter pushes back his chair and looks up at the ceiling, as if still tracing the path of mud from street to sea. After a long pause, he continues: "Of course, the real question for you is this: How much mud was there before European settlement? Is it a new feature of our landscape? Do our travel routes cause it? Did Native Americans experience mud or did they remain sedentary in spring and on higher ground? Do good sod and shadowed forest canopy equal quick thaw and no mud? Plowed fields and many roads equal seasonal mud. Would it be reasonable to extrapolate that white settlement is the problem? What does your canine naturalist think about that idea?"

I resist the urge to point out that he has asked seven questions, not one. Still, they seem like good ones, so I tell him we will return home and see. He eyes me and Ari skeptically, then returns to his fishnets. I promise he won't be disappointed.

And he's not. In fact, we are both surprised to learn that Potter's joking connection between dogs and mud is closer to the truth than we might have thought. In his outrageously interesting book, *Dirt: The Erosion of Civilization*, David R. Montgomery contends that pre-colonial Native Americans had at least an intuitive sense of mud season and the boons of avoiding it by dispersing their cleared spaces and keeping to higher ground this time of year. The first colonists were a different story entirely. They arrived in North America expecting the Mediterranean—after all, the new colonies were at roughly the same latitude. Perhaps thinking they could build this temperate region and defy meteorology, they cut down trees and fashioned their settlements. In the process, they removed the plants capable of processing spring runoff. What they were left with was a climate not only cold, but now muddy, too.

If Montgomery is right, then maybe we really have domesticated mud season through our own actions. And though it might seem something of an ecological stretch, I'd go so far as to suggest that mud season and dogs have a great deal in common. Our transition to fixed, agrarian societies ultimately created both. Mud exists because we tilled the land, set up houses and barns, established roads and dumps. We have domestic dogs for many of the same reasons. Of course, we didn't plan on a mud season—and we certainly didn't willingly encourage it. But some historians say the same thing about early dogs. And both have flourished—at least in volume—during the development of our civilization. The real difference, it would seem, concerns the values we have assigned both.

As a collective culture, we have chosen to embrace the inconveniences of rearing and cohabitating with dogs. We tell ourselves that we enjoy setting our schedules to the whims of their play cycles and digestive tracts; we budget out money and time for their recreation. And we do it all with a smile, certain that we're better off for the experience. Not so with mud season. We grumble and curse and create colorful epithets to express our displeasure over the goo our development has created. If mud even deserves a place on the tea cake that is our current Great Chain of Being, it's surely a very low one.

But Potter has a point: These are anthropomorphic responses to mud. His salamanders and tree frogs really do seem to benefit from this unsightly season. Ari's species, of course, does not depend upon a vernal pool in any way, shape, or form. But she certainly benefits from it where recreation is concerned. She has come to believe that her pleasure depends upon her ability to make her way through each puddle, either porpoising through haunch-deep muck or swimming a smart little doggy paddle.

I know that all dogs are programmed to swim instinctually, but I somehow believed there would need to be an introductory period before Ari took to the sport. Not at all. Her little body floats with ease, and on cue her chubby legs churn circular strokes the minute she encounters water deeper than her shoulder. The only thing that needs work is facial posture: For reasons unknown, she insists upon drinking whenever paddling. What results is my own little fairy-tale chimera: half bear cub, half alligator. She gapes her jaw wide with each stroke, continuously swallowing gulps of water and muck. By the time we return to the car, her little belly has become Buddha-like in its distension. She is undeniably adorable, and I find myself quietly encouraging the behavior, despite my sustained dislike for the season.

Back at home, we take extra bathroom breaks outside to compensate for all the hydration. Still, Greg and I begin finding a resurgence of wet spots on the living room carpet. She's sneaky, this little dog, and knows better than to pee inside when we humans are paying attention. The minute our focus is averted, however, all is fair in her moral code. And since she seems capable of teleporting herself into the living room while the bipeds are momentarily unaware, there is little I can do to correct the behavior, other than up our visits outside even further. Which, to be honest, is fine by me.

After the past week or so, I'm ready to admit that I really enjoy the visits first to the vernal pool and then Ari's favorite bathroom spots in the yard. The appearance of a real spring is just too delicious to ignore, as is this giddy puppy. She is finding her place in the natural world, which is what I've always wanted. Even better, she's allowing me to come along for the ride—and it is becoming a pretty gleeful ride, even with the mud and the stink.

When Ari experiences unbridled joy, it's infectious in the best possible sense of the word. She grins widely, showing off her new grown-up teeth. She zooms back and forth between found object and adoring human. If I don't make the connection soon enough, she takes my hand in her mouth and tugs me over to the puddle or the leaf or whatever else she finds. I can't help but love that. I even laugh occasionally at her clotted coat and sooty paws. I still don't want to be *in* mud, but I find myself increasingly tolerant about being *around* it. And so we walk and paddle and gape our way through the first half of the month, not caring nearly so much that we—like most of the house—are encased in messy swaths of stinking, industrial-grade clay.

By the end of May, we are two months into our naturalism project. I'm still no expert on doggy values, but I feel prepared to draft a preliminary caninaturalist manifesto based on our time in the woods.

The finished policy reads as follows:

1. Never go around anything you can jump over or wiggle under.
2. Noxious materials exist to be felt and experienced firsthand.
3. To that end, any surface becomes positively embellished when caked in ooze.
4. All creatures exist solely for our amusement.
5. Everything—and I mean *everything*—is edible.

I feel confident in asserting these conventions because they so clearly dictate Ari's behavior in the woods. She now derives great delight from scooching under logs and splashing through puddles; if there happens to be an animal living in that log or puddle, that's considered an absolute windfall for the pup. For my part, I'm doing better with the wiggling and squelching—and I'm even mostly amused by both, provided a hot shower awaits shortly after.

Still, the last of these canine rules has me concerned. As the snow disappears from even the shadowiest places, two seasons of potentially edible treasures have emerged. Each walk, Ari returns from a brief foray into the brush with a new example of what lies just beyond the trail. A few days ago, it was an entire piece of breakfast pizza: an enormous, congealed palimpsest of dough, eggs, cheese, and sausage left by a winter hunter. It's a useful reminder for me that this land is far from pure wilderness. For Ari, it's pure heaven.

In the case of the slice of pizza, she worked diligently to free it from the underbrush, then sidestepped wildly with this forest booty—which was considerably bigger than her head. She walked awkwardly, trying to balance her small frame against the huge slice, and then tripped over its dragging tip. As she did, her little back legs splayed out, causing her to roll to a stop only after she was well out of reach of the pizza. I snatched up the slice and tossed it, Frisbee-like, into the woods, then promptly attached the puppy to her leash so that she couldn't go off in pursuit. It took hours for her to forgive me. And in that time, I think she might have been plotting new tactics for maintaining her forest booty. If so, the strategizing seems to have worked.

On our walk yesterday, Ari remained out of sight longer than normal. I began to worry, calling her name and fearing that she had either gotten lost or into trouble. Luckily, she is a good student in school and mostly understands recall. At the sound of her name, she bounded out of the woods, dragging along with her an entire leg of a white-tailed deer. This treasure—which spanned from thigh bone to hoof—measured nearly three feet long and was massive by puppy standards.

Ari beamed with her find. *Look!* she seemed to say. *Look at this thing!! We can eat off it for a whole week and never get hungry again!!!*

I wanted to appreciate her enthusiasm and the thoughtfulness behind her desire to share. Still, I found it impossible to overcome my very human response to this festering limb: *yuck*. It may not have been a medieval plague victim on a corpse cart, but this leg certainly headlined my list of undesirable dinner options. I once again pulled rank and disobeyed my primary directive: Today, *I* get to dictate our time in the woods. And that time will most certainly not include a rotten deer leg.

Ari seemed both perplexed and offended when I demanded that she let it go. As Don Hanson explained to me during our first meeting, dogs are opportunists. If they see food, they need to eat it. Now. Leaving behind as big a find as this isn't just poor form, it could be tantamount to suicide under extreme conditions. Ari's hardwiring wasn't about to let that happen. I knew this. But my disdain for decomposing deer parts wasn't about to let her bring it with us. So I resorted to the theory that socialization trumps all else. I did my best to look disapproving. This was not all that difficult, since the deer leg looked like a prop from a zombie movie, and I was more than leery of getting anywhere near it.

Ari hesitated slightly when she saw the frown on my face: hadn't she just brought a delightful treat for us to share? I disagreed. She raised an eyebrow and looked hurt, almost. Still, I refused to be wooed by the puzzled expression and fetching blue eyes. "No, Ari," I said firmly. "No." As I repeated myself, I moved slightly toward her, forgetting her mastery of my body language. The combination of the word *no* plus my forward movement had already resulted in confiscated breakfast pizza; Ari wasn't about to make the same mistake twice. As I continued toward her, she bolted, trailing the deer leg awkwardly behind.

She didn't go far, but she created enough distance between us to ensure I wasn't going to rob her of her deer leg. I stopped and sighed. As I did, she stopped as well, eyeing me over the enormous leg, which still hung comically from both sides of her jaw. I tried taking another step forward, but she could read my expression and knew that I was not about to revel in this ghastly treasure. She bolted again. On and on we went until, finally, the brittle joints of the deer leg gave way and crumbled into three separate parts. We both stared at the leg, wondering what would happen next.

In a tactical error, Ari made her choice and reached for the hoof, which lay detached from the rest of the leg. In spite of myself, I felt smugly delighted: By my standards, this was the least offensive part of the leg; by dog standards, it was undoubtedly the least useful—or pleasurable. One hundred yards later, I found it resting unceremoniously on the trail, forgotten. For the rest of the afternoon, Ari pretended not to see me gloat. That did not lessen my pleasure.

Still, any victory of my moral code over hers is not so easy when it comes to Ari's favorite natural delight: red fox scat. With the newly receded snow, it's everywhere and utterly distinctive—about two inches long and roughly the diameter of a Magic Marker with stringy, tapered ends. Ari absolutely *lives* for this scat. She also has a preternatural ability to ferret out the slimy excrement from every mound of leaves and drooping bough of pine. Each time, she gobbles it up eagerly before I can tug her away. I'm appalled she deems this a delicacy, and I tell her that this is one of multiple reasons why we should never have a kissing relationship.

All joking aside, though, I worry about the puppy. Although she's fleshed out some since we adopted her, she still seems frail to me. What's more, she has suffered occasional bouts of diarrhea from the moment we brought her home. When Greg and I return home one night to find the puppy and her crate streaked with liquid feces, we are devastated. I gently coax the pup out of her soiled crate and dab her with the softest towel I can find. I promise her this will never happen again—that we took her away from that ramshackle shelter so she would never have to spend another day like that. Her eyes seem to look right through me, and she retreats to the corner of the room where she spends the rest of the night, looking very small. The next day, I cancel my morning classes so that we can go to the vet.

For most animals, such a visit would be another moment of trauma. But not this pup. Ari *loves* the vet's office—almost as much as she loves scat. There, countless humans so dote upon her with biscuits and sweet nothings she never notices she has been weighed, inoculated, or probed. On this particular day, the puppy wags her whole body with delight when we enter the clinic. When the receptionist strokes her chin, Ari pees on the floor. I am embarrassed. She, on the other hand, is oblivious and deliriously happy.

We are soon greeted by Dr. Erin Rutherford, who begins our appointment with basic questions about our home life—diet, sleeping arrangements, training, that sort of thing. She is delighted to hear that we have begun a positive reinforcement training program at Green Acres, and she gives me a book on the subject. "Dog training has changed dramatically in the past ten years," she tells me. "Positive reinforcement is definitely the way to go. Good for you for enrolling."

Ari and I beam with the praise. But when Dr. Rutherford and I walk the pup over to the scale, we're both disappointed to see that she weighs in at just over thirty pounds—only two pounds more than she weighed in April. From what we know of her parents, the pup ought to be much bigger than this by now. I tell Dr. Rutherford I'm concerned Ari isn't absorbing enough nutrients and calories. I admit my suspicion that Ari's woodland snacks are to blame for the underlying condition, but I also worry this might be the sign of a more serious illness.

"It probably is just the scat," says Dr. Rutherford. "For a lot of dogs, it's a delicacy. And not just fox excrement: dog poop, litter box bits, horse manure—you name it, they'll eat it."

I turn up my nose. "Why?"

Dr. Rutherford tells me that no one is entirely certain. "Mother dogs will do it sometimes as an instinctual way to keep the location of their litter secret. Some researchers think that puppies just acquire it as a learned trait. Other people think dogs find the taste appealing. The scent is definitely likely to catch their attention. And as for fox, they eat a lot of rodents and carrion. I'm sure their scat has a vivid bouquet."

Plenty of animals—both dog and otherwise—seem to agree about the appeal of fecal bouquet. As far as they're concerned, such stink signals one very tasty blue plate special. Termed "coprophagy," this preference for scat has a food pyramid all its own and based on the nutrients within certain feces. Historically, humans used this to their advantage: Why go to all the trouble of digging a latrine if Spotoclus is willing to dig in for his evening meal? At least a few human societies still make ready use of the tendency—either by wiping soiled hands on the coats of dogs or allowing puppies to, as Raymond Coppinger puts it, "substitute for baby wipes."

Aside from the ick factor, this relationship appears to be a good example of mutualism—a symbiotic relationship in which both parties benefit. The problem, according to Dr. Rutherford, is the other organisms involved. In addition to some nutrients, scat often contains microbes and parasites that also go undigested. Quite a few of them can be fatal to both dogs and humans. Over time, humans have created cultural taboos to help keep us away from these nasty little bugs. But dog society has made no such provision.

"That's why we tell our clients that it's always best to keep their dogs on a leash short enough that they can avoid such temptation," she suggests gently.

I chew on my lip: I want my dog to be healthy, but I also want her free to investigate and frolic.

"That's a choice you'll have to make," Dr. Rutherford concedes. "In the meantime, we can give you some anti-parasitic medication. Heartworm tablets can also help with some of the bugs. That'll probably solve the problem."

But when I hand Dr. Rutherford the bag containing Ari's stool sample, she frowns.

"This has an awful lot of mucus in it to be a parasite," she observes. "I'd like to run some tests. Why don't you wait in the waiting room. It won't take long."

I don't like the concerned tone in her voice.

Fifteen anxious minutes later, the veterinarian returns—verdict in hand. The final analysis of my baggie reveals that Ari is suffering not only from a parasite, but also from ulcerative colitis, a severe inflammation of the large intestine that creates ulcer-like sores.

"We see this a lot in shelter dogs," says Dr. Rutherford. "Especially young ones. Was she under a lot of stress there?"

I think back to the pound's rank pens and constant noise. "Without a doubt," I say.

This response seems to confirm her diagnosis. She gives me an encouraging pat. "Most of the time this condition heals itself on its own—once dogs are able to relax in a stable environment."

Before we leave, Dr. Rutherford asks if I have any other concerns. I tell her about the way Ari's hind legs seem to slip out from under her when she runs. I know that huskies are prone to hip dysplasia, and I'm worried that this might be an early symptom. Dr. Rutherford feels Ari's hips, rotating them in their sockets and checking her extension.

"They seem fine to me," she says. "Maybe just a little underdeveloped. That's also common with shelter dogs. I'm sure she'll build up the strength in time. Let me know if they don't improve. We can do a more formal evaluation then."

We thank her for her time and head to the car. The last two diagnoses have made me simultaneously furious and protectively tender. I'm angry about the mistreatment this innocent dog has already endured: the din and dirt of the shelter, a lack of mobility from spending her first three months in a cage, an evening in a soiled crate. I worry she is not well served by what I think are the benefits of domestic life.

And maybe she's not. As much as we would like to believe we are in a mutually beneficial relationship or even one that benefits the canine species, many scholars speculate that we actually do a fair amount of harm. Whether through neglect and abuse, or even just through the controlled reproduction of breeds, we not only compromise dogs' evolutionary development but also create situations in which they can be hurt or even killed—all because of our sense of value. We damage the biological success of dogs by molding their evolutionary patterns into our lifestyles: We breed dogs for our chosen temperaments; we prize attributes that compromise a dog's ability to exist independent of us; we try to ignore or extinguish instinctual traits when they're not convenient for us. All of these things end up hurting the biological advancement of the canine species. For the most part, we humans don't mean to do so—we just don't see things from a dog's point of view.

This fact makes me wonder about the effect of Ari's new life with us. I spend our car ride home in deep contemplation as I puzzle out what our relationship means. Is domesticity the best thing for her? And what about our caninaturalism?

Woozy from her inoculations and the car ride, Ari lies on the seat next to me, resting her chin on my lap and quivering from time to time. I keep my hand on her shoulder throughout the drive home, experiencing my own discomfort. We adopted this dog because we wanted to give her a good life, and I feel now more than ever that I have somehow shirked this duty. I tell her I'll do my best to make it up to her. In return, she licks my hand hopefully.

The Ties That Bind

[june]

"You two are DINKs," my friend Andrea says to Greg and me. We are lounging in their side yard, enjoying some early summer sun with her husband, Chris, and their dog, Bentley. It's a gorgeous afternoon—just enough warmth to sit outside without a coat, but not enough to kickstart the biting insect season.

Andrea's comment rouses me from meteorological reverie. I raise an eyebrow. Have I just been insulted?

"Dual-Income-No-Kids," she explains, smiling. "DINKs."

I'm still wondering if my feelings should be hurt. Greg and I love kids—we just have chosen not to have any of our own. Between environmental concerns and deliberately hectic schedules, children don't fit into our life's plan. We're at an age where that tends to draw criticism from others, and I gird up for some now.

"Relax," Andrea laughs, casting a weary glance toward a pile of soccer cleats, ballet leotards, and iPods—all clearly visible inside the house and left by her three teenage daughters. "It's a compliment. You're adults who are still fun to hang out with. It means you still have time to play."

In the dog world, it also means that we are a very small, very insular family. That's fine by us, but I sometimes wonder what that means for our developing canine naturalist. After all, if Ari were a wolf, she would probably travel in a pack of at least five members—and possibly as many as twenty. Even the far more solitary coyote, who spends much of the year traveling alone or in a single pair, tends to pack up in groups of six or seven for hunting purposes.

Of course, Ari is neither of these animals. Yet the impulse to hang out with other dogs continues in her. Having mostly recovered from her colitis and parasitic infection, she is more exuberant than ever. Each time we visit Green Acres, we are reminded that this puppy is nothing short of a gadfly. She may not need a group of other canines to help her secure food, but she seems to require plenty of social interaction.

That's part of what has brought us to Andrea and Chris's house today. As much as we humans enjoy one another's company, it's dog social time I'm really after. So while the bipeds chat about summer movies, the canines get down to the business of friendship building. Bentley is an interesting candidate. He's a peculiar mix of basset hound and terrier who looks like a full-sized Benji with a severe case of allergies and legs amputated at the knee. But as far as Ari is concerned, he's perfect.

They begin to play at once. Although Ari is already a bit taller than Bentley, he is more than twice her length and weight—a real freight train of a dog. He uses this to his advantage, relying on his low center of gravity to fend off the springing puppy and occasionally knock her off balance. Ari loves the attention and somersaults around the yard each time he nears. She then rights herself and alternates between attacking Bentley's rump and his front end. I can understand the confusion—they're far enough apart that they may as well be separate entities.

"We washed Bentley today," Chris says, looking on and smirking. "I took the back end, Andrea took the front, and our hands never met."

Bentley, oblivious to his unique physique, is instead working hard to undo the bath. He capers with Ari around the perimeter of the yard, wrestling with the pup on the pale grass and rolling in dust with pleasure. After an hour or so, both dogs are blissfully exhausted and lie panting—their bellies stretched long to absorb the cool dampness of the ground. It's lovely to see Ari so tired and content. On the way home, she curls up in the backseat and falls right to sleep.

Here is another canine lesson I have learned: If Ari had her way, our lives together would be one long orgy of canine group time—nothing but wriggling, romping, barking dogs. This makes perfect sense, given her upbringing. Both domestic dogs and their wolfie kin establish baseline social behaviors between five and twelve weeks of age. During this time, they'll decide who they want to be with and in what context. Around ten weeks of age, most wolf pups learn that hanging out with extended family has some real benefits—and they'll continue to do so throughout their lives, eventually indoctrinating future generations in the practice.

Dogs aren't much different. In his landmark study *The Ecology of Stray Dogs,* Alan Beck reports that most feral dogs he observed tended to live in groups averaging about 2.46 members apiece. These social groups helped primarily when it came to securing food. Domestic dogs don't need to form hunting packs, but they do learn social behaviors and bond deeply with either humans or other animals. That bond is particularly powerful for primitive breeds like the husky, which is part of why they are so successful at pulling sleds—a truly group effort. It's true for other working breeds as well. Herding dog pups live almost exclusively with sheep during their socializing period; the sheep become the puppies' lifelong pack and, thus, well worth protecting.

These tendencies are why behaviorist Patricia McConnell stresses the importance of socializing all puppies before fifteen weeks. During this time, they also learn what to hunt or hug. Because Ari was born and raised at a shelter, she spent her socialization period around not only dogs but also cats, a few birds, and a homeless lizard. The effects are pretty clear. At our house, we like to joke that Ari has a *play* drive instead of a prey drive. She's never tried to harm a living creature, but she goes out of her way to frolic with them. Robins, goats, squirrels—especially squirrels—are all friends in the making, as far as she's concerned.

Of course, Greg and I are not much different. Like all primates, we humans crave social interaction. To that end, we like eye and body contact, verbal affirmation, and a sense of connection. Still, the way our two species go about actualizing these instincts can be very different. Greg and I can seek out social stimuli whenever we choose—whether we drive to Chris and Andrea's house or give our families a call. But Ari's life isn't set up that way. At our house, she mostly has two humans and a cat to choose from. I worry this makes her sad. It's still not clear how Ari views me and Greg—whether she buys into the whole pack hierarchy idea, or how she understands our relationship with her. She dotes upon us when we return home each day and loves to prompt games. She knows that we control her food source and that we are able to offer some protection. But are we her kin? That's hard to say for sure.

It's even more difficult to determine how Ari views our cat—though few living creatures would blame her for this uncertainty. Cam is what my friend René calls "special," as in *we're too polite to say she has behavioral problems.* Greg and I adopted Cam two weeks after we moved in together. She was just six weeks old, and our first few months with her were like a dreamy Hollywood romance. Visiting friends couldn't get enough of her, what with her gray and black stripes, her four white paws, her big green eyes. She was impossibly clever and undeniably sweet. But then, somewhere around her six-month birthday, Cam developed what, at the risk of anthropomorphism, can really only be described as a social anxiety disorder. She came to view anyone other than me, Greg, and Kinch as her mortal enemy. And she meant it. Instead of simply lashing out whenever someone tried to pet her, Cam sought out people, preemptively initiating acts of war. She tried to chase our favorite neighborhood toddler out of the house. She trapped Greg's mom in the bathroom. The list goes on and on.

Cam's problems have not tempered with age. Now six years old, she's bad enough that we have to lock her in the basement whenever company arrives, where she growls and cries and swipes from under the basement door in furious protest. To her credit, she has made exceptions for clan members. Cam and Kinch, for instance, had a kind of understanding that allowed for domestic armistice. After Kinch died, Cam seemed to spend a surprising amount of time looking for the beagle, and she seemed genuinely sad when she couldn't find him. We were relatively optimistic, then, that Cam would accept another dog in her life. When we set out to select one, the folks at the vet clinic suggested we adopt a puppy: A mature dog, they predicted, might retaliate against acts of tabby aggression. A puppy, on the other hand, would quickly learn to leave the cat alone.

The problem is that Ari and Cam clearly do not see the wisdom in this plan. Cam has found little in this exuberant puppy that reminds her of her grouchy old hound friend. And our hopes that a worst-case scenario might be Cam giving Ari a good swipe or two on the snout—thus teaching the pup to steer clear—have proven misplaced. Instead, the puppy seems to find Cam's aggression impossibly alluring. When Cam raises a paw to swipe, Ari interprets the act as an invitation to play. She responds by pouncing on the tabby, causing Cam to lash out and then scamper away. The puppy lumbers after her, delighted with the pursuit and an opportunity to seek out play-prey.

This does not sit well with Cam. After three months with the new canine addition, Cam has conceded that the usual display of hissing and swiping will not deter this dog. She surprises us all by surrendering and retreating into herself. In the past few weeks, she has become visibly morose and nervous, pulling out tufts of fur we later find on the bed and couch. We're left with a piebald tabby—mottled swatches of black and gray stripes interrupted by angry islands of pink skin. She looks terrible and is clearly distressed.

Greg and I both worry this might be a serious condition. We talk about our options, which are very few. Cam has a red flag on her file at the vet's office, signaling her fierceness. The vet techs wear falconer's gloves and fencing masks when they try to handle her. She, meanwhile, nearly goes into cardiac arrest from the stress of the visit. If she's sick now, will taking her into the clinic do more harm than good?

I call the vet's office and describe Cam's condition. Laurie, the office manager and a longtime vet tech, relays my report to Dr. Rutherford. The response is nearly instantaneous: We need to put Cam on Valium.

I am flabbergasted. "Is she serious?" I ask. "Is this like a feline mother's little helper?"

It's not clear whether or not Laurie gets the musical allusion. "Kind of," she says. "It'll help mellow her out."

I ask her to explain what, specifically, this means.

"Well," she says, "mostly Cam will just be really groggy all the time. She'll probably sleep most of the day. The rest of the time, she'll just be kind of . . . well, you know. Kind of . . . dreamy."

I tell her I need to think about this—that Greg and I want to discuss the ethics of antidepressants and our much-adored cat.

This seems to strike her as odd.

"Okay," she says reluctantly. "But we'll have the prescription all ready for her as soon as you want to pick it up."

I thank her and repeat that I'm not ready to take that step.

Over dinner, Greg and I discuss the prognosis. I tell him that I am torn: As Cam's primary caregiver, I feel an obligation to help her any way I can, but I am not comfortable with the idea of sedation. Though it seems a potentially inappropriate comparison, I remind him of my paternal grandmother. Born before psychology had achieved much sophistication, she suffered from bipolar disorder and schizophrenia—two diagnoses that were made far too late in her life to be of any good. Instead, she spent portions of her adulthood in hospitals enduring ice baths, electroshock therapy, and other misplaced treatments. When I knew her, she was on an exhaustive number of drugs including lithium and a host of other pharmacological heavy hitters. She functioned—and even retained a glimmer of her wit and humor—but mostly she moved through life in a haze. I always felt as if there were a substantial screen—reams of filmy fabric—that separated her from us.

I understand that pet cats and grandmothers are not the same thing. Still, I am wary of the effects of drugs. And I constantly return to the issue of ethics. What is more defensible: keeping another being sedated without approval, or doing nothing and prolonging the obvious mental discomfort of that being? Neither position sits well with me. So I try my best at another basic human response: denial. I tell myself that we're all just a little stir-crazy after the mud and rains last month. Maybe Cam's condition is just exacerbated by a kind of kitty seasonal affective disorder. If so, a little sunshine and fresh air are bound to make a difference. Until Mother Nature can provide these panaceas, I try to keep the two animals separated as much as possible.

Happily, this is relatively easy. We're still in that delightful meteorological limbo—late enough for a little summer sun, but too early for the deluge of mosquitoes and blackflies. It's a good time to be a dog. And since mine is starting to get her sea legs when it comes to the automobile, we begin spending more time out and about together—working on our socialization and trying to give Cam some quiet time.

The first Saturday of the month is temperate but gray. Ari and I drive into town for a trip to the local farmers' market and then my college campus for a woodland walk. We're already known at both places. I suppose that Greg and I stand out a bit in this community, where the median age is well over forty and our few contemporaries already have multiple children. Ari stands out, too, but more so because she is a real attention hound. At the market, she mugs for the crowd, spinning on the length of her leash and cocking her head as people coo over her dramatic eyes and soft fur. One farmer, who seems particularly taken with the pup, offers to sit with her while I finish my marketing. For a moment I worry we will be inconveniencing her, but her expression tells me this is as much favor to her as it is to me.

When I return a few minutes later, I find Ari sampling the farmer's wares. A masticated carrot and radish lay in pieces around the farmer's lawn chair, and a very contented puppy rests nearby, an early snowpea clutched between her paws.

"She likes them," says the farmer proudly, who then looks at the half-chewed vegetable smorgasbord strewn about. "The peas, I mean."

"She has good taste," I respond. "They're my favorite, too."

This compliment earns us a complimentary bag of peas for the road, which the pup and I share as soon as we return to the car. The pods are small and slender—the perfect size for both human and dog mouths. I dole them out for us as we drive up the hill toward campus—one for her, one for me. Ari grows impatient with this system, gobbling up her share quickly and trying to bury her snout in the bag. I don't know what these taste like to her, but to me they are pure summer: verdant, sweet, and light incarnate. Our weather may be lagging behind, but the vegetables know what's what.

Once we arrive at school, I stow the remaining peapods in my pocket and park at a gravel lot near the athletic fields and away from any traffic. Leash-free, Ari bounds from the car and cavorts across the soccer field, spinning figure-eights and other loose geometry on the shaggy field. She stops every few minutes to make sure I'm watching—partly for security, mostly because she wants an audience. She knows I am more than happy to oblige. After making eye contact, she intensifies her routine for both our amusement.

The sky hangs low and thick today, acquiescing only to the occasional rush of sea air from the nearby coast. This cloud cover makes the light flat, compressing hues and contrasts until they become nearly indistinguishable. The pup couldn't care less, and she continues her leaping and spinning around the field. But it does mean she's late to notice a swallow-like bird—the same color as our leaden sky—swoop down out of a large spruce tree to join in the fun. Fearlessly, the bird dives down within striking distance of Ari, then pulls up just out of reach. When Ari stops, puzzled, the bird circles back, completing first one, and then another flyby just above the pup's head. Ari's surprise soon turns into eagerness. *Is this a game?* she seems to ask.

Deciding that the next few minutes will be more fun if the answer is yes, Ari balances on her hind legs and paws at the air. The bird drops down just out of reach, then quickly rises in the air. As it does, it looks back at the pup, who is trying unsuccessfully to levitate. If birds could laugh, I'd swear this one was snickering. Forget about the bashfulness we assign much of the avian world—this is one brazen little bird.

While Ari leaps about with her new friend, I consult our tattered field guide, eventually identifying the visitor as a female purple martin. They are known in the birding world as among the most acrobatic of all swallows—and the most playful. I certainly see why after observing this one. She dips again, buzzing just past the upturned snout of the pup. Ari leaps higher; the martin zooms in, then executes a snapping roll. As she does, the pup bucks in the air, kicking out her hind feet like a donkey. The bird keeps her altitude low, cartwheeling through turnabouts and slips, then ascends high into the air, only to drop down again. Ari tries to do the same from the ground, though she's no match for the aerial prowess of this flying ace. Still, she gives it her best, staying close to the martin and following her about the field. She wants desperately to catch up, but the martin stays just out of reach. Eventually the caninaturalist stops, then looks at me.

It seems like only yesterday I was chasing Ari around our kitchen table, preparing for our first walk. Two months later, though, Ari is old enough to realize what I knew then: namely, it's no fun to play tag when you're always *it*. Her exuberance for the martin begins to fade. When it seems as if the pup has tired of the game entirely, the bird swoops in again—even closer this time—and spins mad, low-lying circles around the field, chattering back at the caninaturalist as she does. The increased boldness of the bird incites Ari, and she begins her chase again. Eventually, though, the pup looks frustrated. She's being taunted—and she knows it. This martin isn't about to let her catch up, let alone get the upper hand. Ari trots back to me and sits on her haunches. *Game over,* she seems to insist. The martin gives another few flybys, just in case. But the pup is firm: She's not having fun anymore, and she doesn't like being a plaything.

Once back inside the car, I gently try to suggest that this might be how Cam feels every day in our house. I ask if maybe Ari has learned something about what it might feel like to be a persecuted tabby. But she's not interested in my attempt at Old Testament parenting. In a huff, she hops up to her perch near the hatchback window, resting her nose between her front paws and sighing heavily. Even canine naturalists, it seems, have limits when it comes to enjoying nature.

By the second week of June, bug season has begun in earnest—alternating between mosquitoes in the cool evening and pernicious little blackflies during the heat of the day. As a result, Ari and I shift our long walks to early morning to avoid the worst of either pest. The recent warmth has brought out early maple and beech leaves—pale arrowheads with tidy edges and a will to grow. They blend with the thick morning sun, giving the impression that we are swimming through a bottle-green pond. I am lulled by the light and tempted to try an easy backstroke on the trail.

Ari is not so easily wooed. She has experienced firsthand the joys of actually paddling through these woods; drying muck must seem paltry by comparison. After a few forays into the diminished pools she seems to prefer the ease of a well-packed trail, where she is not burdened by the drag of evaporated goo. Still, she can't resist the prospect of a brushy detour to investigate a scent every few yards or so.

Each time she wanders off, I call her back to the trail. She responds by casting me a cavalier glance over one shoulder, then returns to the project at hand. I take this behavior as a declaration of independence. Ari is clearly becoming an adolescent—and just as temperamental as any teenager. On any given day, she oscillates between infantile play and adult sternness in an instant, though she still clearly prefers the former to the latter. She also has a newfound confidence when it comes to asserting herself on our walks. On days like today, even some of my most enthusiastic attempts at recall are met with a cool stare. What emanates from those steely blue eyes is nothing short of pure will.

At dog school, Joel warns that this developmental phase—although mercifully short—presents challenges to the dog-human relationship. Just like many human early adolescents, "tween" dogs like to test limits and boundaries. The prospect of pleasing adults becomes quickly replaced by the desire to assert their developing selves. Joel says this means that Ari will be inclined to ignore or resist otherwise learned commands like *come*.

"Now is definitely the time to be strategic outside," Joel cautions. "Shake up your routine to keep her guessing; otherwise, she'll anticipate patterns—and resist them."

I tell him I'll do my best.

And so, as we make our way through these forested walks, we engage in a strange version of Russian roulette. Every few minutes, I call her. It's a game of chance—and she knows it. Will she get a treat? Reattached to the leash? Both? Neither? The odds keep her guessing, and for now the gamble represents the best opportunity for a compromise. On leash, we share control—both choosing when to stop and explore. When not on the leash, this lanky adolescent may trot ahead, headstrong and sure, believing she is in charge of her own destiny.

Which, of course, she mostly is.

Late in the week, we step out for our early-morning walk. Ari insists upon loping a good twenty feet or so ahead of me, but she is considerate enough to look back periodically. The rest of the time she engages in idle investigation, burying her head in newly sprouted ferns and checking the atrophied vernal pools. This study has no clear focus—and why should it? We've almost reached summer vacation. The birds are singing, the sun is out, and we finally have time for proper recreating.

Suddenly, though, Ari's path becomes deliberate and accelerated. She's racing down the trail with positive focus—a dog on a mission. But what is it? I come up over the rise and catch sight of a long, narrow missile flying just out of her reach. Is it another martin? The pup and I seem to ask this question simultaneously. For her part, she's definitely forgotten that the last martin encounter ended in frustration. Today, she just wants to play: Her ears are up, as is her tail, and she bucks in the air, hoping to engage a new friend. This bird, however, hasn't heard of the new sport of dog taunting. It is not amused by her overtures and, instead, continues a beeline down the trail corridor.

The pup's pace slows only when the bird angles upward, a move that gives me enough of a look to see that it is a hairy woodpecker, complete with telltale red head patch. It continues upward, eventually perching on a hollow white pine trunk, where a few tiny gray heads pop out in boisterous greeting. I change my pronouns: *It* must be *she*, for she has just returned to her nest. Mom has an impressive bug bounty with her—perhaps a dragonfly or grasshopper. She sticks her head into the nest and then removes it quickly—once, twice, then a third time. After that, she pauses—perhaps to catch her breath, to reposition her bug store, or to give the little ones time to digest. They want nothing to do with this intermission, and two bold gray heads soon wiggle out of the hole, each attempting to snatch the remainder of the insect from the larger woodpecker. Mom relents—she knows a losing battle when she sees one.

Ari and I are both enthralled by this display of domesticity. As soon as we return home, I round up our bird books and devote myself to a long morning of woodpecker life histories. I want to know about this mother pecker and how she takes care of her own family. Never one for erudition, Ari takes a piece of kindling from the woodstove and commences a whittling project instead. Sensing that the pup is occupied—at least for now—Cam emerges from behind the sofa and agrees to help with my research. She curls up in my lap and purrs contentedly. With her shortened fur and newly exposed markings, she doesn't look so different from the woodpecker—just a lot less maternal.

As it turns out, my assessment of the woodpecker reveals a tremendous gender bias. I had assumed that the adult bird I saw was a female. Why? Because mammalian mothers are the primary feeders of their young? Because years of TV-watching instilled this pop-culture mythology deep in my psyche? I suppose either these reasons would make my assumption perfectly reasonable. But in this case, it was also perfectly wrong. In many woodpecker families—including the hairy—the male (who sports the characteristic red patch on his head) is the primary incubator of eggs. Once hatched, the young spend their evenings brooded by Dad while Mom sleeps in her own tree chamber nearby. And while she makes plenty of trips back and forth to feed the kids, these pale in comparison with those made by Dad, who takes up to ten flights an hour to keep the little ones fed. For all this trouble, Dad gets little thanks. His kids will howl vociferously at him as he departs, all the while sticking out their tongues menacingly and mostly behind his back. I try to imagine this display in human terms—a pack of toddlers biting their parents and making evil faces while their father tries to pour another bowl of Cheerios. It's a pretty disturbing picture.

Luckily for them, adult hairies are remarkably adroit at food gathering, and this efficient homesteading affords them a life of luxury and recreation not often seen in the animal kingdom. Ornithologists repeatedly point out the birds' propensity for lying in—waking much later than other feathered creatures, and often lounging about the tree cavity or sunning themselves lazily on a branch before even thinking about breakfast. Like martins, they are also known for their great love of play—drumming just for the musicality of it all, inciting chases with other birds, tossing up clumps of grass and catching them, and generally acting like nature's trustafarians.

I love these tendencies in the woodpecker. And so, armed with new insight on the avian world, Ari and I return to the woods in search of the easygoing birds. For three days we visit the white pine tree, hoping to catch another glimpse of a busy dad. We try different times of day, braving the cloud of mosquitoes that take turns at my bare arms and legs, then Ari's thick coat. We stick it out as long as the buzzing and biting will allow. But with no dad in sight, the nestlings scream from within their tree trunks and refuse to emerge. Ari quickly bores and grows restless, preferring to paw at decaying branches nearby, sending them up in satisfying sprays of mulch-sized pieces.

I'm equally as twitchy, having gained a dozen or so red welts from the mosquito cloud. So we continue on, widening our loop in hopes of seeing a hairy parent. Still no luck.

But now that we know what to listen for, we begin to find broods everywhere in the forest. In one afternoon alone we find four—all with perfectly round entrances and unrelenting cheeps. At the last trunk, Ari endures the racket for a minute or two, but even she seems agitated. She flattens her now tall ears against her head and gives the tree trunk a corrective, scolding bark. When that does nothing to pacify the infants inside, she turns her back and trots dismissively down the trail. I follow, wondering if Ari is quietly commiserating with woodpecker parents across the globe.

Being a parent is hard—whether it's in the woods of North America, on the coast of the Galapagos, or in any number of human locales. I say that, of course, with absolutely no firsthand knowledge. Still, after talking with Andrea and watching these woodland creatures, I feel prepared to make that judgment vicariously. Ari doesn't have firsthand knowledge, either, and that's how it's going to stay. Just shy of six months old, the pup is on the cusp of sexual maturity. Although her bones will not fuse for another year, Ari is nearly full grown at forty pounds. This is half the size we had imagined she would be, and she still doesn't even get close to filling out her extra-large bed and house. Still, her growing willfulness and desire to distance herself from us outdoors is a sign that she might be approaching her first estrus period. Time to act. The idea of her in a torrid love affair is not at all appealing, nor is the fact that dogs who go through a reproductive cycle are more likely to contract mammarian cancer. I contact the vet's office yet again, this time to set up an appointment for Ari's hysterectomy.

When I call, I expect them to schedule the appointment a few weeks away—long enough for us to get comfortable with the idea. But Laurie tells me they have an opening two days later and urges me to take it. I reluctantly agree and am given a list of instructions for the next forty-eight hours: light meals beginning today, no food the day before, no water beginning at midnight. Any disregard of these rules, Laurie warns, may result in complications during the surgery.

She runs down a list of precautionary questions.

"Is Ari allergic to anesthesia? Does she have any ill effects with it?"

I tell her I have no idea—Ari's just a healthy kid; we've had no cause to sedate her.

"You understand that there are serious risks involved whenever an animal is anesthetized," she warns. "Some never wake up."

This is not what I want to hear. We have no choice but to spay Ari. We can only hope that she will be fine.

The night before her surgery, the three of us go for a late walk. For once, I feel no sense of urgency or lingering responsibilities back home. This will be our last caninaturalist outing for a while, and I want it to last as long as possible. I'm more worried about the pup than I let on. I want to do something momentous—just in case.

Electronic pulsing from the pond across our pine grove advertises that it's just the place for such an excursion. The spring peepers got off to a late start in May, so they're just now winding down with their nocturnal orgies. We walk to the neighborhood fire pond in search of these boisterous frogs. Even in this, the decline of their mating season, the sound is deafening—a single, piercing pitch out of the range of even a coloratura soprano. The din has a throb to it—one that reverberates in my inner ear, sending static all the way down my spine. How must it sound to this wolf-eared dog, already more attuned to volume and pitch? Greg and I take each other's hand. We have entered an alien landscape and need reminders of that which is familiar.

Donning headlamps, the two humans crouch at the edge of the pond, looking for amorous amphibians. We spy a crayfish and a single, skimming frog. Both glide just above the pond floor, making feathery kicks with each stroke. Ari wades in up to her belly and stares intently into the water. *What's in there?* None of us is sure. The water seems oily in its blackness, reflecting our light and shrouding the pond goings-on in secrecy. Meanwhile, the din of the frogs continues. It is more than deafening. Ari retreats from the water and hangs tight, leaning her shoulder against my leg.

"How many?" Greg asks. His voice is high and forced over the peeping. Still, it's hard to hear.

I ask him to repeat what he just said.

"How many? The frogs. How many of them do you think there are?"

I look up, casting my headlamp into the trees, as if this narrow beam of light might reveal the masses. It doesn't.

"I don't know," I say. "A hundred? Or maybe just a few dozen *really* loud frogs singing in symphony?"

Try as we might, the three of us cannot find more than that one peeper. We duck and weave our way through the brush, peering into cattails and stands of trees. I am aware that this behavior is highly peculiar—and very much unlike me. It feels exhilarating, though, and I'm proud of us for making the trip if for no other reason than because it is an utterly uncharacteristic thing for me to do. Ari, on the other hand, remains alert and guarded—uncertain why we're out at night and what is causing this amazing din. She continues to stick close by, venturing only a few steps into the pool before once again attaching herself to my side. If this was to be a celebratory walk in her honor, I'm pretty certain it's not having the intended effect. She seems relieved when we circle back to the dirt road.

On our way back home, Greg and I crouch beside one of the last remaining vernal pools—nothing more than a residual puddle, really. There, illuminated by our two headlamp beams, rest hundreds of little gelatinous orbs. Roughly the size of a small marble, they are nearly transparent, save for a telltale black dot in the middle of each. Many rest singularly, although we also find much larger, brain-like masses. These are salamander and tree frog eggs, laid to incubate in this joint nursery while their parents return to upland woods and await their delivery. We are impressed, and at least two of us are glad for the nocturnal mission.

The three of us return to our own woodland house. Once inside, Ari stands impatiently while I remove her leash, then she trots to the kitchen, awaiting her evening biscuit. We're too close to her surgery time for a snack, so I shake my head. She looks confused. When the biscuit tin remains closed, she cycles through the tricks she has learned at school: sit, shake, lie down, bow. Still nothing. She sighs—either frustrated with me or wondering why she is being punished—and makes her way slowly upstairs to bed. A few minutes later, her guilty owner settles in as well.

Swaddled in sweatpants and flannel sheets, I read about the reproductive practices of amphibians out in their cold liquid beds. It seems a harsh place for coupling, and studying them makes me feel very much a sexual voyeur. I can't help it, though: Amphibian sex is outrageously interesting. Frogs, for instance, mate through a practice known as *amplexus*, which translates from Latin as "to braid." Poetic as that sounds, the reality of their courtship lacks lyricism—let alone romance. From the time they thaw, peepers rush the mating ritual. They're the first to arrive at the pond—often showing up too early and turning into frogcicles on icy tree branches. Once established, males are so zealous in their attempt to jumpstart the process that groups of them will mob a single female, drowning her in the process. Most males have also developed large calluses on their thumbs that allow them to hold females more firmly. As a result, a pair of mating peepers will remain entwined for up to four hours—much of it underwater. While they are submerged, the female will lay anywhere between eight hundred and eighteen hundred eggs.

I finish reading this chapter on frog sex and look at the sleeping pup on her dog bed. "Be glad you're not a peeper," I whisper. She doesn't stir. Neither does Greg. I, on the other hand, cannot get to sleep. The sheer volume and endurance of the amphibian reproductive project overwhelms me, and I have a series of fitful dreams about plaited bodies and oozing piles of egg sacs overflowing ponds and pools.

The next morning, we all arise out of sorts. Ari is hungry and anxious; I remain distracted by amphibian reproduction; Greg claims he was repeatedly awakened by a wife executing frog kicks in her sleep; Cam does her usual glowering between pulling tufts of hair. We make a miserable household and try our best to stay out of one another's way. Ari and I need to be at the vet's office by eight o'clock for her check-in, so we have little time for anything other than a quick walk. Once back inside, she hovers by the spot where her food and water dishes are usually located, wondering what has prompted this continued ban on food. I give her my best look of empathy and a few long strokes down her back.

Greg and I are both fretting. Ari doesn't know what's ahead of her, other than another day with no food and two unexpectedly nervous humans who keep hugging her and telling her to be strong. By the time I go to leash her up for the car ride, she seems leery of us. Greg can tell I'm apprehensive, too, and he gives me a big hug before we leave.

"Call me at work," he says, "as soon as you hear anything."

I smile, feigning stoicism, and head out the door.

At the vet's office, they've seen too many tearful, overwrought good-byes to allow for much ceremony. Instead, a new vet tech takes Ari's leash from me and ushers her back into the hidden part of the clinic. I remain at the front desk, where I ask nervously about their schedule.

"We're doing three or four of these procedures today," Laurie says. "I think Ari's in the middle. She should be awake by three. You're welcome to call."

Later that morning, I nod my head thoughtfully as students share their perspectives on Robert Frost. I do not hear a single word they say. Instead, I am trying to imagine Ari's surgery preparation and hoping she is not terrified. After my last class, I race home, forgetting that there is no need for a bathroom break in the yard. Instead, I sit on the kitchen table, staring alternately at the nearby phone and my watch. 2:38. 2:45. 2:49. Time has never moved so slowly. Cam circles my legs, confirming that the coast is clear. I give her a tight hug—too tight. She protests and wiggles out of my grip.

At 2:52, I phone the vet.

"I'm calling about Ari," I say as soon as Laurie answers. "How is she?"

"She's *fine*. No trouble at all. Just a little groggy."

"Really?" I want more reassurance.

"Of course. And she's a doll. She was wagging her tail before she was even fully out of the anesthesia. Everyone thinks she's a real sweetheart."

Laurie repeats what I have already committed to memory: They will keep her overnight to confirm that there are no ill effects from the medication or the surgery itself. They also need to make sure she does not pull at her stitches, which could still cause her to bleed to death. And of course, she needs to rest—she is going to be very sore.

Driving over the next day, I become impatient at red lights and drivers observing speed limits. Once at the office, I take my place in the small line of people there to collect their recovering pets. When it's my turn, the vet tech grins.

"Ari?"

I nod.

"She's a little ornery sometimes, isn't she?"

I nod even more enthusiastically. "Why?"

"She's been trying all day to remove her stitches. We had to put on a restraining device. Don't worry—she'll just have to wear it for a day or two. And we added some surgical glue, too. That should make it harder for her to yank them out."

She goes back to retrieve my dog. When they emerge, Ari seems miserable—a space-age cone has been tied around her neck with an Ace bandage. She looks like Astro Jetson. Even worse, she's lost all sense of physical perspective and promptly bangs the cone into the doorjamb. This causes her to stop in her tracks and sigh dramatically, lowering her head until the cone thuds against the linoleum, which prompts yet another sigh. Her technician politely pretends not to notice the tragicomedy of the scene, and I get the sense this has happened repeatedly on the short walk from the kennels to the reception area.

"Oh, pup," I say. "You poor thing."

She sighs yet again. The technician hides a giggle.

Before Ari can be released, I receive our post-op instructions. We are told to limit her activity and keep her incision clean for a week. I raise my eyebrows at the improbability of either. *Are they serious? Keep this dog away from muck and vigorous exercise?*

"I know," Laurie says. "It's going to be hard with this one. Just do your best."

We struggle our way out the office door and meet our first real challenge at my tiny hatchback car. When Ari tries to step in, she catches the bottom of the cone on the driver's seat. When I try to lift her up, we bang it against the roof. A few more tries are equally unsuccessful. Eventually, by cradling her in my arms, I am able to load her like a missile into a payload. We begin our drive home. At each stoplight, people in adjacent cars point and chuckle at my space-age dog. For once, she does not enjoy the attention.

Back home, I call Greg to inform him about the extraterrestrial presence in our house.

"Oh, no," he laughs. "Poor puppy. Is she embarrassed?"

"Wouldn't you be?"

By the time he returns two hours later, Ari has not only removed the cone but hidden it as well. Greg finds me on my hands and knees, trying to fish it out from behind the couch. A groggy but nonetheless triumphant dog looks on from across the room. Using a broomstick, I am eventually able to slide the cone and bandage back out from the couch. Greg tries to reattach it, but the pup scampers away. We are faced with a choice: run the risk of inciting vigorous activity by trying to reattach the cone, or take a chance that Ari can't bite through the surgical glue.

We opt for the latter, though we make a point of checking on her every hour that night. When I visit during the wee hours of the morning, I find the pup quiet and subdued. She curls alongside my leg, resting a paw on my hand much like she did as a young puppy. It's painful to look at her shaved belly. The incision is bright pink—an angry worm running down her abdomen. She has also been tattooed—a circle and descending cross, the international symbol for woman. Through the circle is a thick X. Semiotic translation? Once a female, but no more. Over breakfast later that morning, I begin theorizing about gender definitions in contemporary culture. Greg rolls his eyes and, instead, makes jokes about the thick ink, calling Ari a biker chick.

During the spring months, we don't get much company: We're usually too busy working to see friends, and our out-of-state relatives know better than to visit during winter or mud season. Once summer arrives, however, we become a very popular destination spot. This year, our first visitor is my mom. She fell and broke her ankle earlier in the year, causing her to miss a girls' trip to Florida with several of her friends. To make it up to herself, she's decided to visit us while my dad travels on business. Over the phone, we make plans for her visit. I remind her that we are hemmed in by Ari's bladder schedule and will need to plan any day trip accordingly. I can tell my mother doesn't care for this restriction.

"It's a *dog,* Kate," she says.

"*She's* not an 'it,'" I correct. "And she's much more than just a dog. You'll see."

"Umm."

"You're going to love each other," I say hopefully. "Besides, you two have lots in common. You can compare hysterectomy scars."

Her silence speaks volumes.

I'm curious about how Mom's trip will change dynamics. She represents the first addition to our pack since the pup arrived, and I wonder if it will change Ari's behavior. It's certainly going to change our approach to naturalism. My mother prefers her nature served up on a sidewalk or incorporated into a picnic somewhere. Crawling around ponds in the dark or sniffing moss isn't really her thing. Up until now, it hasn't really been mine either, and I wonder how she'll interpret the change. I steel myself for critique. Greg, remembering the sniping that accompanied earlier visits, lays low with the recovering pup.

In advance of Mom's arrival, my dad sends a grainy photograph: my paternal grandfather and one of my great-uncles on Christmas Day 1938. The two boys are standing side by side, dressed in wool caps and pants, striped shirts, and thin, hooded coats that zip in the front. They are standing before a weathered barn; each holds in front of him a dog standing on its hind legs. The boys are hooligans—that much is clear from their jaunty poses and mischievous smiles. The two canines are narrow and lanky, indiscriminate farm dogs—perhaps part Lab, part hound, maybe a little shepherd. Held by their front paws as one might hold a small child, the dogs look part human—satyrs from a bygone era.

The image charms and surprises me. I call my dad.

"What do you know about these dogs?"

"Not much. I know your grandpa used to throw corncobs at a goat."

"Was he mean to dogs, too?"

"He liked dogs. We had a dog."

This surprises me even more. Between my grandmother's illnesses and my grandfather's seeming pragmatism, I never picked them as pet people. "Growing up, you had a dog?"

"Blackie. He was the family dog. We used to wrestle."

"What kind of a dog? How did you find him?"

"I don't know. A collie mix maybe? He was black with long, shaggy hair. He wasn't real tall. I was eight or nine when he got him."

"When who got him?"

"Dad."

"Grandpa?" I ask, as if my father might have had more than one patriarch in his life.

Dad laughs at my disbelief. "He was working at a gas station. The dog showed up and hung around for a couple of days. He seemed friendly, so your grandpa started feeding him his lunch scraps every day. Eventually, Blackie just came home with him."

"And?"

"And that's pretty much it. We'd go play together in the woods behind the house."

I ask him to put Mom on the phone.

"My turn?" she asks warily. They have grown accustomed to unexpected interrogations that eventually make their way into print.

"Did you know Dad had a dog?"

"Of course. I did, too, you know."

"But Dad's dog. Did you meet him? Was he still alive when you started dating?"

"No." There is a pregnant pause. "I think your grandfather accidentally ran him over."

"Oh."

I grow silent. My father made no mention of this. I worry that I have upset him by broaching the subject.

My mom intuits this response. "It's been almost fifty years, sweetpea," she jokes. "I think he's recovered by now."

I'm not so sure, but I can tell the matter is closed as far as she is concerned. "Okay," I say. "Tell me about your dog, then."

"Mistakenly Mine," she says, her voice suddenly wistful. "We called her Misty. She was a gorgeous, pedigreed golden retriever. We bought her as a puppy, and friends from the club adopted her littermates. It was great fun. Misty was really *my* dog, and Mother sent us both to obedience school. She was very gentle and very smart."

"Grandmother? Or the dog?"

I hear an exasperated sigh.

She continues. "Of course, there were other animals at the house, too. Your aunt's dog Cricket used to appear in the society pages. We had Pixie and Dixie the cats, and MiMi and Folly, too. But everyone loved Misty. Your great-grandmother used to take her erranding. They'd come home in her Thunderbird, Misty sitting in the passenger seat, her fur flowing in the wind."

I hang up thinking about the breadth of these two stories—somehow, they seem to encompass so much about my parents' backgrounds. And it's clear that, no matter how different the tale, both of them adored their dogs.

Why, then, didn't we have a dog when I was growing up? I call back my folks to ask.

"Dogs limit your mobility," my dad says.

"We wanted to be mobile," my mom agrees.

"What on earth does that mean?" I ask. I am surprised by how petulant I sound. It's as if I have become an eleven-year-old all over again.

"You know what that means," says my mom. "We moved around for your dad's work. We like to sail and travel and take long vacations. Having a dog would have made that difficult."

They're right, of course. While I was growing up, my father was working his way up the corporate ladder, which meant we had lived in four states by the time I was fourteen. Besides, my brother and I never really wanted a dog. I pined for other critters and contented myself first with hamsters and toads, then with horseback-riding lessons and our family cat. Meanwhile, we did take all sorts of family vacations. They were fabulous, cluttered events filled with piles of tennis rackets and fishing poles, swimsuits and banana-seat bikes.

To my parents' credit, this is where my interest in naturalism first developed. Despite already rearing us in the pastoral heartland, they insisted on additional outdoors time each summer—weeks at camp, the family vacations, hikes in the nearby state park. There, they taught my brother and me to love nature. And they obviously love it, too. Even so, these excursions seem unlikely to me in hindsight, and I find it inconceivable that the current manifestations of my folks slept in cotton sleeping bags on the forest floor.

This is what I tell Greg in advance of Mom's arrival. I'm nervous, aware that these visits haven't always gone well.

"People change," he responds. "You have, right?" His lips are drawn tight—my complaining and fretting are wearing on him.

I grimace, returning to my task of scrubbing the kitchen floor with a toothbrush. It is an inexplicable act—my mother endured eighteen years of my clutter and will not be fooled. That only makes me more agitated. I look to Greg to give me a sense of balance, but he has come to appreciate the value of neutrality. He says my mother and I are burdened by history and an inability to see that we have both evolved. This makes him visibly uncomfortable. Still, when I ask him to cancel a scheduled kayaking trip to play intermediary, he agrees. For that, I am most grateful.

In my cleaning spree, I move on from the kitchen to the pets. The rotten-snake dog assesses the determined look on my face and disappears. It takes a well-marked trail of dried liver to get her into the tub. Even so, I can't find the toothbrush I used on the floor for the rest of the day, and I suspect she's buried it in the clutter now stashed underneath my bed, lest I decide to apply it to her.

Once the house and canine are prepped, I pick up Mom at the airport. Despite the wistful Mistakenly Mine stories, I know she's not much of a dog person. And so I arrive armed with a litany of instructions and helpful hints, all garnered from dog school.

"Remember to turn your back if Ari jumps up on you," I tell my mother. "Dogs are very sensitive to rejection. Always reward good behavior and ignore bad."

I reach behind the seat of the car, pulling out a small stack of artisan dog biscuits wrapped in a blueberry-print ribbon. I picked these out especially for her, thinking their craftsy appearance will appeal to her.

"Here," I say, "these are your own personal treats. You can give one to Ari whenever she does something good." I hand them to my disbelieving mother.

"Oh, please," she says. "You have got to be kidding me."

The earnest look on my face tells her I'm not. She sighs and puts the biscuits in her purse. She will do her best to cooperate. I vow to do the same.

From the minute we enter the house, Ari is obsessed with my mom. She breaks every rule she has learned, rising up on her hind legs to paw at my mom's waist, hopping onto the guest room bed, chewing one of Mom's books, and trying to steal food off of the dinner table—anything and everything to warrant notice. My mother tries her best to be patient, but I can tell she is displeased. I jettison my positive reinforcement project and begin scolding Ari, but it does little to abate her.

My mother will also not be censured. Over dinner, she regales us with stories of my high school classmates who are now having children. She does not attempt to veil the implication. I tell her that Greg and I are woodpeckers, not peepers. She looks at me as if I am insane and then gently explains that we are neither tree-clinging birds, nor reptiles. I remind her that peepers are amphibians not reptiles, and more importantly, we have much more in common than she might believe. My mom raises her eyebrow as if to say, *I birthed this creature? How is that possible?* My look asks the same. Meanwhile, Greg becomes focused on cutting his crab cakes into small, symmetrical cubes. We all finish our meal quickly.

As Greg and I wash dishes after dinner, a drawn voice—half resignation, half wariness—comes from the guest room.

"Hello?" my mom says, drawing out the second syllable long and demonstratively. "Hel-llloooooo?"

I go back to see what is the matter. There, I find mom trapped between her own Scylla and Charybdis. Ari lies curled up on the guest-bed pillows, play-growling and flashing her front teeth. *Let's wrestle,* this expression says. *We'll snarl and bite each other on the arm. It'll be fabulous!* Meanwhile, the half-naked Cam stands in the doorway, hissing with real aggression. My mother looks from one animal to the other and then asks me politely what she should do. We both laugh. This is an absurd place to spend one's vacation.

The next morning, Mom surprises me by offering to join me and Ari on a short stroll out in the town forest. She's trying to make up for the tension the previous night. I appreciate the gesture, and promise to show her some of the things we've learned. My canine sidekick is elated. Now healed from her hysterectomy, Ari wants some real romping time. I let her off leash so that she can release some of her excitement. Immediately, she races up and down the trail corridor, still eager to impress her new friend. As she executes some of her best swan dives into the remaining mud puddles, I watch my mom grimace, no doubt mentally transporting that mud back to our home. I tell her that's what dogs do. She responds by rolling her eyes at both of us. Ari remains oblivious and steps up her activity. She whizzes past us, turns on her back feet and returns, this time kicking up some thick gray water that lands on our pants. I hear a disapproving sigh. My mother is not pleased, and we all decide that perhaps this will be our first and last community walk.

When we return home, Mom makes a point of asking for laundry soap and soaking her slacks in the bathroom sink. She spends the rest of the morning flipping loudly through a magazine in her bedroom.

The rains return later that day, layering the area with low clouds and occasional drizzle. Greg retreats to his office at work; mother and daughter decide to head to the coast for some sightseeing and shopping. We're going to be gone longer than four hours—Ari's maximum bladder time—so we leave her tied to a long run next to the oversized dog house. Placed beside a large apple tree, it's the most idyllic place in the yard and was a favorite spot of Kinch's. Still, I am apprehensive about this decision. The few times Ari has been tied outside before, Greg and I were within earshot. She clearly didn't enjoy the experience, but then again she didn't get herself into any major trouble, either. We decide that she will be fine: She has food and water, an extra-large shelter, and the shade of a tree, should the rains end. Still, I cast a worried look at her as we pull out of the driveway, my heart breaking as I hear her yowl at us to come back.

"She's fine," my mom reassures me. I am not comforted.

An hour later, the two humans arrive in Camden, one of our favorite coastal towns. Despite the looming threat of more rain, we are here to practice avian indolence: dining out for lunch and collecting souvenirs for Mom to take back to friends. Over lunch, though, the conversation once again returns to lifestyle choices. She says she does not understand why Greg and I are opposed to raising a family. I remind her of our jobs, our interests, our ideologies. The last one rankles her—she thinks I am criticizing her choices. I clarify: We don't think the environment needs to sustain another human. There are more than enough already.

"So just have one child," she suggests. "Then you're not adding to the population. You're just replacing one of you. It's a zero-sum."

I remind her that this would be true only if the rest of the planet adhered to the same rule. "Besides," I say, "it's just not us. Being parents, I mean."

"Sometimes decisions are bigger than two people," she replies. "But I have always supported your decisions. I'm just sad for my own reasons."

I can see she is replaying her own life at my age. My maternal grandmother died of breast cancer while we were living in Arizona. My mom was just twenty-eight at the time and did not make it back in time to say good-bye. She received word of her mother's death while she switched planes in Chicago. Afterward, she dedicated much of her adulthood to raising my brother and me, not returning to work until we were both able to take care of ourselves after school.

"It was hard," she says, "raising children a long way from home. There were lots of changes, adjustments, separations, and inconveniences. It was difficult at times, but I did it for my family."

I nod. "Greg and I don't want to have to do that. Neither one of us. Having a dog and a cat and a cabin in the woods suits us just fine."

This brings us to a standstill. We agree to a silent truce and window-shop, slowly working our way down damp streets and letting the lunch conversation fade. It doesn't entirely, but we at least manage to dull some of its sharp edges with other stimuli. After a few minutes, we're making small talk again.

Meanwhile, the drizzle increases, forcing us inside. As we enter a shop, Mom studies my worried expression, once again intuiting its meaning.

"Ari has a house," she reminds me. "I'm sure she's gone inside."

I am still not convinced. I look at my watch meaningfully, but she doesn't catch the gesture or, if she does, she pretends not to notice.

When we return home two hours later, I race to the doghouse. There I find a frantic and tangled puppy. She has not thought to go inside her house and certainly hasn't been engaged in any inventory of the outdoors. Instead, she worked fiercely and unsuccessfully to release herself from the long cable. Her struggles have shorn a huge swath of bark from the tree, and the trunk now stands completely bare from its base up about twenty inches.

"Oh, dear," says my mother, the archetypal gardener. "You'll need to wrap that trunk if it's going to survive."

I do not notice the tree, except to wonder if my puppy has been injured in the stripping of it. Ari is agitated—a mess of wet fury, worried eyes, and frenetic movement. I wonder once again how this dog will survive with such a thoughtless, neglectful caretaker. I unwind the cable from her front paws, and we lead the rain-soaked, anxious pet inside. For once, she consents to be wrapped in a towel and does not squirm away as I hold her tight. I resolve that this experiment will not be repeated—that she will not be left like this again while I so cavalierly sip clam chowder and browse for pottery. My mother stands, looking on silently and assessing the situation as only a mom can.

"That look," she attempts, trying to read my expression. "It looks . . . it looks like . . ." She pauses, trying to place it. "It looks like a mother's," she says wistfully, her eyes actually moist.

For the rest of the week, my mom seems to demonstrate a newfound tenderness toward Ari. We steer our conversations from family dynamics to less volatile topics like global politics and religion. These are heated debates, but they lack much of the sting present earlier in the week. We all seem grateful. Eventually, we'll have to address some of the words exchanged during the trip, but this doesn't seem to be the time.

As Greg and I give my mom a hug good-bye at the airport, her face grows stern. "You better keep sending pictures of that puppy," she tells us. "I want to show everybody my grand-dog."

A Walk in the Park?

[july]

July is the height of vacation season in Maine. On the first day of the month, I call my mom to see how she has been. It's been two weeks since she visited, and I still haven't heard from her. When we speak, she is polite but distant. I worry our debates cut deeper than I thought. We chatter about superficialities—our flower gardens, the weather, my dad's travel. I tell her I am about to embark upon a three-day trip aboard the *Angelique,* a stunning tall-masted ship. This piques her interest, and she asks me to tell her more. I explain that each year, these classic sailing ships carry nearly ten thousand vacationers in and out of the islands in the Penobscot Bay. The ships are known not only for the unadulterated views they offer, but also for their conservation of Maine's island network.

What they're not known for is being dog-friendly, so Greg agrees to take Ari with him on a river trip. He'll return for a few days to restock his supplies and rendezvous with me; then the three of us will return to the mountains together. It's a makeup trip for the expedition he canceled in June and a chance for us to spend some good time together.

I return from my nautical adventure invigorated and purged of any care or woe. Greg's clenched jaw tells me his trip has been considerably less cathartic. He listens politely as I spin yarns about knots and island life, but I can tell his mind is elsewhere. After he casts a third tired look in the direction of Ari, I begin to catch his drift.

"The pup," I ask, "what is it?"

His voice is resolute. "She's crazy. I just don't know what to do with her."

I look again at Ari, who is curled up and snoring in a nook near the woodstove. Her nose and whiskers twitch lightly as she enters a REM cycle. She is the model of docility. "She doesn't look out of control," I say gently.

"That's the thing about her," Greg says. He has the aura of a conspiracy theorist. He lowers his voice and narrows his eyes, casting them in the direction of the sleeping dog. "She can *change*."

I try not to laugh. "You mean like a vampire?"

"Vampires don't change. You're thinking of werewolves. And that's what we have here." He considers the hyperbole and decides it is too much. "Sort of a werewolf," he corrects. "More like a wolf in sheep's clothes. Or a coyote in dog clothes. You know what I mean."

I have no idea. But I soon learn.

While I was cruising the coast and making new friends, Greg and Ari arrived at his favorite riverside campground on the banks of the Penobscot River—a truly wild place in the northern half of the state filled with thick forest and miles of unsettled white water. There, they met with other paddling chums, a handful of children, and a persnickety cat named Friendly. The grown-ups agreed to a staggered kayaking schedule so that kids, canine, and cat could be supervised at all times. During their downtime, Greg and Ari took a quick swim in the river and wandered about the campsite, chatting with new friends. Ari was unleashed, and that seemed to suit them both fine. When it was Greg's turn to paddle, he left Ari and her leash in the care of our friend

Brent. For about an hour or so, Ari hung close to Brent, wading in the river with him and even taking a three-mile hike. That, she decided, was enough domesticity for one day.

"Brent said you could see it in her eye," Greg says. "A little switch was thrown somewhere. She turned into a wild dog."

"Ferocious?" I try to picture this snoring little creature turning into a werewolf. Even knowing her propensity for willful mischief, it's impossible.

"Not ferocious," Greg explains. "Just *wild*. Totally uncatchable."

Apparently when people began returning to the campsite after a day of adventure, Brent decided it would be safest to leash up the pup. But Ari wasn't about to go gently down that road. Each time Brent moved toward her, she'd scuttle just out of reach. When he took a step back, she'd crouch forward and give a play-bark, trying to lure him into lunging at her. When he did, she'd leap away. He tried bribing her with bologna slices, making a little trail of them around the campsite, but she managed to steal all the lunch meat before he could grab her collar. He tried acting disinterested and went to read a book. She accompanied him, making sure he knew she was tantalizingly close but would not be caught.

"This went on for three hours," Greg tells me. "*Three* hours. Brent was about ready to kill her, he was so frustrated. And he works with *prisoners* for a living."

"I know where Brent works," I remind him. "And don't forget, the fundamental difference here is that most prisoners can't escape. He doesn't have to worry about catching them."

Greg fails to see the humor in this last observation. "Brent calls her coy-dog now, you know. He thinks she's going to run off with her coyote forebears. He says we better watch out."

After four full months of canine research, I am positively brimming with information on the subject of wild dogs. I eagerly unleash a stream of what I am certain is fascinating information. I tell Greg that evolutionary biologists have, in fact, confirmed reproduction between domestic dogs and eastern coyotes. Radio-collared coyotes have been observed instigating play with domestic dogs for years now—wrestling, pouncing, and play-biting, all using universal dog cues that say *This is a game*. A well-known study followed one hapless coyote male who tried repeatedly to mate with a golden retriever in

Nebraska. In the end, she seemed fairly receptive, though her owners certainly weren't. They chased the coyote away. A few months later, he was shot and killed by a hunter.

This tale sounds to me like the canine world's version of *West Side Story*. It makes me wonder how the pup would do in her own interspecies musical. I tilt my head, humming "I Feel Pretty" and trying to assess Ari's likeness to Natalie Wood. This causes Greg to clear his throat with great purpose. My new enthusiasm for esoteric biology and classic Broadway is not mutual. Reluctantly, I return to the drama at hand.

"So," I ask, "what happened? You got her on the leash somehow."

"When I got back from paddling, Brent was leaving another giant trail of bologna slices around the entire campground. It was, like, two pounds of lunch meat. But coy-dog wasn't interested. She had met another dog by then . . ."

Aha.

". . . so we waited until she was distracted by that dog. And then we tackled her."

Oh, dear.

Greg is clearly frustrated and probably embarrassed by this latest show of independence. The looks he casts in the pup's direction are not warm ones. But as his voice rises, Ari stirs. She sighs and rubs her snout with both front paws, then flips onto her back and resumes her nap. My heart leaps up at this sight. How could you not love this dog?

Still, I know Greg is right. We have a bratty adolescent on our hands—and right on developmental schedule. Even with her hysterectomy, Ari is a hormonal machine right now. And that makes her a danger to herself. She has the will and strength of a mature canine, but none of an adult's common sense. There are good evolutionary reasons for this shift: It marks a dog's independence and ability to exist away from her litter. Still, in the human world, it's a recipe for disaster—or a serious accident—if she decides to go romping in a busy street or the wrong person's yard. Consequently, Greg and I agree that, caninaturalism or no, this dog will remain leashed until she graduates from this phase. All three of us hope that commencement day will be very soon.

The next afternoon is the start of Fourth of July weekend, but in keeping with our agreement, there will be no independence for this young dog. Instead, we pack up her tie-down and lead line, suit her up in harness and leash, and then head back to the Penobscot River. As we set out, I joke that perhaps Brent will be able to work his rehabilitative magic on this inmate. If not, maybe he can lend Ari a tin cup to scrape across the bars of her jail cell. Greg gives me a tired look in return.

But in truth, even dealing with our delinquent dog can't really dampen Greg's spirits. We are on our way to join our friends Mike and Jean, along with their three-year-old daughter, Olivia, on the Penobscot. This time, we'll be camping in the shadows of Katahdin, Maine's highest mountain: a craggy, sleeping dinosaur with a slight curve in its spine and folds of granite running down each enormous flank. The five tribes making up the Wabanaki Nation have long considered this mountain holy. Out of respect for this sacredness, they do not climb the mountain but instead conduct annual religious ceremonies at its base, paying tribute to Katahdin and its spirits.

For most visitors, however, Katahdin is far less a spiritual place than it is a mere cardiovascular challenge. The crown jewel of Maine's Baxter Park, a two-hundred-thousand acre wilderness area, Katahdin sees thousands of tourists each year, making it one of the most popular recreation destinations in the area. Because the alpine landscape is so fragile, the park limits the number of permits it offers for hiking, camping, and climbing each year. They are awarded on a first-come, first-served basis beginning January 1. Regardless of winter weather, dozens of intrepid hopefuls spend their New Year's Eve camped out in front of the state park headquarters, awaiting a chance to summit the grand mountain or cast their flies and match wits with brook trout eight months later.

Today, the long line of vehicles crawling toward the park confirms that popularity. It also makes for very slow going. As Greg navigates the traffic and Ari sleeps in the back of the cab, I count cars and trucks. There are two distinct types of vehicles here: large trucks with ATVs, fishing poles, and gun racks; and sporty cars overflowing with kayaks, backpacks, and LEAVE NO TRACE bumper stickers. Collectively, they represent the confluence of cultures that meet each summer here in the North Woods: conservationists and preservationists; conservatives and liberals. But for the most part, the politics of red and blue America blend smoothly here, creating what political pundits call a purple response to the environment.

I'm most interested in the history of outdoor recreation around Katahdin, and I consider this something of a literary pilgrimage. In 1846, twenty-nine-year-old Henry David Thoreau took a break from his time at Walden Pond and ventured up this way with five companions, including Wabanaki guide Joe Polis. Thoreau later immortalized the trip in a collection of three essays collected posthumously as *The Maine Woods,* a wonderfully lyrical account of life in Maine's North Woods. I have the book tucked in my backpack and fully intend to read aloud at the campfire until someone objects. Thoreau loved this place—and so do I.

Despite their lofty ideals and rhapsodic prose, Thoreau's party failed to summit the great mountain. We, too, will fail in this endeavor, albeit for very different reasons. The area that is now part of the official park was made so by a gift from former governor Percival P. Baxter. A great nature lover and outdoor enthusiast, Baxter also had a prescient eye for the future of conservation and land use. Foretelling what would become very real issues of land preservation in the second half of the century, Baxter bequeathed the park to the state in 1931, designating it a wilderness and wildlife sanctuary. Because it is not part of the state or national park systems, Baxter Park is free to create rules and policies based on the late governor's view of nature. One such rule forbids dogs from entering the park. As a result, we and the coy-dog will camp just outside its boundaries.

I'm curious about this rule, so we stop by park headquarters to speak with Heather Haskell, the park's interpretive specialist. She seems conditioned to questions regarding the dog policy and offers me a rehearsed—but friendly—explanation.

"Percival Baxter was a great animal lover," she assures me. "He had a series of Irish setters all named Garry. You know, Garry I, Garry II, Garry III, Garry IV, and so on. He even built a miniature governor's mansion on the property for his dogs to occupy. One of the Garrys died while he was in office. Baxter actually lowered the state flag to half-mast. People protested, but he didn't care. That's how committed he was."

I nod appreciatively, but she still hasn't said anything about the policy. I try to ask more directly. *Why no dogs?*

She seems uneasy, and I get the sense that she has been challenged by aggressive dog owners not willing to leave Pooch at home. I tell her we don't object—we're just curious.

"Well," she begins, "the park is a sanctuary. Early on, domesticated animals like dogs and horses were allowed in. But over the years, Baxter began to realize a few things. He was making the park for wild animals. Dogs can interfere with that. They chase squirrels, run down deer, and cause stress to the animals. Some people say, then, that they just won't take their dogs on hikes. But if you leave your dog at a campsite or in the car, the dog's upset and barks all day long. That's no good, either. Eventually, we just said no to pets altogether."

I ask her about the response they receive to this policy. She admits that it varies, and that some visitors feel very strongly about bringing their animals with them on vacation. "And not just dogs," she adds. "We've seen hamsters and snakes and parrots on shoulders. We have to say no to all of them. Even if they're domestic animals, they can spread disease. And it goes both ways—if your pet runs into a skunk or a porcupine, it can really wreck your trip."

The caninaturalist and I are not totally persuaded, but we thank her for her time and information.

As soon as we arrive at our campground outside the park, Ari immediately proves Heather Haskell right. The pup lunges at the end of her leash, pursuing a red squirrel. Ari adores these little rodents, and back home she plunges into the brush each time she catches sight of their herky-jerky movement. Tail wagging furiously, she offers each squirrel in the town forest a quick play-bow and then takes off in hot pursuit of another new friend, never once considering that the affection may not be mutual.

Here at the campsite, she seems elated that her rodent compatriots have chosen to join us. She spins with pleasure and wags her whole body at the specimen glowering from a large pine tree.

Like Cam, this furry critter is quick to reproach Ari. As the pup draws near, rump wagging hopefully and leash trailing behind, the little squirrel pokes its head out of a nook in the tree and scolds—loudly. It chuffs an angry squawk that is half cheep and half hiss from deep within its tiny body, causing its entire torso to convulse from the effort. I'm glad Heather can't see this obviously stressed rodent—she might push for a ban on dogs in nature altogether.

Even Ari recognizes this squirrel's sound as one of distressed antagonism. The sound of the angry chuffing gives her pause, and she sits on her back haunches and cocks her head, wondering why the squirrel isn't enjoying the game as much as she is. The squirrel continues to berate her. Ari tries her best to mimic the chuffing, perhaps hoping that a medley might lure her new friend out of the tree. No luck.

As the escaped caninaturalist tries to engage the squirrel, we humans work on our own tactical maneuver, which consists primarily of trying to steer Ari away from the squirrel. Crouching low, we make our way to either side of the tree, where we can tackle her if need be. The pup doesn't notice our advances, but the squirrel does. She halts her tirade against Ari just long enough to assess us. *Whose side are we on?* The squirrel can't tell. She gives us a quick reproach, just in case. Miraculously, Ari doesn't notice this division in the squirrel's attention. Instead, she paws at the ground, hoping this will attract her new friend.

It does, but not in a friendly sort of way. The squirrel works its way, headfirst, down a section of the tree and screams at Ari even more loudly. Ari takes this as a hopeful sign and rises on her hind legs, placing both front paws on the trunk of the tree. Meanwhile, Greg has taken matters into his own hands. He dives down and swoops up the pup as if she were a football. Mercifully, he refrains from an end-zone victory dance.

Not that Ari would probably notice either way. At our campsite, the caninaturalist seems to fancy herself part cop, part delinquent; she's much too busy embodying both to be bothered by us. I watch her carefully as we set up camp, wondering how she feels about the trip. Other than the aborted adventure with Greg, this is her first time really camping. As the humans pitch our tent, we set up a long run for her, and she gets busy sniffing around the campsite without so much as objecting to her cabled incarceration.

A few minutes later, our friends arrive. I pull in Ari, worried that her enthusiasm will be too much for little Olivia, but the pup is surprisingly subdued around the toddler. It's as if she somehow understands Olivia's youth and fragility. Instead of mauling Olivia with her usual display of spirited greetings, Ari sits sphinx-like next to her new friend, enduring an assault of floppy pats to the top of her head without so much as grimacing. By dinnertime, Olivia and Ari are great comrades. The former gathers mounds of leaves and acorns and dirt, offering them all to the pup on a bright red plastic shovel. Ari dutifully takes each scoop, holding its contents in her mouth until Olivia turns her back and she can spit out the forest detritus without offending her new buddy.

The two play this game for hours. Best as I can tell, neither seems all that interested in the fact that we have left the comforts of our homes in order to sleep in the woods. It makes me wonder if they even register the distinction. Kinch certainly did. As far as he was concerned, we embarked upon pure wilderness each time we went camping. This necessitated a decided shift in behaviors, too. Kinch would hunker down in survival mode as soon as we arrived—burying his food into secret caches and barking at every rustle in the trees. This was a dog running on pure instinct. He didn't want to be petted, and he certainly didn't want to play. We were, he seemed to insist, in crisis mode. That the humans didn't acknowledge as much clearly infuriated him. He became a self-appointed sentry and team leader, shuttling us this way and that. No time to recreate—we just needed to endure. God willing, we might just get out of that campground alive.

In retrospect, this behavior makes sense to me. Having been on the lam after getting his hunting-dog pink slip, Kinch knew from an early age that wilderness isn't always your friend. Ari doesn't seem to share this sense of nature, and here at the campsite she eats dinner with her usual abandon, eventually settling in with us around the campfire. Still, she is more vigilant than usual: Even as her eyelids begin to droop, her ears remain alert and home in on any sound. When one piques her interest, she gives a threatening growl or two before settling back in. This delights Olivia, who clearly sees through the tough-dog exterior. She begins joining Ari in the guttural barks. I refrain from pointing out that no creature, no matter how timid, is likely to be intimidated by this pair of wild things.

By 10 PM the fire begins to die down. Mike and Greg wrap up their plans for the next day's paddling, and the four of us stare quietly into the fire. I admit that I'm exhausted and excuse myself for the evening, leading Ari over to our tent. Inside, it takes her about five minutes of shoving her nose into the taut canvas before she understands that, all appearances to the contrary, we are actually *inside*. She makes several circles around the circumference of the tent then finally nestles at the foot of my sleeping bag, delighted to be finally sleeping like a pack. Her happy snores punctuate the cool night air, making me feel close and safe.

The next morning is characteristically glorious. No matter the heat and humidity of our home in the foothills, we can always count on temperate summer days in the North Woods, where the average annual temperature is thirty-eight degrees Fahrenheit and snow is possible year-round. As Greg and Mike don their paddling gear, Ari and I offer to drive them to the base of Ripogenus Dam, a massive hydroelectric producer that churns out more than three thousand cubic feet per second of roiling white water. Once there, the two paddlers shoulder their tiny boats down toward the river. Ari and I watch them walk toward the hydroelectric station. As soon as they are out of sight, we drive a mile or two down the logging road, where we'll have a good view of their adventure, safely atop a fifty-foot cliff.

This cliff forms the terminus of what paddlers simply refer to as "the gorge." In it, the river drops seventy feet per mile. Pushed by the dam floodgates through the narrow rocky tunnel of a gorge, the water creates hair-raising waves, holes, and *very* few eddies. It's taken me years to arrive at the mental place where I can watch Greg and his tiny boat navigate these waves without fearing for his life.

Today, I divide my time evenly between contemplating life as a widow and observing my dog observe nature. Ari begins by sniffing the little cliff upon which we are perched. After reading the urinary messages left by previous canine visitors, she has decided it's okay for us to be here—at least for now. She then commences a study of some spindly white cedar roots that have somehow found purchase on this smooth granite.

I don't know how old these particular trees are. Still, even a year or two of clutching this unforgiving rock seems a noteworthy feat to me. Ari is considerably less impressed. Bored by the lack of smells, she seems frustrated that our walk has stopped here, where we are hemmed in by a precipitous drop on three sides. With no other obvious mischief to cause, she paws at the cedar roots, trying to pull them from the rock. They don't budge. Any tree that has learned to withstand water and wind and a lack of soil surely won't be deterred by a forty-pound puppy. Still, she hacks away, eventually removing a few strips of their thick outer covering. I take her paw and reprimand her gently, pointing out the cedar has enough of a challenge without her destructive tendencies. She resists this admonishment by nipping at my nose. But at least she gives up on her warfare against conifers and instead, contents herself with a survey of the scene below.

We are standing on over fifty feet of rock: a combination of limestone (cedar's preferred mineral composite) and granite. Both have been washed smooth by the coursing river below. Does this impress the pup? Hard to tell. But she seems even more alert than usual above the roiling rapids. As for me, I try my best to ignore the fact that the same river capable of slicing granite is currently carrying my husband and his very small plastic kayak through its surges.

After we have been watching for about ten minutes, a flotilla of red commercial rafts makes its way down the last wave of the gorge. As they go by, the faces of the rafters—each of whom has paid about $150 for this trip—range from abject terror to nervous glee. They have just completed one of nature's most impressive roller coasters, and unlike the ones at amusement parks, there are few controls here other than current and the bored-looking guides who serve as rudders in the back of each raft. The guides have made this trip every day for the past two months, and even nature's extreme pronouncements can become routine. But the paying customers are dutifully awed by the experience, most forgetting to give a single stroke of their paddles. The guides eddy out the rafts directly below us to regroup. A few customers return my thumbs-up with tentative waves.

Unable to smell or hear the rafters below, Ari is only mildly interested, and she soon returns her gaze upriver. A few minutes later, we watch as the red rafts are followed by a dozen others—this time light blue—filling the onetime logging river with its newest commodity. Following on their tail are Greg and Mike, both riding out the last of the wave's current. Greg spies us up on our perch and paddles over. He is swathed from head to toe in black neoprene and shouts a hello that is more seen than heard. Even so, Ari begins to wag her tail furiously—launching into the figure-eight rotation she normally reserves for Greg's return home from work. She recognizes him—that much is clear—but I can't tell if she's made this identification based on sight or sound. She barks at him to join us. After it's become clear that he's going to remain down in the river, she moves dangerously close to the edge, trying to get a better look. I worry that she might leap off in a desperate attempt to unite the pack. I hold her leash more firmly and tell her not to go too far. This earns me a dirty look, which seems to say, in conventional adolescent-ese, *Ummm, hello? Give me a break: I'm, like, not a moron, you know.* Apparently the dangers of height, if nothing else, register with this dog. So, too, does the inanity of adults.

From below, Greg shouts something, but once again I can't make out the words. I shake my head and shrug. He moves his paddle into one hand and points up with the other. There, Katahdin rises ethereally up and out of the morning mist. It is quiet and serene, and the sight of it blocks out the raging sound of moving water. I swear I can see the mountain gods stirring from their sleep, and for once I am glad not to be climbing its flank. Somehow, doing so just seems too ordinary. From here, I feel like I am part of something serenely spiritual. As we stand in the distant shadow of this sleeping giant, I silently thank Percival Baxter for his foresight.

Back home, we launch into a full investigation of the ecological effects of our recent trip. Turns out all three of us are more of a nuisance than we thought. Although white-water rafting and kayaking appear to have minimal impact on riparian ecologies, the rest of our trip was far from guilt-free. Campsites like the ones we inhabited often obliterate up to 90 percent of some species, like forest-floor spiders or fragile vegetation. The damage is instantaneous and difficult to repair: Within as little as two years, a low-impact camping site can sustain damage to its soil and vegetation that would take better part of a decade to repair naturally. Even small clearings like picnic areas in parks have been known to effect substantial change on wildlife patterns, ultimately creating what some scientists call semi-natural landscapes. There, animals commonly associated with urban landscapes (like pigeons and rats) tend to flourish at an accelerated rate, while other species, including many native animals, decline.

Canines don't help matters. By their nature, dogs are crepuscular, which means they prefer to hunt primarily at dawn and dusk. This is particularly true at the height of summer, when a dog's inability to sweat can become a life-threatening problem, particularly during the full light of day. Nevertheless, a recent study in California using infrared cameras revealed that domestic dogs—either accompanied by human companions or on independent jaunts—tend to visit wilderness areas primarily during the daytime. Scholars speculate that this visiting time is most likely the effect of dogs' willingness to internalize our circadian rhythms. The rest of the natural world isn't so charmed by this shift in scheduling. As a result of dog visiting hours, large wild mammals have been forced to shift their circadian patterns, ultimately becoming night-owls in an attempt to avoid the recreating canines and their humans.

But which is the bigger nuisance—dogs or people? A group of scientists in Colorado sought to answer this question by examining the "flush" distance of wildlife (that is, the proximity they allow before running away and the distance they run when they do). To do so, they considered three variables: a human hiking alone, a human hiking with a dog, and a dog walking alone.

What they found was a series of responses rooted deeply in genus evolution. Most birds, for instance, couldn't care less if a domestic dog wanders past—so long as that dog doesn't give chase. When the dog is accompanied by a human, however, the birds are quick to leave the area. Animals like mule deer, bighorn sheep, and marmots, on the other hand, showed a much greater likelihood of bolting when confronted with a dog than a human.

The reason for these responses? Wildlife biologists speculate, once again, that it all comes down to our relationship with *Canis lupis*. Wolves regularly dine upon animals like deer and usually pass up birds for more ambitious prey. Over millennia, hunted mammals have learned that their survival depends upon an exaggerated flush distance when confronted with a large canid. It doesn't matter that said canid might be a coyote or bichon frise; he still has enough wolf DNA to resemble a threat, even if it's just a theoretical one. Birds, on the other hand, have discovered they don't need to waste the energy when they see something resembling a wolf. Most canids just aren't a threat. Humans, however, like to take their eggs, put their breasts on a spit, or use their plumage to make silly hats. So when they see one of us coming, they're not likely to stick around. The study's conclusion? When it comes to dogs and humans, we both tend to get in the way. And since most unaccompanied dogs don't read signs or heed park policies, they can be a pretty big annoyance for wildlife.

These findings make me reconsider the negative effects of our project—not on Ari this time, but rather on the natural world. Is it possible to go outdoors and really *leave no trace*? The answer seems to be no. Still, not going outside doesn't seem like a very appealing option either. How do people handle this dilemma?

State and nonprofit agencies have tried a variety of responses to the impact of dogs on nature. Some state parks are limiting dog-walking hours to just a few each day so that wild animals might have more freedom of movement. Other places, especially populated cities, have created specially designated dog parks. There are seven hundred of them in the United States; New York City alone boasts more than forty such canine getaways.

Still, most domestic dogs and their human companions get their nature the cultivated way—by walking and romping in one of the hundreds of urban green spaces existing across the country. Many were envisioned and designed by a single man with a singular vision: Frederick Law Olmsted. Born in 1822, Olmsted watched the rapid urbanization of North America firsthand. His response was to create the appearance of nature in the built environment. The results persist—and flourish—from Manhattan's Central Park to San Francisco's Pleasure Park, and countless additional parks in between.

Olmsted was a self-identified dog lover. Childhood pictures often show him standing next to a dog resembling a Brittany spaniel; as an adult, he and his family owned many dogs through the years. One of his favorites was a giant Newfoundland named Neptune. He also kept a smaller and more travel-friendly dog named Judy as a companion on his trips around the country. Even with so much canine love in his life (or maybe because of it), though, Olmsted recommended that many urban parks consider leash laws. Dogs, he warned, could really compromise the landscape of a park.

Contemporary park managers have come to recognize the foresight of Olmsted, and they are experimenting with creative ways to manage the dog presence at their parks. In Portland, Oregon, for instance, park officials estimate that dogs deposit around five tons of poop each summer in a single park. As a result, they instituted a trial "doggy loo" to accommodate the canine visitors. Human companions collect the waste and deposit it in a modified portable-potty; it's then siphoned and sent to a wastewater treatment plant.

At first, says Gay Gregor of the Portland Parks Department, some humans resisted using the new loo. "People really wanted their plastic bags and garbage cans," she explains to me during a recent phone call. "That's very wasteful: It's bad for the environment, and it's expensive. Some people have suggested that we provide biodegradable bags. This seems like a good idea, but our research suggests that it wouldn't work in this situation."

So how are people taking to the new system? Gregor thinks it's catching on. The treatment company empties a nearly full loo every week, and she says the Parks Department is doing its best to make it convenient—for dogs and humans.

I ask how they do that.

"We provide several different kinds of scoops, including short-handled shovels," she says. "That way, everybody can get involved!" The enthusiasm in her voice suggests using the loo has the potential for one big party. I file this idea away under yet-untried soiree themes.

Portland may be somewhat unique in its doggy loo, but plenty of other cities are trying programs to open up urban nature for their resident canines. The oldest park in the country—Boston Common—is experimenting with leash-free zones and hours in downtown Boston. The Common, first established around 1634, began as a place for livestock grazing and military encampments. At that time, there were all sorts of dogs around. Later, it was used as a site for public executions, a historical function in which I am particularly and personally interested. As my mom likes to remind me, one of our ancestors was hung there for being a witch. Actually, she was a Quaker—but colonial Puritans didn't like splitting such theological hairs. Contemporary Bostonians don't do much hairsplitting, either, but their Common remains one of the most visited examples of urban nature in North America. It's also near Henry David Thoreau's old stomping grounds. I decide we have to visit.

Ari remains surprisingly subdued for most of the three-hour car trip. But once we get about twenty miles outside Boston, she's alert and eager. She paces between the front seat and the back, trying to take in the thickening traffic and tall buildings. Eventually, she drapes herself over the driver's seat, resting her front paws on my forearm and sticking her snout out the cracked window. We pass a Massachusetts state trooper, and I wonder if we can be ticketed for ungainly dog poses. Luckily for us, the answer appears to be no.

Our driving directions to Boston Common take us through the narrow streets of Chinatown. We've encountered a very different kind of gorge here: The granite rock walls are replaced by skyscrapers and the white water with a constant torrent of people. There's much to see and smell, and the pup does her best to catalog it all. She's never been in a city before, and I suspect it overwhelms and intimidates her. As if to prove me right, she stays close to me after we park the car, crouching against my legs and looking around nervously. The arrogant adolescent has been humbled: It's my meek puppy here with me now.

As we enter the Common, we are greeted by a deafening chorus of *Oh, look, a DOG!!!* sung by about two hundred grade-school children. Ari smiles nervously and wags her tail, but she continues to lean against me. Still, she's intrigued by the kids, who are all dressed in identical orange shirts and bright yellow hats, complete with exaggerated bill and lots of orange feathers. "We're ducks," one of them explains. "Quack," he adds for emphasis. "Quack! Quack!"

Ari gives one of her half bark, half whines. She's not sure how she's supposed to respond to this giant flock. They look like pals, but they're not behaving like any other creature she has encountered. She barks again; the children quack in response and then waddle toward the duck pond.

We say good-bye and walk deeper into the Common, past a group of three college-aged guys. As we pass them, I hear one tell his buddies that a woman just walked by with a blue-eyed fox on a leash. Urban definitions of nature, I am quickly learning, are clearly relative.

That's even true when it comes to what constitutes a park. Bostonians have a conflicted relationship with their Common. Some scorn it, calling it the city's largest—and dirtiest—vacant lot. Others relish its verdant fields and shady groves, calling it an oasis in an otherwise crowded metropolis. There's something to both interpretations. The Common is worn in places, and it's certainly not pristine. But it's also lovely in its green coolness and mature foliage. I marvel at the height of its elms and oaks—home to many of the same bird species we have back in our pine woods. And at this hour of the day—barely 10 AM—there's a peacefulness to the place also very much like our town forest.

We watch as a monarch butterfly alights upon a park bench. Ari is momentarily transfixed, but she's soon distracted by an enormous gray squirrel, who scurries up a tree. Much larger and less bellicose than its red cousin, this squirrel can only be described as succulent with its beefy flanks and round belly. I can hardly blame Ari when she lunges at it. Somehow, the rotund squirrel retains enough rodent nimbleness to race halfway up the tree trunk when pursued. Ari tries to follow, getting about two feet up before remembering (1) she is attached to a leash and (2) she cannot climb. She looks like the Looney Tunes coyote, suspended in midair before plummeting back to the ground. Still, she's regained some of her confidence: Having forgotten about the city surrounding us, she drags us merrily from tree to tree in search of other mega-squirrels.

Our serpentine course takes us near the visitor center, where two unleashed little white dogs frolic in a sunny spot of the Common, chasing each other and a few dry leaves.

"Do you see that?" asks a voice behind me. "The city's rat population is really growing!"

I turn and find myself facing a young man dressed in colonial attire, including a large felt hat and white stockings. He introduces himself as Patrick Gilson, an eighteenth-century Irish highwayman turned Boston butcher.

"There's only one highway in colonial Boston," he explains. "So I wasn't getting a lot of work as a robber. The eighteenth-century meat industry is more profitable. But less rewarding."

He asks if we would like to purchase a tour of the Common, but I decline and explain our specific reason for visiting.

"I call it canine naturalism," I say.

"Boston is a great dog town," he insists, rat comment aside. "We're really dog-friendly in all the neighborhoods."

When he's not a colonial meat man, "Patrick" is Chad Clayton, method actor and sometime waiter. "We have a lot of certified helper dogs visit my restaurant," he says. "They're our favorite customers. You see them all over downtown, too."

I remind him that we're here for urban nature. "What about the Common?" I ask. "Is it nature?"

"Nature or natural?" he asks.

A philosopher highwayman. I'm impressed. "How about the first one?"

"Well," he says, "there's nature here, isn't there?"

I can't argue with that.

He asks what we've observed.

I'm embarrassed to admit that my sensitive, astute dog—the one who noticed the first trout lilies of the season, who adores lichens and finds hidden woodpecker chicks—has eyes only for squirrels.

"You mean falcon food."

Huh?

Patrick-Chad tells me that the Common boasts a resident peregrine falcon famous for swooping up squirrels in front of sensitive tourists. He says he's also seen owls, turtles, and a coyote while working as a guide.

I ask if he's had much interaction with dogs in the Common.

"Well-behaved ones can run around off leash," he says. "I think that's good. It adds to the atmosphere. Back in the day, dogs were here all the time. So were sheep and cattle."

"Do you get many dogs on your tours?"

"Actually, I've never had a dog on a tour. But I like to end each one with a little dog story. Do you want to hear it?"

Of course I do.

"Well, leading up to the Revolution, Boston grew so quickly and got so dirty that colonists tried to ban all dogs over twelve inches tall to keep down the mess. Everyone had to follow the rule," he says. "Except for Sam Adams. He had a giant Newfoundland named Queue. Queue only attacked Redcoats, so he was allowed to stay. During his life, Queue was stabbed, shot, and set on fire."

"Did he die?" I ask.

"Doesn't everyone?"

I grimace at the would-be philosopher-king. He relents. "Eventually. But not from any of those. His heart gave out when he was seventeen."

I nod, dutifully impressed.

Ari, meanwhile, has been enveloped into the marketing strategy of Patrick-Chad's co-workers. A man in a three-point hat and doublet threatens a tourist family that this fierce British cur will gnaw off their legs if they don't agree to a tour. The family takes a look at Ari and purchases four tickets. We thank the highwayman for his time and return to the greenery.

By now, human activity is in full swing around the Common. A large Mennonite choir vies for audiences with a heavily pierced girl holding a guitar bigger than she is. Bands of tourists make their way from monuments to pretzel carts, and dozens of suited workers spend their lunchtime beneath the large trees. No falcons or turtles, but plenty of pigeons, sparrows, and squirrels. And of course, more recreating dogs.

An attractive gay couple with a poodle approaches us. The dogs hit it off right away. I tell them Ari is a little overwhelmed with this much stimulation.

"She's a country mouse," I say. "It's her first time in the big city."

"So is Sofie," they say. "She lives in New Hampshire and visits us two weeks a year." This is apparently a settlement agreement from a past relationship. The couple are doing their best to give Sofie a good vacation. "That's why we came down to the Common today. We were hoping to find some dogs off leash to play with."

I explain Ari's belief she is a coyote and apologize—without Greg to help me get her under control today, I doubt I'll ever see her again if I let her loose.

A young woman with a Baby Jogger and a yellow Lab approaches.

"They look promising," I say. But no luck—according to the woman, the Lab has caught one too many squirrels to be trusted. Ari looks jealous.

The Common is getting hot and crowded. The pup is panting and is so overwhelmed that even a romp with the poodle isn't all that appealing anymore. We say good-bye and head back to the car.

On the way home, I make a quick detour to the town of Concord. We stop at Sleepy Hollow Cemetery, a deliciously cool and shaded knoll overlooking downtown. When it was first established, Thoreau, Emerson, and other transcendentalists imagined the cemetery as more park-like than anything else. Townspeople would stroll, picnic, or even listen to bands there. Now it's another pilgrimage site for fans of the writers who, along with Hawthorne, Alcott, and others, are buried there. Ari and I walk to Author's Ridge, where they rest below giant pines and maples. Ralph Waldo Emerson's grave is a giant uncarved chunk of pink granite—just like the rocks we stood on at the Penobscot. Thoreau's is much humbler, just a small marker in his family's plot. Reverent visitors have embellished it, however, with a bounty of pinecones, maple leaves, and sunflowers. Ari sniffs each offering thoughtfully. To this collection, we add a small stone from the river. Perhaps, I tell him and the pup, it once rested atop the great mountain neither of them has climbed.

Grief

[august]

A posting in the local newspaper advertises a general-interest meeting for a new dog park in our neighboring town. The notice reads: "Picture dogs gamboling off-leash, playing joyously in open, public space. For many dog owners, this would be a dream come true. For those who are afraid or resentful of dogs, it would be a nightmare. In a well-functioning dog park, it is a safe and responsible reality every day of the week." I'm hooked at once. Ari and I both want this to be our reality, so I plan to attend the meeting.

Donning shoes and sunglasses, I meet the expectant look of a young dog now accustomed to daily trips in the car. She cocks her head in the direction of the front door as if to say *Good idea! Let's take a trip*. I shake my head, which causes her to slouch across the length of the doorway—a furry roadblock. I'm not wooed and leave her in the care of Greg and our friend Scott. Dogs gamboling in coastal town hall buildings and disrupting meetings are not mentioned in the ad. I also worry the fearful and resentful crowd mentioned in the notice might also be at this hearing. Even if they're not, my adolescent pup is no practitioner of parliamentary procedure.

When I arrive at the meeting, I'm both surprised and delighted to see how many other humans in the area have similar fantasies about canines in public spaces. Like their dog friends, they tend to move around and group up in corners, so it's hard to keep an accurate count. I estimate, though, that at least thirty people have turned out on this gorgeous summer day. The meeting is informal and has a kind of a support-group feel about it. *Hi, my name is Kathryn and I want my dog to run free. Hi, I'm Dale. It's been two months since my dog played outside with other dogs.*

Hi, Dale.

The stories I overhear throughout the evening are both gloriously familiar and sometimes tragic: tales of dog antics and escape artists even Ari would admire, coupled with a few horrible stories of dogs hit by vehicles or kidnapped. It's a sober reminder of love and loss. Everyone present seems to agree about the importance of safe spaces for our four-legged friends. I volunteer to help with construction and canvassing, then spend the rest of the meeting fantasizing about safe dog saturnalia by the time the first maple leaves begin to fall. I can't wait to tell the folks back home.

But when I arrive, Greg and Scott are too busy chasing Ari around and through the house to notice I've returned. As far as the pup is concerned, everything is a dog park—particularly this place right now. She's in no mood to stop and learn about easement permits and new designs in water fountains. She's in sheer ecstasy—cavorting about and beaming at the two grown men stumbling behind her. *Park, schmark,* she seems to say.

If asked, I suspect Greg and Scott would have other choice words right now, but probably of the less printable variety.

Both athletic, the two men are physical complements: Scott is long and lean, a dancer turned soccer player and coach. Greg is broad and muscular from years of football and far more diligence at the gym than his wife can muster.

They embody wellness. That, of course, is of little consequence when trying to catch a juvenile dog.

Their expressions tell me that they have no time or patience for this game. The two are supposed to be preparing for the last kayaking adventure of the season. Scott has flown from his home in Colorado especially for the trip, and the plan is to spend a few days catching up before the two paddlers depart. Scott is an easygoing kind of guy. A kindergarten teacher by day, he is well accustomed to the sights and smells of young mammals and can tell you stories about the bodily functions of six-year-olds that would give even a registered nurse pause. I've often joked that Scott's school district ought to import him into health classes at the high school: A few anecdotes from him, and abstinence may very well become a viable form of birth control for teenagers.

This is all a long way of saying that Scott is not easily put off by anything, particularly anything of the olfactory variety. I can't understand, then, why he would be exclaiming in loud peals of disgust every time he comes within ten yards of Ari.

"*Man!*" he shouts each time he approaches the gallivanting dog. "*I mean, mmmaaannnn! That is a wicked bad stink!!*" This is followed by one of a series of guttural noises—mostly unique combinations of vowels like "eeeoooooffff" or "uuuuuaaaaaggg."

Greg, meanwhile, looks as if he is trying to lasso Ari rodeo-style with one of his kayak straps. As a college professor, he is accustomed to considerably fewer bathroom messes than those seen in a kindergarten classroom (though probably more than you'd expect). Regardless, he isn't about to get as close to the pup as Scott.

I stand next to my car, frozen in amazement. I'm too far away to understand what about Ari is so rank, but the scene before me is so vividly cartoonesque, so absurd in its exaggerated chase and theatrics, I find myself looking around for confirmation that this is in fact my home, my husband and friend, my spiraling dog. As I do, the threesome completes yet another lap through the house, then across and over the front porch. While Ari and Scott dart past, Greg stops near the bumper of my car.

"You're not going to believe this," he says.

I fight the urge to admit I already don't.

"Ari's been fishing," Greg says, struggling to catch his breath, "for dead things."

Before I can ask him to clarify, Scott limps back up the edge of our yard and toward the car.

"That dog is *pun-gent!*" he shouts—drawing out the last word as if he were at a pig call in the Deep South. "I'm talking *ripe!!*"

The two men have both resigned from their pursuit. It is more profitable for them to alternately reflect and commiserate on their failed attempts than to continue. As they recount Ari's new adventures in aquatic necromancy, Greg casts me the occasional look that says—as vividly as Scott's use of all capital letters—*Your dog, your problem.*

Point taken.

I go inside for Ari's leash and tin of biscuits, then set out through the yard and into the woods. I clamor over the rock wall, past the yellow No Tresspassing signs, and onto our neighbor Risto's property. Several hundred yards later, I finally spy my dog. Or what looks like my dog. It's hard to tell, since all I can see is an inverted quadruped whirling its paws in the air as it flops from side to side. I creep closer, hiding behind a large birch tree.

From my surveillance station, I can see that the object of Ari's current infatuation is a giant—and once bloated—dead koi fish from Risto's pond. As I watch Ari smear its now oozing decay into her thick fur, flashbacks from the past two weeks come rushing to the surface: Greg mentioning that he had seen something bright and large floating in the center of Risto's pond; Ari returning from unsupervised woodland jaunts with wet feet and matted fur, smelling of pond water and something slightly fishy; her increasing attempts to bolt from the front door. This has clearly been a project of some planning and initiative on her part.

I can't say I entirely blame the pup. Before it was mashed by her writhing, the fish was a lovely mix of oranges and reds, and it probably measured about twelve inches in length. Even from her vantage on the edge of the pond, Ari would have seen the appeal of its limp form floating atop the water. She must have worked for days, nudging it toward the shore, before gingerly carrying it to this prime rolling spot, right in the middle of the trail, where it could explode in a pageantry of unthinkable decay.

If Greg's memory is correct, this fish has been dead for more than a week. That's a lot of time for it to become disgusting. As a child, I once stepped on a two-day-dead sunfish on the beach at my family's house. Bloated, the fish yielded under my bare foot with the kind of *pffflllttttt* that made whoopee cushions famous. The sensation and resulting smell have been enough to make me wear flip-flops on that sand ever since.

What's happening in front of me now makes that childhood memory seem as rosy as a Hallmark movie. Other than its skin, the entire fish has turned into a thick, greenish black paste, which my dog is now insinuating throughout her coat. From fifteen feet away, I can smell the process as vividly as if I were actively taking part. Ari grunts with orgasmic pleasure as she flops this way and that, coating every inch of fur on her thick back. As she does, she rolls her eyes halfway up into her head and shudders with ecstasy. I'm shuddering, too, though for very different reasons.

It takes no small amount of effort to right this writhing dog, and she seems dazed as I pull her away from the fish. Forget airplane glue; these fumes are truly far out. I try some of Scott's guttural exclamations. They seem more than appropriate in this setting.

Koi means "love." I try telling myself this as I drag our coy-dog back to the house. With one hand wrapped around her leash and the other senselessly plugging my nose (as if such a feeble act could combat the stink), I repeat the statement like my own Shinto chant. *Koi means love. Koi means love.* It doesn't help.

Scott refuses to enter the house once we force Ari inside. Cam scuttles into the basement. How can we blame either of them? This smell is so powerful it has mass—a thick coppery cloud that hangs low and thick everywhere the pup has been.

We wash her. Once, twice, three times. The copper cloud in the bathroom begins to dissipate slightly, and we can once again see across the bathroom. Still, the stench is overwhelming. Greg gags violently. I begin to yearn for the common aroma of rotten snakes. That at least had an earthy bouquet to it. This stink, on the other hand, is preternatural. After two hours thumbing through a thesaurus, I still can't find a phrase in the English language vivid enough to do it justice. Frustrated, I leave the table and make my way upstairs just in time to see a flailing dog burying her stinking back into my side of the bed, wriggling her way across my pillow. It makes me want to cry, but all I can muster is a feeble "ppfffllltt."

Several days later, Ari and I arise for our early-morning walk, only to find a white-tailed deer lying on the side of the road in front of our house—a casualty of the late-night accidents all too common in this area. The doe's eyes are clear and glassy; her teats still show droplets of milk. She can't have been killed more than a few hours ago. I reel in Ari, fearful that she'll try to roll like she did with the koi fish. But the pup shows little interest in doing so. In fact, upon seeing the doe she promptly stuffs her tail between her legs and hesitates, taking in a few wary breaths as she makes sense of the scene. Clearly, this doe is a different sort of object altogether. I let Ari approach. She stands before the deer, cautiously sniffing at its nose and stomach. The pup seems subdued—leery almost.

This doe is certainly not the first roadkill casualty we have encountered on our walks; still, it's the first time I've thought to stop and let Ari really study one. I think I've always assumed she would interpret the animal as food or a toy. But she does neither. Instead, she shies away from the doe's head and returns to the udders, taking a few nervous sniffs before scuttling away. She approaches again, stretching out her neck so that she can get a better sniff without coming too close. I kneel down for a closer look. The doe's lower abdomen is distended and blue, heavy with milk still contained in her body. I suspect Ari can smell this lactation and is attracted by it. In fact, she looks as if she might try to nurse. This action sparks a new and urgent revelation about the body before us.

"Oh, no," I say to the dead doe. "You have a baby."

I look up for signs of the fawn. There are none. We traipse through the woods along the road, looking for clues. I let Ari dictate the way, figuring her chances of finding anything are better than mine. Still, there's no sign of animal life either one of us can discern.

Later that morning, Greg and I appoint ourselves ungulate undertakers. We don heavy work gloves and carry the carcass into the woods where it can decompose peacefully. In just a few hours' time, the deer has changed radically. Her one exposed eye has been eaten by crows, leaving only a portion of a raw socket. Her other eye is cloudy and dull. The birds have also been at work on the tender tissue of the deer's orifices, opening up the body cavity for further intrusion. Greg and I lift the limp body—rigor mortis has only begun to set in—and carry it awkwardly into a stand of trees. Though small, the deer is surprisingly heavy in her moribund state. We don't make it very far into the trees before setting her down heavily. I wish, for her sake, we could have been more graceful—or at least ceremonious—in this little procession.

We look everywhere for the fawn, knowing perfectly well we will never find it. Fawns are masters of disguise. They curl up their legs underneath them and even to a careful observer flatten their bodies against the ground. With their dun coloring and white spots, event to a careful observer they take on the appearance of downed leaves. My hope that Ari might smell the baby is also unlikely: From birth, baby deer are all but odorless, which also helps them avoid detection. All we can really hope for, then, is time. Fawns begin to eat grass at around two weeks of age. By two or three months, they are weaned from their mother's milk. Baby deer that age still lack the street smarts to avoid dangers on their own, but they can sometimes survive by hanging around an established herd. So will this fawn make it? Or will it stay in one place, waiting for its mom until it dies—either from malnutrition and an exposure to the elements, or via one of several predators in the area?

The question of this particular fawn's survival boils down to its birthday. If it was born in early May or before, it might be okay. But such an early birth is unlikely here in northern New England, where most does fawn in mid-June. That means, realistically speaking, there's little chance this particular baby is two months old. In fact, it's probably just a few weeks old and barely able to digest grass, even if it has the wherewithal to try. Even under the best of circumstances, the rate of survival for wild fawns is less than 40 percent—and that's *with* Mom nearby. Things don't look good for this little one.

Despite the statistics, I dedicate our early-morning walks to search and rescue, looking for any sign of the fawn. We find none. Like most baby deer, it has been too well schooled by its mother to be found. Chances are, it will die as a result. I find myself playing a grisly game of wishful thinking—that the cool nights or the active coyotes around the area will make this process quick and relatively painless. That the frailty of the fawn will hasten this inevitable conclusion.

Ari does not sense my somber mood. Instead, she capers about on the end of her leash, playing in the high grass that grows alongside the road. Part gazelle, part kitten, she pounces after leaping high and tight. She spreads her front paws wide and pats the grass—hard. She buries her snout deep within the tangled foliage, then overlays the same space with those big front feet. Most of the time, she surfaces with only a blade of grass in her jaw. But on our Sunday morning walk, when she comes up, she has a small gray-brown object in her mouth. I give it a half look. Turkey feathers? Scat? When she drops the object on the road, however, I see it move. I look closer. It's a large meadow vole, an animal bigger than a mouse, with a wide, domed head. For now at least, our specimen is very much alive. It looks wise. Or it would look wise if it weren't terrified and injured. The vole shakes—perhaps seizing from an internal injury—and drags one of its hind legs limply behind it. I don't know what to do. Leave it to die? Put it out of its misery? Let Ari do that for me? Cowardly, I choose the third. Ari picks up the vole, then places it down. It goes to move, and Ari sets her white paw on top of it. She doesn't seem to want to kill it. I can't tell if she knows she is hurting it. I try to pull her away, but she lunges forward yet again. This time, the vole, whose back leg seems to be broken, rolls awkwardly onto its back—much like Ari does to show she is submissive before other dogs. The vole keeps its face directed toward me and Ari, never once breaking eye contact. It raises a front hand to shield its face.

This is an expression of abject subjugation. It's the same one made by abused children and beaten prisoners—by anything, in fact, with hands and enough sentience to fear the unleashed power of another. I am heartbroken by what I take to be the pleading of the vole. Ari and I exchange looks of wonder: *What do we do now?* Neither of us seem to know. Meanwhile, the vole is still cowering on the road. I doubt it will survive its time in Ari's jaw, yet I can't bear to leave it here, where it will be run over by a passing car or die of its injuries in the full light of day. Why are we suddenly surrounded by so much death?

With Ari's leash wound tight around my fist, I lumber into the ditch, where I find oak leaves wide enough to cover my hands. I place the leaves over the vole, hoping to move him without causing further injury. But this vole, dying or not, refuses to be picked up again—by *anything*. He drags himself into the ditch, soon disappearing in the brush.

Ari and I walk on. One of us continues searching for more voles; the other keeps replaying that look of desperate submission. The vole's face was unnervingly communicative. That awareness saddens me. I dub him the king of the voles. I do not care that this is egregious, anthropomorphic fantasy. I saw those brown eyes; I felt that desperation. There was wisdom in that domed head.

The next day, we go out in search of the vole but can find no trace of it. Farther down the road, Ari does find a recently killed bird, but she's no more interested in it than she was the dead deer. Maybe it's because neither of them really seem all that dead—not in the rotten, decomposing way of the water snake or the koi fish anyway. Biological theory supports this idea.

Forensic scientists often divide decomposition into six discrete stages, with evocative names like "black putrefaction" and the more jargony but nonetheless descriptive "butyric fermentation," which is sometimes explained as the "smells-like-cheese" phase. In each of these stages, a new band of grisly actors is invited to the feast, beginning with the bacteria in our own gut and ending with beetles that possess mandibles capable of gnawing on dried meat and skin.

What particularly interests me about this six-staged process is the orderly fashion in which everyone enters and exits it. Flies wait for the second stage, after the bacteria has done its heavy lifting, before they lay their eggs and raise their maggots; beetles remain scarce until the fourth. Even within each insect genus, there's a clear progression. For instance, the green-bottle fly is the first to arrive, since it is attracted to the feces and bodily fluids often released from orifaces upon death. The grim flesh fly comes later, when the body has become more rank. After them, many species of moths appear to dine upon remaining hair and skin, or use the decimated corpse for their own breeding ground.

In each instance, the genus or species waits until its designated time, arrives promptly, works efficiently, and then leaves before the next stage has begun. Evolutionary history ensures they understand and keep these scheduled appointments.

So to what stage have dogs been invited? And do they keep to their designated reservations? Ari and I review her interest in the various dead things around our neighborhood, hoping to deduce clues. If the vole and recently killed doe are any indication, the stage of initial decay does not interest the pup. Any degenerative processes during this stage occur from the inside out and with little evidence to entice a curious puppy. In fact, at this stage the corpse is less than not interesting to her: It hardly seems to exist. Without the animation of life—the smells, movements, communication—or the process of death (smells, smells, and more smells), the body is inert and amorphous, a non-thing. I'd go so far as to say that gravel is equally interesting to my pup.

The koi fish and water snake, on the other hand, were somewhere between putrefaction and the early stages of butyric fermentation when the pup encountered them. Ari's interest with them at this stage was entirely olfactory. She wanted to smell—and ultimately *smell like*—the corpses. She didn't need to see them and she certainly wasn't interested in tasting them. Instead, they existed either as a social novelty item or disguise—depending upon what theory of rolling you adopt. It's not until a dead animal transitions into the final and dry stages of decomposition that Ari considers it edible. This is true with the leather-like skins of animals she finds in the woods and, with the possible exception of her deer leg, every other dead animal (or dead-animal part) she has encountered.

Still, she clearly distinguishes between that which is dead and that which is alive, even before it reaches putrefaction. The same awareness has been observed in many domestic dogs. This observation has led both pet owners and scientists alike to wonder what death means to canines. Stories abound of dogs who demonstrated emotions resembling grief or alarm upon discovering the body of a deceased family member or companion animal. Skeptics could claim that these displays are as much in response to a change in routine or loneliness as they are mourning. But as Ari has demonstrated repeatedly this month, dogs certainly seem to grasp the difference between a living and a dead thing. Does she understand death itself, though? Or is she interpreting cues like a lack of responsiveness on the part of the deceased, or my behavior around the dead animal?

The answer to that question depends entirely upon whom you ask. Harvard neuroscientist Marc Hauser contends that animals can't really know death, since they don't really know themselves—at least not in a Cartesian or metacognitive sort of way. Still, he does acknowledge that animals vary their response toward any creatures behaving unlike "normal living individuals." Since most dead animals don't act like living ones, a dog's behavior will necessarily be wary or excitable when faced with the deceased.

Jeffrey Moussaieff Masson, on the other hand, seems to suggest that Hauser's interpretation of animal behavior is really just splitting existential hairs. In his book *When Elephants Weep,* Masson argues that the depression and suffering experienced by animals after one in their community dies can really only be considered grief. He makes a persuasive case, pointing to the number of instances when a captive animal has starved itself to death immediately after the death of its mate. Lest we consider this a purely biological or reproductive function, he also includes reports of formalized bereavement practices such as fondling bones or refusing to leave a window after a human companion has died. Siding with Masson are a whole host of writers and scientists who have observed everything from dolphins to mother elk engaged in elaborate gestures of what can only be called mourning—baying over carcasses for days, transporting dead bodies in group formations.

I want to believe they are right. But does Ari really know what it is to mourn? Based on our evidence so far, I don't really know. Unfortunately, we're all about to find out.

Cam is sick. Sometime during the past week, what seemed like a few random hairball incidents have become a more serious condition. She vomits early each morning—a gaspy, gut-wrenching sound that awakens Ari and then, by relation, me. I race to get to the vomit before Ari, lest the puppy eat it. Is she doing this to help disguise Cam's illness? Or simply because there's enough that resembles cat food in this steaming pile to make it seem appetizing? I can't tell for certain. For her part, Cam slowly starts to give up on keeping food down. I notice that I am refilling her dish less and less, while she becomes more and more listless.

I worry what to do with my beloved cat. She still hasn't been to the vet, and I haven't accepted their offer to put her on Valium. The argument that such a visit would prove too traumatic loses ground each day as she appears weaker and more lethargic. I spend two days wringing my hands and following her around the house, looking for signs of improvement.

Meanwhile, Greg and Scott are about to leave for their trip. We talk about what to do.

"I could stay," Greg offers. I can tell he does not want this option. Scott visits just once a year, and the kayaking season is about to end. Plus, he thinks I'm worrying over nothing. *Animals are resilient,* he always says, *they do a fine job of taking care of themselves.*

I do not believe this. And I want him to stay. But I say he should go, thinking myself brave and generous. I feel a twinge of resentment when he agrees.

Scott and Greg depart early Saturday morning. I tell myself that if Cam is not better by the end of the day, she and I will make an emergency visit to the clinic. She curls up under the covers on my side of the bed and does not move. She has not eaten in a day or two. I doubt she's had anything to drink. By 9 AM I've aborted my plan to wait out the day; I call the clinic, explaining her symptoms. Laurie recommends a cat-sized dose of an over-the-counter anti-nausea drug. This seems absurd—both that I would consider giving Cam a syrupy pink liquid intended for adult humans and that administering the drug would even be possible with a temperamental cat. Still, I agree to try and say I will call their office if Cam's condition does not improve.

That evening, Andrea is hosting a birthday party for Chris. I do not want to go. If Cam worsens, I want to be with her. Still, our small-town pharmacy does not have the medication prescribed by Laurie, so I have to make the drive across the river and into the city anyway. I'll only stay at the party a few minutes, then get back to the animals.

The pharmacy is enormous and brilliantly sterile. The air-conditioning is set high and hermetic, making me wonder if doctors could perform open-heart surgery on the floor of the blood pressure medication aisle. I suspect there would be little risk of infection. Even if there were, finding a hundred different antiseptics would not be a problem here.

I stand for what feels like hours in the aisle marked DIGESTIVE, staring at the confluence of SICKNESS & NAUSEA and DIARRHEA drugs at the pharmacy. I have never before purchased medication for a cat, and none of it makes sense in this context. Most of the liquids are peppermint- or lemon-flavored—two of Cam's least favorite tastes. Others have properties not mentioned by Laurie: stool softeners, anti-heartburn, and the like. I don't know if this is okay. After much deliberation, I select four or five boxes: capsules and gels, liquids and tablets. Surely one of them will be right.

Chris and Andrea are deeply respectful of my concern over Cam. Still, it's his birthday party, and we all know it would be selfish to convert it into a wake for a sick tabby cat. I sit quietly in their side yard, petting Bentley and nursing a beer. I tell myself I will stay for an hour: no more, no less. But when a mutual friend starts telling stories about the at-home veterinary surgery performed by her pediatrician father on her childhood cats, I decide I've had enough. I kiss Andrea and Chris good-bye. I need to get back.

The drive home normally takes three quarters of an hour. I'm back in less than thirty minutes. Cam staggers down the stairs to greet me and winces when I pick her up. She's obviously uncomfortable. Still, she places her striped head under my chin and rests it there—our daily greeting. When I set her down, she walks away gingerly, and I do not see her for the rest of the fitful night.

The next morning, Ari bounds around the house with her usual enthusiasm. I scold her each time she approaches Cam, and then take her for a long walk to give the tabby some peace. When we return, Cam has resumed her spot under the covers. She hisses when I peer under them to check on her. *Go away,* she is saying. *This isn't about you.* After the fifth time I peer in, she rises and limps deep into my closet. There, she loses control of her bladder.

This is serious. I contact the vet's answering service and tell them I think we need emergency attention. I try to lure Cam back out of the closet, but she'll have none of it. She is vulnerable—her instincts are telling her to hide from everyone.

Dr. Matt Townsend calls back twenty minutes later. I have not met him before, but he has the same quiet calm and empathy of Dr. Rutherford. I like his quiet familiarity with hysterical cat owners on Sunday afternoons. I explain Cam's condition, and he agrees I should bring her in immediately. I go downstairs to fetch her crate but soon think twice about trying to cram her into it. Instead, I inch deep into my closet and wrap her in a towel; then we head to the car. I put the crate in the backseat—just in case. During the ride, Cam weaves between my legs on the floorboards, then clambers to climb back to the passenger seat. She cannot jump, and her hind legs seem impaired. I worry what this might mean.

When we enter the clinic, she gives a halfhearted growl and swipe at Dr. Townsend; she no longer seems committed to anything but survival. As she seethes on the exam table, we talk about the possibilities of her condition. Several years earlier, Cam suffered from what seemed like a severe bladder infection. I wonder aloud if this could be related. Dr. Townsend offers to do tests—an ultrasound, an X-ray, some blood work. They'll be expensive, he apologizes. I can tell he finds the monetary side of his job distasteful—as he does the decision-making process families endure as a result. How much is our pet worth? What expense can we justify on behalf of him or her? Checking account balance aside, I can rationalize just about anything at this point.

Dr. Townsend gives Cam a sedative, then begins the battery of tests. He does not like the resolution of the ultrasound, so we splay her on a cat-shaped black board in their imaging room. After he completes the X-rays, Matt leaves me in the exam room with the still-sleeping Cam while he develops the images. When he returns to the exam room, I know instantly that the news is not good. I don't like the calm resolve on his face or the gentle way he asks me to come look at the film. Still, I follow obediently.

We stand before the illuminated screen, which shows the negative image of my cat's long, lean torso. He points to her kidneys, explaining that they are grossly enlarged.

"But what concerns me the most," he continues, "are these." He points to jagged white masses emanating from the organs and moving outward. Her kidneys are riddled with stones and what look like tumors. She is in kidney failure and has been for quite some time. Dr. Townsend speculates that she has been suffering from the stones throughout her life—part of a genetic defect never diagnosed. The question now becomes how far the disease has progressed.

"Basically, her kidneys aren't functioning," he says. "That means she's not clearing out waste and it's building up. Depending upon her level of toxicity, she may have another few years of life." He lets this sink in. I understand that I am not to feel overly hopeful.

"Even if we can save her," he continues, "her life can be functional but it's also going to be considerably shortened. She'll have to eat special food, and she'll need her system flushed out regularly with intravenous fluid."

Matt takes me back to the still-sedated Cam and shows me how to inject her with a large bag of saline solution. This will become our weekly routine if she survives the next seventy-two hours. I nod diligently, but I'm not actually paying attention. As her body begins to absorb the large hump of fluid, we talk more about options.

"We'll get her blood work back first thing tomorrow morning. Then we'll know," Dr. Townsend tells me. "If the levels are high, there won't be anything for us to do." He pauses. I know what he is about to say and I do not want to hear it. "You'll have some decisions to make then," he says. "You will want to consider euthanizing her."

I nod again. "Of course," I say. "I don't want her to suffer." My voice doesn't sound like my own, nor does this statement of resolved stoicism.

We put the sedated Cam into her crate, and Dr. Townsend recommends I purchase pureed baby food for her to eat.

"Chicken or turkey," he says. "And try warming it in the microwave. The aroma might entice her to eat."

At the grocery store, I break down into tears in the checkout line. I've taken two tiny servings—one turkey, one chicken. I know it doesn't make sense to buy more, but I feel like I've issued a death knell for Cam by showing such little consumer faith. The clerk seems both concerned and leery of this inexplicable display of emotion. She asks if I want help out with my two microscopic jars of food. I'm tempted to say I do.

Throughout the long drive home, I vacillate between more stoicism and sobbing. Cam begins to stir, and I tell her to be strong. She begins to object to her incarceration in the crate. I take this to be a hopeful sign and nearly cause multiple accidents by leaning over to look into her carrier.

Greg's truck is in the drive when I return. Only then do I check my watch. I've been gone for hours and have given neither him nor Ari a second thought. Greg, on the other hand, has quickly deduced from the missing cat carrier and wife that Cam's condition has worsened. He meets me at the car. I don't want to relay everything that has happened in the past thirty-six hours; I don't want to recount the conversation with Dr. Townsend. I wanted him with me during this time. But I can't say that, either. It's just not fair. And besides, I am too distraught over Cam.

We take her into my office and shut the door so that Ari cannot bother her. Greg croons at Cam and strokes the front half of her—where her fur is still glossy and thick. This infuriates the puppy, who hates to feel excluded. She begins to throw herself against the door, yowling and scratching to be let in and united with the pack. I can't stand for that. Not now, when Cam may be dying. Her eyes are glassy and barely responsive. For the first time, it seems entirely possible that she may not make it through the night. I cannot bear to think of her dying alone, and so I retrieve my sleeping bag from the basement and tell Greg I want to sleep with her in the office. He says he understands and retreats to occupy the puppy.

That night, neither Cam nor I sleep much. She folds herself into a sphinx pose, trying to be vigilant, while her head droops from time to time. I watch her and whisper that she'll be all right. She purrs when I do. Mostly, though, she just stares at a point somewhere beyond the horizon. I study her, trying to memorize each contour and line. I want to see this countenance for the rest of my life. I fall asleep briefly around three o'clock and am awakened about forty-five minutes later by the sound of Cam lapping at the bowl of baby food. My heart leaps. Maybe she will be okay. Maybe she is finding a way to rally.

I have to go to school for a meeting first thing in the morning, and when I return—hopeful that Cam has continued to improve—I find Greg crying softly in the office.

"No," I say, as if correcting him. "She's going to be okay." I don't believe this. But I so want to think it's true.

"Matt Townsend called," Greg whispers. "Her numbers are off the chart. There's nothing anyone can do."

I look down at my beautiful little cat. Her eyes are unseeing, as if she has retreated deeply within herself. She is dying. Quickly. And she is in pain.

We call the vet's office. The receptionist has already been briefed on our case. I ask between gaspy tears if Dr. Townsend can euthanize Cam. He's been so kind to her. He knows her. The woman explains that he is in the field at a dairy farm in the next county. She promises she'll call and see. When she phones us ten minutes later, she tells us that he will meet us at the office in two hours. These are the longest of my adult life. We sit next to Cam in the humid room, ignoring the pleading puppy on the other side of the door. Cam doesn't seem to notice any of us. She's just concentrating. Or enduring. I can't tell.

Just after eleven, we wrap Cam in her favorite fleece blanket and take her to the truck. On the ride over, she curls herself around my leg and rests her chin on my foot. She wants me to protect her. She feels safe with me. I want her to be angry with me. To fight and resist. But it's too late for that. For the first time in her short life, she is feeble resignation.

Greg and I sit in the parking lot with Cam for several minutes before entering the clinic. I resist the urge to run away. To wrap this little striped cat in her blanket and take her somewhere else where she can spend the rest of her life in peace. But that, too, seems cruel. There will be no more peace in her life. We walk inside.

They're expecting us, and quickly usher us past the waiting area and into a private room. Cam burrows into my arm. I cry, telling her it will be okay. The lie makes me weep harder.

Matt Townsend enters the office and introduces himself to Greg. He is considerate and polite. He tells us he is very sorry. I know he means it. He explains what will happen and asks us to sign a consent form, then leaves to prepare the drugs that will end Cam's life. First, he administers the same sedative she received the night before. This time, though, she resists its effects, raising her head jerkily each time she hears a noise. She does not want to go to sleep. I think she knows it's forever this time. Dr. Townsend leaves us for a few minutes, then returns with a young, pretty vet tech, who nods shyly at us. This is hard for them, too.

They shave Cam's front forearm and swab it with alcohol. The drugs will be administered intravenously and will be instantaneous. Even with the saline infusion last night, she is dehydrated and it takes them several tries to find her vein. "Come on, sweetheart," Matt whispers. "Don't make this hard for us." She consents. A minute later, she is gone.

The four of us stand awkwardly, looking at the floor.

"This is your room," Matt tells me and Greg. "No one else will use it for the rest of the day. Take as much time as you need."

He leaves with the technician. They have dozens of patients to see today. Behind the door, I can hear them greeting a new dog or cat. The sound is very far away and yet uncomfortably close. I want the world to shut down—just for a minute.

Cam's beauty has returned in her death. Her eyes are clear and moist, no longer dilated with discomfort. I stroke her head and ears, then run my finger along her paws. It is inconceivable to me that she is gone. Greg cries behind me. Cam is his cat, too, and he has not seen her worsen over the past two days. Her death must feel even more jarring to him.

After some time, we wrap her limp body in the fleece blanket and take it to the truck. It feels heavy on my lap. Popular wisdom has it that the human body loses twenty-one grams in death. But Cam feels heavier, as if her life has been replaced by lead. Throughout the long ride home, her body sinks deeper into my lap until I wonder if I will be able to lift it. I remember the weight of that small doe. Cam feels at least that heavy now. Maybe more.

Back home, we leave her in the truck and take shovels into the woods. There is room enough near Kinch's grave, dug almost exactly one year earlier. We are surprisingly familiar with the routine. I set to collecting stones while Greg struggles to break tree roots and heavy earth. This grave will be smaller and shallower than the beagle's. Perhaps because of that, or because we are becoming adept at the process, we dig Cam's in a fraction of the time. I walk slowly to the truck and collect her swaddled body, taking it back into the woods. But kneeling before the opened earth, I cannot release her. I cannot place her in the ground, where she will decompose in the dark and the cold. I hug the blanketed form closer to me.

"Take your time," Greg says, placing his hand upon my shoulder. "We don't have to rush."

I clasp her body to my chest. Even in the weightiness of death, it feels familiar. I will never hold it again, and this thought slays me. I rock back and forth, cradling her as if this will somehow bring her back. For a moment, I think that we don't have to bury her—that there must be some way to keep her with us. But then I think about the fish and the doe and all the other dead animals we've watched decay. I can't see Cam endure a similar process.

Tibetan Buddhists have a class of individuals known as bone breakers. Called *domdens,* their jobs are to grind bodies into meal so that they might be consumed by vultures and, thus, transported high into the sky. I want to give Cam the same feeling of liberation. But I am no *domden*. I cannot break this little body. Instead, I lower the blanket into the jagged hole, smoothing her swaddled form and making sure she is tucked in tight. We spread the dirt upon her—a carnal sweep that cakes our hands and sweat-soaked arms. There is power in this process of burial. I don't think I ever understood it before this moment. When Kinch died, I was more concerned over the poignancy of Greg's grief than I was my own sadness. But this time is utterly selfish. I know only the heartbreak I am feeling and the shred of comfort I find from balling my fists deeply in the cool dirt then packing Cam's body in that same solidity.

We pile stones on top of the earth, building them into a smaller version of Kinch's warrior cairn. Then we return, briefly, to the sunlight of our yard, where we pick bouquets of daisies and black-eyed Susans. One for the new small grave; another for the larger one that has settled over four seasons.

As we walk back toward the house, I spy a triangular face peering out from the kitchen window. Tall, black-tipped ears; thick tawny fur; blue eyes and a grin. She barks a greeting and whines impatiently. We are still excluding her, and she's had enough.

I do not want to see this young dog, so exuberant and curious. I do not want to feel the thickness of her life, or be reminded of her endless pursuit of my now dead cat. I resent both: the former because it reminds me of what Cam no longer has; the latter because I worry it hastened her death. I walk away from her when she greets me at the door, then retreat upstairs and fall asleep.

Greg takes Ari on her evening walk and wakes me to ask if I want dinner. I do not. I want Cam—that's all.

Later that night, I curl into a cat-sized ball on the futon in my office. The TV is on, but I do not notice. Instead, I stare straight ahead, watching my own grief. I have always believed in euthanasia—for all creatures. Greg and I swore we would use it as a way to end terminal illness when discomfort outweighed vitality in any of our pets. We've even wished for the same in our own demise. But sitting here in the shadow of Cam's death, I find myself burdened by responsibility and guilt. Two months ago, I chose not give her antidepressants because I objected to her lack of autonomy in the decision. Under this logic, then, what right did I have to end her life? Who am I to say that, given the choice, she would have preferred a hastened death to another few days of mitigated existence? I worry that I have done the wrong thing. I fret that I have taken a life not mine to take. I beg forgiveness from anyone able to give it, then try contenting myself that I made the right choice. But did I? I don't know. I return to the original questions.

I had no idea the aftereffects of this decision would be so hard. The circularity of my reasoning continues for hours as I hop wildly through the various stages of grief. When I finally stir, I notice for the first time that I am not alone in the room. Ari has been with me, too—curled up under the desk and observing me nervously. She is uneasy and seems timid, folded tightly in the back reaches of the desk well, where she might be safe.

From what?

Me, I suppose.

I look down at her warily. My emotions are raw and short-circuiting right now. The introduction of this dog put an obvious strain on an obviously troubled cat. Cam died half naked and pockmarked because she was so rattled by the presence of this puppy. If I hadn't been paying so much attention to Ari, I might have noticed that Cam was sick when there was still enough time to save her. Forget about wanting to resent this dog, I want to blame her outright. I turn my full attention toward her. She curls into a tighter ball, as if willing herself to disappear entirely. But she does not leave; nor does she turn her face away. Instead, she stares at me from beneath the desk. She looks hopeful. She is watching my face carefully, as if to anticipate what I am going to do. As far as she is concerned, I am highly unstable right now—just shy of a crazy person, really. Whether or not she knows Cam is gone, she knows that I am—at least the version of me she has encountered for the past six months. Still, we have pledged to live as a pack. She looks as if she might be reminding me of as much. She cannot understand why I am withholding my affection. Has she done something wrong?

I have no way of knowing, of course, if this even resembles her actual thought process at this moment. But the faintest suggestion that she might be entertaining these ideas is enough to stir me from the depths of my grief. I am mourning an animal dead and buried, while a living creature cowers near me. This is not grief; this is cruelty.

I look at Ari again. She raises her head and tilts it ever so slightly. It's enough, though: For the past several months, I've been studying her body language, too. She's asking if it's all right—if she has permission to come over and say hello. How could I say anything other than *Yes, yes, oh please, yes!* And so that's what I do. She asks again. *Are you sure it's all right? Are you okay?*

I'm not okay—not yet. But I love this dog, all the more because she is here to love. I pat my thigh and whisper quietly to her. She unfolds her limbs and rises from the desk. For once, she does not resist when I wrap my arms tightly around her. I need to do this. She knows that. And it's okay.

The New Transcendentalists

[september]

For the next several mornings, I wake up face-to-face with a blue-eyed dog. This isn't the cavorting puppy or even the bratty adolescent demanding a romp outside. This is the concerned face of a friend—or even a family member. Each dawn, I open my eyes to find Ari sitting next to me on the bed, peering down and waiting for me to wake. When I do, she looks deep into my eyes, unblinking. She does not look away or urge me to rise. Instead, she sits and watches and waits.

It takes me a very long time to get out of bed these mornings. There, I can pretend nothing is wrong. Once I am fully awake, I will have to acknowledge again that Cam is dead. Delaying that admission brings a false hope I'm willing to champion, even if it is foolhardy. I linger as long as I can, aware that I am being observed and recorded by my subdued dog.

Ari has always been a morning kind of girl—impatient to get the day started. She's quick to pounce on my belly or lick my face if it means we might head out for a walk any sooner. And if that isn't enough, she's certainly not opposed to pulling off my blankets or nipping at my nose to accelerate our morning. But not these days. These days, she just sits, bearing witness to me and the grief that has so utterly changed me. At least, that's what her behavior looks like to me.

The reality of the matter is that no one really knows for sure if dogs understand human emotion. Scholars are split on this issue, but most at least acknowledge that dogs read human cues. So whether or not Ari rightly interprets the cause behind my malaise, she certainly understands that I'm not quite the same person I was a week ago. And just as she seemed to understand that being around young Olivia up at camp necessitated a new way of being, she gets it that I need a kinder, gentler version of life for a while.

And so each morning she cocks her head and coos at me when I linger in bed. When that doesn't work, she pats my arm with her paw, eventually allowing it to rest there. Such a simple, comforting action. Does she sense that I derive solace from it? I don't really know, but it's just so easy to believe she gets what is happening—at least in the sense that I've slid into a deep sadness.

Maybe she does understand. Just recently, I told a colleague of mine in Korea that Greg and I had adopted a jindo mix. He was delighted to hear it. But he also wanted us to take that adoption extra seriously. "Jindos are very sensitive dogs," he wrote to me. "Very smart, very astute." These days, this young creature occupying my house is proving him right. On our morning walk, Ari shows she can do what Joel and I have long since deemed impossible: heel, with her shoulder parallel to my leg. She spends the whole morning stroll like that, never once leaping ahead to greet a squirrel or bird. Instead, she watches me and offers that utterly lovable open-mouth grin: *Hey, friend, we're having a pretty okay time, all things considered. Right?*

Maybe.

Once back from our morning walk, Ari drapes herself like a blanket across my legs. I reach down and touch her back. It helps—at least a little. But I'm feeling impossibly greedy and want more, so I call my parents back home to share the news about Cam. They will make me feel better—I know it.

Between the two of them, my parents buried more than a dozen animals during my childhood: goldfish, hamsters, bats, chipmunks, and any other creature that died in a place where I might find it. Each death was commemorated by an elaborate funeral, including readings from *The Book of Common Prayer* and much wailing on my part. My parents endured it all with the kind of stoicism generally saved for natural disasters and war. Most recently, they had to cope with the death of our not-so-imaginatively named family cat, a calico named Cali, whose very long life ended while I was in graduate school. It took them three months (and several threats from a dear family friend) before they summoned the courage to tell me Cali had died. Given my protracted grieving processes over animals much farther down the Great Chain of Being, I can hardly blame them.

My mother can be the archetypal magna-mater—maternalism incarnate—when the need arises. This is one of those times, and she senses it as soon as I call. She refrains from making a single joke about my maladjusted cat or from mentioning the numerous times when Cam threatened her life. Instead, she just tells me how very sorry she is. The tension over her recent visit has evaporated, and she is doing what she does best.

As Mom listens patiently, I explain the source of my sorrow: I cannot reconcile Cam's death with the way that she died. Mom assumes that I am referring to the shortness of Cam's six-year life, which is paltry by most domestic cat standards. It's true: I am saddened by her abbreviated existence. Unequivocally so. But there's something else at stake, I say: metaphysical culpability.

I can feel my mother raise an eyebrow, even across the phone line. I try to explain this feeling of profound guilt.

"I have taken the life of another sentient being," I say. "And not just any animal, but one forced to live in my care. Is that defensible? Is it right?"

She seems perplexed by my interest in arguing environmental ethics. Wasn't this call a request for emotional empathy?

I tell her I see the two as identical. I want her to understand this.

"What about Cali?" I ask. "How did it happen? I mean, did you euthanize her?"

She pauses. I can't tell if she is trying to remember or looking for the right words. Maybe both. "I guess we didn't really have to in the end," she says slowly. "She was too far gone. She died before the vet could do anything."

"So that's different," I say. I want my grief to be more real.

"Is it?"

"Yes," I insist, though not entirely certain I can say why. "You didn't have to choose."

"I had already chosen." She sounds defensive. "That's why we were at the vet's office to begin with."

This is beginning to feel like competition. I don't want that.

"I just miss Cam," I say softly, recanting.

"I know you do. It hurts. A lot. And I'm so very sorry."

Perfect mother words. I'm not entirely placated, but I am grateful.

We promise to talk again soon. In the meantime, my mother's empathy really does make me feel better: as if her understanding has legitimized my grief, or at least given me permission to mourn. So I do. And this freedom to do so really helps. Over the next week, I find ways to pocket my grief where I can still roll it around in my palm and feel its strength, but more privately. I attend pre-semester committee meetings and professional development sessions, where I quietly tell a few sympathetic colleagues about Cam's death. When I do, I sound reasonable once again.

Back at home, though, the feelings are still immediate and raw. My walks with Ari have lost their pizzazz. At night, Greg wakes up to the sound of my muffled crying. He wraps his body around mine and speaks softly into my hair. He doesn't tell me it's going to be all right. Having endured the loss of Kinch a year earlier, he's too smart for that. So instead, we lie in the cool of early-autumn darkness and weep, wondering if we have done the right thing. The sound often wakes Ari, summoning her to the bedside, where she places her chin on the edge of the bed and furrows her brow. *Oh dear,* she seems to sigh. *Oh dear, oh dear, oh dear.*

Gradually, these moments begin to dissipate. I rise from bed a little faster each day and no longer feel so lifeless on my walks with Ari. Her quiet concern lessens until she once again feels safe in prompting me to rise. In turn, I agree not to fight it. As the month progresses, we all seem surprised and even a little relieved when our day-to-day routine finds a way of returning. We love and miss Cam, but we have found a way to insert that grief back into our lived lives.

And in time, I find some reflective distance, or at least the cognitive wherewithal to distinguish between grief and guilt. As I do, I become increasingly interested in the theology of the animal world and my decision to interfere. What does it mean that a little striped cat died? Is it any different from a human or a horsefly in terms of universal significance? Does it matter that she died because of my decision?

Such questions have interested theologians and scientists for centuries. And over the decades, the latter have devised all sorts of experiments to investigate the metaphysics of death. The best-known of these were conducted by Duncan Macdougall, the doctor behind the twenty-one-grams theory. Macdougall believed that if he could assign mass to the human soul, he would have quantifiable evidence of an afterlife—or at least proof that something other than air leaves the body when we take our last breath. He proved just that. And as far as he was concerned, these experiments were a tremendous international success.

The *New York Times* first ran his story on March 11, 1907. According to the article, Macdougall found several men "of the ordinary type of the usual American temperament," all of whom were, quite literally, on their deathbeds (which may be why they were able to be persuaded that a scientist needed to trace the exiting of their soul). After exacting their permission, Macdougall used a carefully calibrated bed scale and determined that each man lost approximately one ounce of weight immediately upon his death.

What the *New York Times* did not report, but has since been made known, was that Macdougall—no doubt thinking he was practicing conscientious science—insisted upon a rigorous control experiment to support his findings. To this end, he procured fifteen healthy dogs and dispatched them on the same weighted tables. According to the doctor, not a single canine showed any change in weight at the time of its death. This result, in Macdougall's opinion, proved that only humans are on the VIP list for the *après*-life party happening on the other side of the Pearly Gates. No weight loss, no soul, said Macdougall. The fact that most philosophers and theologians view the soul as a purely *metaphysical* entity (and thus without any weight or physical existence) did not trouble him when it came to the validity of his conclusions. It really wasn't much of a concern for other scientists, either. They were far more interested in getting to the bottom of those missing twenty-one grams than they were transcending the weightlessness of theology.

Since Macdougall's first experiments, researchers have conducted dozens of tests trying to disprove his findings. Just a few years ago, scientists again tried to discredit Macdougall—this time by widening their range of animal subjects. They began by measuring the weights before, during, and after the death of three lambs and a goat. None of these animals demonstrated any weight loss at the moment of its untimely death. But much to the surprise of everyone involved, these same scientists observed that several of the fully mature sheep actually gained weight upon their death—anywhere from eighteen to eight hundred grams, in fact. This makes me wonder if the exiting souls of humans might be taking up residence in the international mutton supply. If we take the eight hundred grams as a viable figure, that means about thirty-eight human souls could cram into a single dead sheep. Not the afterlife Judeo-Christian thought has endorsed, but intriguing nonetheless.[1]

What most interests me about Macdougall is the staying power of his studies and the theories they represent. His original test dogs, along with the more recent goats and lambs, are touted as proof that animals do not have a soul. Ergo, they have no life after death. This notion, coupled with an animal's apparent lack of sentience, is the most common justification for hunting, animal experimentation, and most things on the menu at McDonald's. But this theory doesn't resonate among pet owners, many of whom go to great lengths to celebrate and grieve their deceased animal companions. Take the wonderful story of the Hartsdale Cemetery, for instance.

The oldest pet cemetery in the United States, Hartsdale was founded almost by accident in 1896, when a New York City veterinarian named Samuel Johnson was approached by a grieving client whose dog had just been

[1] Depending upon your theological position, you may be pleased that further investigation has not happened on this front. If it were, I'm quite confident the *New York Times* would treat it with the same sort of delicious irony present in its original coverage. The first article on Macdougall's soul experiments appears above the headline, "Night School for Butchers," which is followed by an account of the fortnightly meetings of master butchers, covering topics that range from "cutting up carcasses" to "sanitary banding" and the taboos of illegal preservatives. As for Macdougall himself, there's irony to be had there as well. In later life he turned toward metaphysics of a different sort and attempted a short-lived career as a monologue performer, favoring readings from *Hamlet* and French existential farces. No word on whether his body lost weight when this vocation ended.

euthanized. A Manhattanite, she could not take her dog's body home for burial. She asked what would become of his remains and was told they would be disposed of as trash. This horrified her, and she begged Johnson to offer a more suitable alternative for her deceased pet. After a little thought, Johnson settled upon a solution: She could take the body of her dead dog to his summer place, a farm in Westchester County. Just a thirty-minute train ride from the city, its apple orchards offered plenty of undisturbed acreage for quiet reflection. The woman accepted Johnson's offer and was greatly solaced knowing that eternal rest might be possible—at least for a lifetime or two—on this secluded farm.

Word soon got out, and a rapidly increasing number of people began making the short train ride to the county: first with bundles looking suspiciously like cadaverous animals, then with flowers and grave markers. Johnson stopped picking apples in the orchard, and more and more people began visiting. In time, the visitors became friendly. They talked about the future of the orchard, the rapidly expanding suburbs, and the distinct possibility that their makeshift cemetery might soon become a new subdivision. To make sure that never happened, the pet owners raised money to buy the property and then created a deed specifying the land would have just one use in perpetuity. Shortly thereafter, the cemetery was formally incorporated.

Since then, Hartsdale has become something of a legend—both for its longevity and some of its celebrity residents, which include a lion owned by Princess Lwoff-Parlaghy (a Hungarian-born socialite and artist), and Robby, the iconic war dog who brought attention to the military's practice of euthanizing its service dogs after a battle had ended.

This cause célèbre is not what motivates Ed Martin Jr., the cemetery's current director, however. Instead, he seems compelled by a genuine concern for people and their pets. And it shows.

Martin is one of those truly affable animal lovers whom people just want to be around. A CPA by training, he stumbled into the world of pet funerals after his father, a granite worker, befriended the previous chief operating officer. She asked Ed Martin Sr. if he would be interested in assuming charge of the cemetery after she retired. He declined, citing his age and worsening health. *But,* he added helpfully, *my son might be just the man for the job.*

At the time, Ed Martin Jr. was splitting his days between accountant work and teaching at a small New York college. He liked the sense of community at the cemetery, where he had visited with his father, and agreed to consider the position. That was thirty years ago, and he hasn't considered another job since.

Martin's initial attraction to the sense of community continues to motivate him today. "This cemetery is visited by a variety of people," he tells me. "They come from all different backgrounds—religion, race, you name it. But they all have a common thread of loving a pet enough to bury it. These are caring people. They don't have to do this. Some people think using a pet cemetery is way over the top, so when they lose a pet many of them hold in their emotions. They're guarding themselves against some comment like, *you can get another dog.* When people come here, they realize this has been going on for a long time. A lot of people have experience losing a pet animal, and they know it's for real."

I want to tell him about my real reason for contacting him—to ask about the souls of domestic animals—but I'm too embarrassed to ask Martin if he believes in an afterlife for animals. Instead, I chicken out and ask if he has advice for grieving clients like me.

"Only from my own experiences and those others have shared with me," he says. "I'm not a psychologist or anything, but I am sensitive to what they are experiencing. I can tell them about what I've felt or what other people have experienced, but only if they ask. Mostly, I try to let them know that they're doing a special thing. For them, it's the right thing to do. What I was told by the former owner is that the function of this cemetery, and perhaps any cemetery, is to try to make people feel a little better. That means treating people properly and keeping the cemetery well maintained. I don't mean to brag, but a lot of people tell me this is the best-kept cemetery they've ever seen—for people or animals. And it does have a special feel. It's not uncommon to see people talking to each other or lingering on the grounds. Sometimes you see perfect strangers consoling each other."

Martin is right about the special feel of Hartsdale, and he'd have plenty to brag about if he chose. The cemetery is just a few acres in size, but meticulous landscaping and groundskeeping give it the quiet, shaded appearance of a much larger park.

"The original creators emphasized a natural setting here," Martin explains. "Like a miniature Woodlawn."

I apologize for having to ask what the full-sized Woodlawn looks like.

According to Martin, it's what anthropologists call a "Victorian Cemetery." Historians also call it a "Rural Cemetery" after the nineteenth-century convention of landscaping graveyards to look like some of the nation's most esteemed parks. I tell him about Sleepy Hollow Cemetery in Concord, and the transcendentalists' interest in making these places usable nature.

Martin says this aspect is important when dealing with the death of any loved one—animal or otherwise. But the funny thing is that this notion of death and community seems to fly in the face of animal instincts.

"I see it all the time," he says. "Both my wife and I had family dogs, and they wandered away at a very old age. I think they sensed that death was coming and wanted to be alone. No one found them.

"In the period of time since I've been here at Hartsdale, several people have scheduled appointments for their dogs to be buried; we get a call back several days later, and they tell us the dog has gone away. There's just no body to bury."

Martin thinks this is proof of a domestic animal's need to tap into its natural instincts.

"Think about it," he continues. "Other than a few raccoons on the side of the road that have died of a disease or been hit by a car, you don't really see dead wild animals. They've gone somewhere secret and alone. Unless an animal has been killed or was in an accident, you don't see them. Death is a solitary moment in nature."

There's a lot to Martin's theory, and Ari and I have already seen lots of evidence of it in the woods surrounding our house. The problem, though, is that our domestication often forces animals to redefine the death experience—whether they want to or not. Like animals in the wild, Cam's first impulse was to hide: first under the blankets on my bed, then deep within my closet. Did she curl up around my ankles in those last moments only because she couldn't get away? And what about the missing Hartsdale dogs? Were they determined to make good on their instinct to die alone?

According to wildlife research, the answer is yes. Sort of.

Wildlife death is frustratingly hard to observe in a natural context. Take dogs' close relative, the red wolf, for instance. Despite tremendous efforts on the part of organizations like the Red Wolf Recovery Project at the Alligator River National Wildlife Refuge (ARNWR), little is known about dying wolves in the wild. The problem, says Diane Hendry of the ARNWR, is that very few wolves are ever old enough to consider retirement or to expire from what we might consider natural causes (like kidney failure).

"Our biologists just don't see many instances of red wolves dying from old age," says Hendry. "They do occasionally see deaths from natural causes such as mange or intraspecific aggression," she offers. "Really, though, vehicular accidents and gunshot or so-called mysterious causes would be the top two reasons for red wolf mortalities."

As outreach coordinator for the program, Hendry's job duties include regularly fielding strange questions from strangers like me. She doesn't seem at all fazed, then, when I ask her where wolves like to die. Instead, she promises to ask her senior biologists and write back to me. Which she does, just a day later.

"The red wolf field biologists have not noticed a location pattern surrounding wild red wolf natural deaths," she reports. "They say it's just too difficult to get good numbers. Radio transmission is unreliable; plus, these biologists are covering a huge area—1.7 million acres. Not only that, but scavenging by crows and just general decomposition means there's not much to find."

Similar challenges confront biologists studying other wild species. As a result, science is left with a lot of best guesses about the death experience of animals in the wild. But most researchers do feel comfortable in asserting precisely what Ed Martin suggested: The majority of animals prefer to die alone. This is true even in animal species like gazelle or starlings who, by their very natures, spend their lives in groups. So why change your level of sociability in the face of death? The answers vary. Sometimes, sick or dying herd animals simply can't keep up with their group; other times, that same group may ostracize the dying animal because it represents a predatory risk. Compromised animals seem to know they're vulnerable to predation or attack, which is why they hide themselves: They hope that this isolation might protect them.

There are a few exceptions—though not many. Jeffrey Masson retells a heart-wrenching scene among elephants. As soon as one elephant showed signs that she was dying, her herd encircled her, trumpeting and touching her body with their trunks, as if trying to rouse her. After the sick elephant died, the herd stayed near, wailing and forming a tight circle around the body. The inverse of this practice has been observed in a variety of whale species. There, a sick or dying whale will sometimes beach itself and then call out to other members of the pod, who follow the distressed animal to shore and, often, end up dying themselves. But as far as animal scientists can determine, these are just about the only exceptions to the solitary death rule. Most of the time, a dying animal just leaves and never returns. Other members of its group either accept or don't notice the departure.

As for human response to the death (and killing) of animals, it has varied over time. Ancient societies and religions demonstrated almost complete indifference to the death of other species, and it's not until the writings of Plutarch in the first century AD that we see any discussion of ethics and the killing of animals. Plutarch was an affable guy, famous for his great affection toward family and friends. This consideration extended toward nonhumans as well. In his well-known treatise *Moralia*, Plutarch argued that being human comes down to also being humane. And that meant a moratorium on pleasure hunting or other abuses of animals for sport, which Plutarch insisted was anything but beneficent.

The British Romantics and New England transcendentalists all adopted portions of his teaching while crafting their own philosophies—many of which included arguments against animal use and misuse. Nonetheless, history has shown only minor blips of collective consideration for animal death—the early Celts, a few romantic Elizabethans, vegans at Woodstock. Aside from these isolated groups, animal death has remained an individualized and oft-ignored consideration for most of us. Unless, of course, you're forced to deal with it firsthand.

As everyone in my house has learned over the past few weeks, personal involvement changes everything about death. We humans need death to mean something—especially when it happens to a creature for whom we have feelings. Just about every contemporary world religion includes a provision for creating meaning out of dying: whether it's a Christian heaven, a pantheistic return to the World Soul, or the intricate notions of reincarnation held by several Eastern religions. Such beliefs offer great solace to their practitioners when faced with an animal's passing.

In my case, though, what I need more than solace is the one thing I doubt Cam could have given in life, let alone death: forgiveness. I need to know that artificial interventions ending her natural life were not only ethically justifiable, but also acceptable to her.

There is absolution in the world of animal medicine, should I want to find it there. Veterinarians and animal ethicists have devised numerous criteria for end-of-life decisions that take into account an animal's potential for treatment and recovery. On each one, it's clear that Cam's terminal kidney failure and obvious discomfort made her the perfect candidate for euthanasia. But that doesn't persuade me I've made the right decision: After all, these are human, not animal, criteria. More than anything, I want to believe that in Cam's world I also made the right decision. And if I could believe that some cosmic bed scale somewhere recorded a slight decrease in her weight—just a gram or two—when Dr. Townsend administered the lethal dose of drugs, that would be nice, too.

It is now mid-September, and we are halfway through our caninaturalist year. As we pass the autumnal equinox, the nights become much cooler. Most mornings, we awaken to a chilling blanket of fog, while towns a hundred miles to our north report their first frosts. At our house, nighttime temperatures still cling to the lower forties—not cold enough for a crystalline morning, but chilly enough to push back Ari's routine several hours.

Each morning, she gently wakes me around six, and the two of us stumble downstairs. As I wait in the warmth of the foyer, she hurries down the steps of the front porch, into the pine grove to pee, and then back inside. The whole process takes no more than five minutes, but her coat still absorbs the chill of the air—and some of its moisture, too. Without even asking for breakfast, she then lights up the stairs and jumps into bed—a new resurgence of her puppy behavior. But unlike our first winter mornings together, she's not interested in playing with or even waking us. Instead, it's our quiet warmth she seems to value most of all, and she works hard to insinuate herself into one of the pockets created by two drowsy bodies. The absence of Cam means she no longer has to vie for space, and we no longer have a reason to eject the pup. To the contrary, I find a kind of bittersweet solace in another furry mammal curled up in the crook of my knees.

Our walking schedule has changed as well. No longer avoiding the heat of high noon or the bugs that arrive a few hours earlier, we linger in the house another few hours: Ari curls up nose-to-tail in her dog nest; Greg dons a sweatshirt before retreating to his loft office; I settle on the couch to write with a cup of tea and thick wool socks. We all agree: We'll wait out the cool dampness before traipsing down the dirt road. Outside, a million different organisms seem to be making the same decision. The morning is quiet, save for the tempered shriek of a blue jay. No squirrel chases; no crickets, crows, or barking neighborhood dogs to stir activity in our cozy mammal den.

By 10 AM, the temperature differential shifts, and it is warmer outside than in. Greg and I open a few windows to let in the newly heated air. With it also come the tunes of an environment stirring: the rising pulse of locust, the dusty sweetness of one last haying. The pup catches both the scent and sound. She raises her head, then cocks one ear and half her nose in the direction of the window. *Interesting,* she seems to say. She rises with a long, stretching bow and shakes off the cool air. *Time for a walk.*

On these lonesome days, we opt for routine. And so, rather than heading toward the woods, we walk down the drive and over toward Stagecoach Road. Adventure is still far from my mind: I want peace and tranquility. A sense of connection. Perhaps intuiting this change in my demeanor, or at least the embers of the season, Ari remains more reserved as well. As much as I treasure her youthful exuberance, I'm glad for this new calm. It's a good time for reflection, and a quietly trotting juvenile dog who looks up and smiles from time to time does a lot on this account. So, too, does the landscape we've come to know as well as our own home.

But in truth, this route is familiar in name and geography only. As plants work through their growing cycles, the visible topography around our house continues to morph and change. Meanwhile, the sun has moved several degrees to the south, casting new shadows on the drive and illuminating patches of ground and brush we previously ignored. Working in concert with all of that nighttime moisture, it has also created a dizzying display of illuminated spiders' webs and browning weeds.

On our Monday morning walk, Ari seems noticeably impressed by this display, and she stops at patches of crystal, cocking her head and just staring. I tell her it will only get more amazing as we complete the arc toward a frosty winter, but she gives me a look that suggests I might be once again showing off. I recant and return to the silence of our midmorning walk.

We make our way to our usual terminus: Martin Stream. Its pools are quiet and cool in the morning shade. But unlike most days, the pool is inhabited this morning—its uniformity broken by a single object floating on the surface. For a moment, I worry it is another carcass Ari will want to embed in her coat. I wind her leash tight around my hand, since neither one of us wants to endure a bath today. But as we get closer, I see that the object is very much alive. And very much an enormous beaver.

Our field guide describes beavers as hefty rodents with disproportionately large skulls. Whoever wrote that hasn't met this particular beaver, whose immense body not only dwarfs his skull but also makes him utterly unlike the pen-and-ink sketch we find in our field guide. Then again, this book also insists that beavers are both nocturnal and group-oriented. Either I need a new guide or this lone paddler hasn't read up on his rodent natural history.

Regardless, both Ari and I are transfixed. This is the first time either one of us has had the opportunity to really study a beaver, and we both seem to have come to the same conclusion: it is an impossibly improbable animal. Observed head-on, this one seems like an overinflated balloon with whiskers. Its flat, narrow face is identifiable only because of the whorl of two nostrils and enormous ocher teeth. I don't know if that's more mythic or comic. Maybe both. The comic Robin Williams once joked that platypuses are proof that God likes to get stoned. If not further proof of this irreverent idea, beavers at least suggest that metaphysics has a sense of humor.

Ari also seems to appreciate the cosmic sway of the beaver, albeit for very different reasons. The one paddling in front of her has impossibly tiny eyes and ears; however, both senses are good enough to home in on my very curious dog. It stares, chuffing amicably at the pup, who returns the greeting. Theirs is clearly a mutual attraction. The pups whines softly and tugs at her leash, trying to get closer to the beaver. I relent and give her the full length of canvas while trying to make myself invisible behind the lip of dirt separating trail from stream. I want to see how the two of them will interact with limited human intervention.

The beaver doesn't seem to care one way or another about my presence; instead, it is captivated by Ari. They watch each other for a few seconds. Then, after deciding Ari is not enough of a threat to warrant a hasty retreat, the beaver paddles over to the edge of the pool and pulls itself heavily to shore. Even with its long bat-winged feet and thick frame, this beaver is remarkably nimble on land and makes its way to Ari in a single heartbeat. They are now just inches from each other, standing nose-to-nose.

I freeze. Never in our entire project has a wild animal approached Ari like this. I watch them closely, ready to yank Ari well away if the beaver shows any signs of aggression or diseased behavior. It doesn't, and so I hold my breath as the pup studies this new creature. She is pure electricity—dancing from foot to foot and reaching out with her nose, only to quickly reel it back in. Intrigue and uncertainty battle in the mind of this dog: *Friend? Foe? Dinner?* It looks like she can't tell. Or perhaps she is merely trying to make sense of this creature by way of comparison: *Hmmm, round like the neighborhood pigs, but much smaller. Compact like Cam, but not trying to claw out my eyes. Another red squirrel? Definitely not. And then there is that exotic, musky smell. Pretty darn alluring, if I may say so.*

The beaver creeps closer. The two animals are now an inch apart. They are entranced, and the rest of the world, including me, has melted away. What they are experiencing is intimacy in its purest form. They are, cognitively speaking, completely within each other.

In *Teaching a Stone to Talk,* Annie Dillard recalls a similar moment in her own life when she locked gazes with a weasel: an experience she describes as

> *a clearing blow to the gut. It was also a bright blow to the brain, or a sudden beating of brains, with all the charge and intimate grate of rubbed balloons. It emptied our lungs. It felled the forest, moved the fields, and drained the pond; the world dismantled and tumbled into that black hole of eyes. If you and I looked at each other that way, our skulls would split and drop to our shoulders.*

This is what is happening before me—what Dillard calls "mindlessness" and "purity of living." Both are states dogs and beavers clearly understand. Ari has no qualms about giving herself over to mindlessness. Or perhaps more exactly, she surrenders to a special kind of mindfulness: one that surpasses mere recognition of the moment and enters a more immediate kind of awareness not interrupted by concentration on the self. A kind of rapture.

Almost every Eastern culture has an account of this state. In Sanskrit, it is called *Dhyāna;* in Japanese, it is *Zen*. In Ari's ancestral homeland of Korea, Buddhists refer to this state of meditation as *Seon*. All cultures agree that this is a high level state of existence and communion. Ari doesn't seem to care whether this is elevated consciousness or not. There is no metacognition or thinking about thinking; there is just the brilliance of experience in and of itself.

I have no idea what this feels like. I want to, though. And that's the paradox: As soon as I consciously want this state, I have interrupted it. And once I do, the rapture disappears. My elation and surprise over the encounter breaks the spell between these two animals, sending the beaver on its way and leaving a stunned pup to slowly regain her sense of the surrounding world.

We hurry home to tell Greg what has happened. He's delighted and more than a little envious.

"I should have gone with you," he says. "I don't know why I thought work was more important." In addition to genuinely wanting to see the beaver, Greg is also feeling guilty about being gone for so much of Cam's final time. I want to allay those feelings and find a way out of our funk.

"Really, it's okay. Our entire species thinks work is too important," I remind him. "That's our problem. That's why most of us will never lock glances with a beaver. Not like this, anyway."

He seems placated by this explanation. But we both want more. We want to know if we can ever approximate the mindfulness of dog and beaver.

Several days later, I'm still thinking about animal metaphysics. I call my friend and colleague Julie Johnson. A licensed clinical social worker and practitioner of ecological mindfulness, Julie has that calm, accepting way of making no question seem silly. She also lives with one of Ari's favorite friends, a rescued pharaoh hound named Sylvie.

Ari and I meet up with them for an afternoon frolic in the woods, and Julie says she swears she can hear a symphony each time the dogs run toward each other on the trail.

"She's so interesting," Julie says, nodding in the direction of Ari. "I don't think I've ever met a dog like her."

From someone else, I might consider this a backhanded compliment. But Julie is too sincere and thoughtful to mean it in anything other than an appreciative way.

"I know," I say. "Greg is convinced she's a coyote."

Julie nods. This does not strike her as at all peculiar or unlikely. "Maybe she has a coyote spirit."

I tell her, half joking, that I've always thought as much. Then I recount our recent experience with the beaver.

"She should meet Fredda," Julie decides. "He'll know what it means."

Fredda Paul is a Passamaquoddy medicine man. Now in his sixties, Fredda spends much of his time educating others about traditional Passamaquoddy ways. Tomorrow, he and his wife, Leslie Wood Paul, will be visiting our college campus.

"You should come," Julie says. "And bring Ari. I'm sure Fredda would love to meet her."

We agree to meet them at the campus fire ring the next morning.

When we arrive, I find two people clearly in love with each other and the landscape. Fredda and Leslie are delightfully unassuming, particularly given how much they know. Both dress for the chilly morning in thick flannel shirts and jeans, their hair pulled back in loose ponytails. They are slight of build and filled with that benevolent ease of people who have established their place in the world. I ask them how they met.

"Leslie came to me in my sleep a long time ago," Fredda says, smiling. "In my dream, my grandmother told me she would be coming. When I awoke, I took out my calendar and marked the day told to me by my grandmother. Years passed. Then, on the afternoon I marked, someone knocked at my door. It was Leslie."

I'm stupefied. I ask if they had met or heard of each other beforehand.

"No," insists Leslie. "I was living in Kentucky learning about herbs. I decided it was time to move on and go somewhere that I could really study. I had a feeling Maine was the place. I just sort of dropped everything and left. When I arrived at Pleasant Point, someone sent me to Fredda's. I knocked on the door and he answered. Then he went inside and brought me the calendar and pointed to the date. It said I would be there."

She asks about me and Greg. "How did you find each other?"

"Nothing so magical," I say. "It was my first day of graduate school. The English department had a reception for new students in this hidden courtyard. You could only get there from a classroom window. One of the senior faculty was helping lower people down. When he set me on the ground, Greg was the first person I saw."

Leslie tells me she thinks that is plenty mystical. I want to hug her for that. But before I can, Ari and Sylvie have begun their own embrace. Both yowl and yip, wrapping their front paws around each other. Fredda laughs.

"Dogs know joy," he says.

I ask if he thinks dogs know nature.

"I do. Do you want to see?"

Of course I do.

Fredda is beginning one of his many seminars, which introduce non-native naturalists to Passamaquoddy herbalism. A group of community members and college students has assembled, and Fredda asks us to join him in making a circle. He explains what will happen during the next few hours, and then begins with a traditional smudging ceremony. After saying a prayer, Fredda lights a small bowl filled with sage and red willow.

"Sage is not native to this area," he says. "So we add the willow with it. The Passamaquoddy believe that this will purify the air. It protects and strengthens." He breathes deeply. "The Passamaquoddy inhale more of their medicines than any other tribe in North America. Do you know why?"

A student cracks a joke about getting high. Fredda smiles good-naturedly. "I know marijuana," he says. "And it has its place. But not right here." The student is impressed. Meanwhile, Fredda waits to see if anyone else has an answer before continuing.

"It's the air," he says, pointing toward the fog that still hangs about us. "Our air is cold and damp. The lungs need dry warmth."

Fredda walks around the circle we have formed, offering each person the opportunity to breath in the spicy smoke or, if we prefer, to wave some onto our faces and clothes. Everyone chooses to breathe. Deeply. When Fredda approaches me and Ari, he offers me the bowl first, then crouches down before my dog. She is curious but remains fixed, watching Fredda intently. He holds the bowl near her nose. She takes a quick sniff and her eyes grow big, alert. Fredda laughs again.

"She knows," he says. The other participants chuckle. Sylvie whines to be included, but Ari doesn't acknowledge her this time. She just keeps her eyes on Fredda.

On the walk, Fredda points out several of the plants most commonly used in Passamaquoddy medicine.

"This is white pine," he says. "*Kuwes.* Can you say that?"

Twenty people respond with *"Goo-ooze"*

"That's close," Fredda laughs. He's too polite to say otherwise. "White pine is very important to my people. It is used as a painkiller and to speed healing. It can be like morphine. But you must never take it from the trunk of the tree, since that can hurt the tree. Only take it from pruned branches—cuts that will help instead of harm."

We nod.

"What does *goo-ooze* mean?" asks a student.

"Sap that heals," says Fredda. "Good question."

We approach a white birch—the most emblematic tree of our region.

"*Masqemus*," Fredda says.

"*Mas-cue-moos*," we repeat.

"You're getting better," he laughs. "*Masqemus* means 'tree whose bark is curling up.'"

He takes a small piece. It looks like thin white paper. He offers it to Ari. She has seen this bark plenty of times and never shown the slightest interest. This time, however, she looks Fredda in the eye. He looks back. She then takes the offering from his hand and holds it in her mouth, as if awaiting further instruction. I'm amazed and do not know what creature has replaced my gadfly dog.

"Birch is good for digestive organs," Fredda explains. "It can cure ulcers and fevers, or can help with kidneys and the appendix, too."

Ari is still holding the piece of bark.

"Dogs know *masqemus* is good for them, too. Rids them of worms. Does she have worms?"

I say I don't think so. Western medicine insists she gets a preventive tablet every month.

"That's okay," Fredda concedes. "*Masqemus* is good for the digestion, too."

He nods at Ari. She chews and swallows the bark.

After the walk, Julie and I linger with Fredda and Leslie near the fire pit. I tell them, shyly at first, about my current interest in metaphysics and my growing theories regarding Ari and the natural world.

"She sees things," I say. "It's like other animals and even plants are attracted to her. I get the sense that she's tapped into something different in the natural world—something almost spiritual. But then again, maybe that's just silly. Maybe she's just a dog with doggy senses." I pause. "What do you think?"

"I think those are white ideas," Fredda says. "Not mine."

I ask him to tell me more.

"For us, everything is spiritual," Fredda explains. "It comes through the Creator and into the world. That's what gives our medicine its strength. Once, my people were constantly connected to nature. It was how you ate, how you made yourself well. There is intelligence in nature, but most people are too distracted to notice. If you are still, you can feel. The wind, a bird, the moving leaves—it can all tell you something. It can show your spirit the way, too. Plants, birds, dogs . . ." He stops and smiles at Ari. "They have things to say. They can make the mind clear. The message is there if you listen. And if you talk from the heart, they will hear. They will know you understand."

I nod my head, trying to process all that he has said.

"Don't think too much," he says. "Go see. You'll understand. I think your dog already does."

I tuck away Fredda's words and think them over throughout the next week. But the fall semester has begun and I'm too distracted by new classes and students needing schedule changes. The following Saturday, though, I decide enough is enough. I load Ari into the car, and we head to a popular trail one town over. I want to see if I can get to the root of what Fredda has said. But it's hard to change your mind-set in a moment, and I'm quickly frustrated. This trail has none of the charm of our morning walk with Fredda. Instead of thick, undisturbed forest, we wander past brush and an absurd number of discarded appliances. I begin to count cedar trees and washing machines. The population of the latter soon wins out. This irks me. Or at least I tell myself this is why I am irked.

I also tell myself I need real nature to find some sense of the spiritual. This place is a marginal space—the kind of compromised landscape that exists on the margins of suburb and society. Sure, it has all of the accoutrements of wilderness—trees and insects, running water and blooming flowers—but they are dampened by the obvious presence of humans. A few candy and cigarette wrappers intermingle with goldenrod; the sounds of the town raceway clog the air. I'm disheartened. Forget metaphysics; everything about this place is just plain physical—and of the most unimaginative kind.

Ari doesn't seem to mind the human intrusion—in fact, as far as she's concerned it just seems to add to the sensory overload of one of our walks. She races back and forth along the trail, trying to take it all in. As she does, she keeps her nose buried in the scents on the trail itself. I, too, forget to look upward. But instead of taking in the scents, I seek further proof that we are not actually in a natural space. I am sulking, trying to find excuses to alienate myself from this place. Fredda would be disappointed.

And just when I have convinced myself that we can find nothing wild in this landscape, we are stopped cold by a giant roar of water and wings. Ari and I both look out onto the stream, where an enormous bald eagle is rising out of the current. The eagle hovers just twenty feet away from us, and its seven-foot wingspan seems more like seventy. The characteristic white cap and tail tell me that it is a sexually mature bird, but I cannot determine the sex or age from where I stand. Frankly, I can't do much of anything other than stare at this immense expanse of wing and life. Despite Benjamin Franklin's protestation that this is a bird of bad moral character, despite the overuse of the eagle for everything from homeland security to car dealerships, this is a hauntingly majestic animal—larger than life in every possible sense of the cliché. Ari and I are both frozen—in shock or awe or reverence, I can't tell—but we stay like that for quite some time, long after the eagle has risen above the canopy and out of sight, long after the sound of racing cars in the distance once again seeps into our consciousness.

And that's when it hits me: I am experiencing mindful communion. At least in the sense that I am utterly inside this bird as it rises from the water. Is this a sign? The fulfillment of Fredda's natural theology? Or is it just a coincidence of time and space—of eagle dinnertime and the noise of a clumsy hiker? I don't know. I decide it doesn't matter. For the first time since Cam's death, I am rooted in the very best sense of the word. As the buzz of the civilized world returns, it somehow seems more distant, more muted than before. Even the disused appliances retreat a little. Nature—at least this time—has trumped culture. And a sense of wonder has replaced my feelings of loss. The pup and I are spellbound—weightless, almost. And we couldn't be happier.

I Wanna Be Just Like You

[october]

Nature is on the move this month, and Ari's keeping watch. The pup has become increasingly vigilant about our homestead in recent weeks, and she spends most of her indoor time wobbling on the thin back of our sofa, where she can peer out our living room windows. At ten months old, Ari looks like an almost grown-up dog: admittedly, a grown-up whose ears are still way too big for her body and one prone to protracted displays of puppy exuberance, but certainly a grown-up far too big to balance on the back of furniture. Still, she persists in this daily enterprise, wobbling and trying to make herself seem feline on the narrow edge of the sofa.

The couch itself, meanwhile, has taken on a new identity of its own and looks far more like an abominable snow creature than it does a piece of forest-green furniture. Across its expanse, thick tufts of tawny fur undulate in the breeze, giving the appearance of underwater vegetation or epic Midwestern fields. Except, of course, for the annoying fact that neither of those landscapes adheres to wool pants or fleece pullovers.

Our new canine vegetation has taught us another important fact about maturing jindo-huskies: They shed. A lot. So much so, in fact, that those in the know refer to this twice-annual molt as dogs "blowing their coats." I wish this were merely an evocative metaphor. Instead, it's the burdensome reality of a juvenile dog turned dandelion top. Thick balls of Ari's undercoat now float continuously through the air in our house, eventually alighting on the carpet, the dining room table, the husband, and, of course, the much-suffering sofa.

In another context, this might be whimsical or even picturesque. It might even be ecologically elegant. If, for instance, Ari were timothy grass or another late-flowering flora, she'd be dispersing her seeds for germination next year. If she were common milkweed, she'd be feeding monarch butterflies and delighting children with her airborne silks. She's not, of course.

Instead, she's a half husky who has inherited her father's immensely effective insulating fur. Like her wolfie forebears, Ari wears two fur jackets: a thick undercoat of short hairs close to her body, and a mantle of coarser guard hairs on top. Together, they keep her body warm in temperatures as low as seventy-five below. Part of why this fur is so effective is that she completely replaces it twice a year. And that, of course, means that she has to lose it then, too. This makes her grumpy, and she pulls at the clumps of fur with irritation. Once she frees a tuft or two, she spits it into the air, sending it into the follicle orbit already overcrowded with other little furry planets. Normally, this kind of garish display would delight Ari. These days, she barely notices, so consumed is she by her mangy appearance. I can hardly blame her: The pup looks awful, and I think she knows it.

I try to comfort her with anecdotes of orthodontia and other ugly-duckling tales from my own adolescence. But two minutes into what I am convinced is a heartfelt anecdote about a very bad decision in ninth grade to perm my hair before a much-anticipated school dance, Ari rises and leaves the couch in a huff. Or rather, a puff. This makes me laugh. I point out the cleverness of this pun, but the caninaturalist ignores me and slinks into the kitchen, where she can lie on the cool tile floor and mope. She's frustrated. And I suspect I'm only making it worse.

Further incensing her is the increased activity around our house. Although the pup has never been all that territorial, the growing movement of animals preparing for winter seems to concern her. She barks menacingly whenever another animal passes through our yard, regardless of whether or not that animal might be a threat. Of particular concern to her right now are three feral cats who occasionally cross our driveway on their way to some secret location. These are clearly not transcendental animals in Ari's book, and there will be no mindful connection between her and them. They are the enemy, and she is reminded of that fact each time they strut across our drive. When they do, Ari raises her hackles, bares her teeth, and acts as if a massive invasion is imminent. Our peaceful mornings have been interrupted by the schedule of these cats, who invariably wander down the driveway just before dawn, somehow alerting my sleeping dog that intruders are lurking and must be barked away.

Where these cats are returning to and how they spend their daylight hours remains a mystery to me. Like most of the wild animals in our area, the cats are too wily to be seen on one of our caninaturalist walks. I must resort, as Ari does, to stakeout positions near the front of the house if I am to learn anything about these felines. And so there Ari and I sit together each morning, watching the kitty debauchers steal home after a long and tawdry night of vole hunting and free love. They are wily and loose, these cats, and far too clever to let us know much about their wild lives.

We're both surprised, then, when we see a small cat resting on the edge of our road early one October morning. As soon as I see the kitten, I stop Ari and make the now familiar gesture of reeling her leash tightly around my hand, thinking she might spook the cat. But the cat doesn't notice us. In fact, it doesn't even move. We walk closer to investigate, only to discover that the kitten—no more than a month or two old, I'd guess—has become another victim of too much traffic traveling too fast on a dark country road. Trussed in a glossy black coat, she is beautiful and sleek, even lying broken in the middle of the road. Ari forgets to be fierce about this creature, who is undoubtedly the offspring of one of the pup's new nemeses. Instead, she sniffs the kitten gingerly, then pulls back in alarm when she reaches the kitten's fractured skull and dislocated eye. Can she tell this was an unnatural death?

Meanwhile our neighbor Elizabeth drives by on her way to work. Her car idles as she looks down at the cat and shakes her head sadly.

"Not another one," she says. Her voice is full of real regret.

"Do you know this cat?" I ask, just in case. "Does she belong to anyone?"

Elizabeth shakes her head again. "I've seen a new feral family around here the past few days, but I haven't been able to get close. I'm sorry."

She apologizes again—she is late for work. Otherwise, she would stay and help.

I tell her I understand. And the kitten is so small, I'm certain I can take care of its burial by myself.

"Too bad," Elizabeth says by way of conclusion. "We've had a lot of these accidents lately."

We agree. Too many.

As I watch Elizabeth's Subaru drive down the long road, I decide I've had enough. Enough death, enough grieving, enough proof of the fragility and fallibility of life in our neighborhood. I turn Ari around and return to the house. Greg looks up from his morning work, surprised by the shortness of our walk and the militaristic determination of my entrance. I tell him about the kitten as I search for a copy of the week's newspaper, which I will need to collect the broken little cat.

Wordlessly, Greg leaps from the couch and puts on his shoes. He takes my hand as we walk down the driveway and turn in the direction of the cat. We kneel down before her. She is nearly weightless, although her condition requires both of us to maneuver her onto the Business section of the paper. We fold the pages as if the kitten were a package about to be mailed, and then we bury her in the rock wall along the side of the road.

Afterward, Greg hugs me. He knows I am still smarting over Cam, and I get the sense he wants to allay any grief. But this time I'm not feeling sadness. I pull away from him, my jaw set.

"We have to help them," I insist.

Greg nods warily. Is this the deranged insistence of a grief-stricken pet owner? The messianic complex of someone who has been thinking about animals for too long? His expression is indulgent, as if worried he might further agitate me.

"Okay, hon," he says slowly. "We can try to figure out something."

"No," I insist. "We have to help them *now*. We have to save them."

The look on my face tells him I'm about to go home and rifle through our closet until I find tights and a cape. The look he gives me in return suggests clothing of the straitjacket variety might be more appropriate. Too late: I will not be dissuaded.

I spend the rest of the morning visiting shelter and cat rescue websites. Greg and Ari take turns sighing despondently from his office. They are united in their apprehension over my behavior. I begin sighing, too, but more out of despair concerning the current state of the domestic cat than anything else.

The Humane Society of the United States (HSUS) estimates that American animal shelters receive anywhere between six and eight million cats each year. Of these, about three million will be adopted. Another three or four million will be deemed unadoptable and then euthanized. One reason might be because, as a species, cats have never fully embraced notions of domestication. In fact, if we think of dogs as often walking that thick line between the wild and domestic, cats might be seen as inching their stealthy way across the tiniest of tightropes. They are, without a doubt, the least domestic of all our domestic animals. Unlike dogs, many cats don't require direct support from us for their survival. Most of them don't even care all that much whether or not we form emotional bonds. Perhaps that is why so many of them fall under the category "feral."

According to the HSUS, there are currently anywhere between ten and seventy million feral cats running wild in the United States alone. If the actual feral population is anywhere close to the higher end of that estimate, that means there are an almost equal number of feral and truly domestic cats (current estimates place the latter population at around seventy-eight million). No matter how you look at it, this is an epidemic problem. Not only do the cats suffer from disease and malnutrition, but their robust numbers have done serious damage to small-mammal and bird populations. Forget about recreating dogs and their effect on nature: The impact of feral cats on natural habitat is so immense that some scholars suggest we place these cats in the same category of zebra mussels, purple loosestrife, and other invasive species. Factor in the threat of disease and the dangers of crossing country roads at night, and you start to understand why, at best, feral cats can expect to live only half as long as domestic cats. Most never even see their third birthday.[1]

The thrust of this information leads me to conclude that the best way our family can help cats and the environment is by working with one of the feral protection programs in our area. I find an organization called Save Our Strays, which places homeless cats in foster homes until they are fully socialized and can be adopted. It seems a wonderfully humane solution to the overcrowding of so many animal shelters and the decimation of local songbird populations. Plus, the organization's success in socializing young ferals seems like an accomplishment worth supporting.

SOS lists dozens of cats available for adoption in our area. I read the bio of each one, looking for clues about who might enculturate the most smoothly into our home. I rule out all tabbies on principle: They look too much like Cam, and I know I will spend at least our first few weeks wishing they were her. I rule out most older cats for related reasons: Given Cam's stress over Ari's introduction, I worry that an older cat will be just as traumatized living with my ebullient caninaturalist. From there, my decision making becomes far more capricious, as I look for well-written descriptions and interesting cat photos. I feel like I am participating in an online dating service. In a way, I suppose I am.

Eventually, I email a foster cat parent named Cheshire. I decide that with a name like that, she must have a good sense of cats. Her email address is that of a local college, and I appreciate the lyrical descriptions of her foster kitties. In my introductory letter, I tell her about the three of us and ask if she knows of a young cat who might enjoy living with such a family.

She writes back an hour later to tell me that she has the perfect candidate for me. Her name is Mouse—a yearling cat who was recently rescued along with her four siblings. Cheshire describes Mouse as very curious, adventuresome, and busy. A real character.

[1] Feral dogs don't do much better. According to Alan Beck, the life expectancy for these hapless canines is 2.3 years.

I ignore Cheshire's coded language about Mouse being "a character," as well as her more overt warning about Mouse's fondness for chewing paper. Instead, I immediately visit the Website featuring pictures of Mouse. There, I find a jester of a cat. Not quite calico, not quite tortoiseshell, Mouse wears motley. Her face is a swirl of black and brown, with a jagged orange stripe rising from her nose to a point on her forehead. She also has the biggest, most speckled ears I have ever seen. Delighted by the cat's carnival-esque appearance, I write to Cheshire and tell her I think Mouse is beautiful. She sends me an adoption application, which I tuck away in my saved email folder. Meanwhile, I creep upstairs to the loft, where Ari is napping and Greg is writing. They both eye me and become instantly dubious.

"You've found something," Greg says.

"Not something," I correct. "Someone."

Two days later, we leave Ari at home and drive to Cheshire's Victorian house. Greg is doing his best to be a good sport, but I can tell he's not entirely enthusiastic. Even as she continues to mature, the caninaturalist can feel like a full-time job. He's pretty sure we don't need to be logging overtime hours. He also knows I'm not about to be dissuaded. We've entered the realm of compromise.

Earlier in the morning, the three of us had gotten together for a house meeting. I laid out my plan, which went something like this: We can undo the karmic debt paid to our recent roadkill victim by adopting a feral cat and bringing it into our home. Not only do the three of us have a moral obligation to do so, but any other response would most certainly tilt the universe toward disharmony. Ari responded to this assertion by looking bored and returning to her command post in the living room. As she pitched and rolled on the edge of the sofa, Greg returned to his pragmatic side.

"We can't help everyone," he said. "Certainly not every creature in nature."

I told him I'm not trying to help everyone—just one cat. And maybe a littermate. Or two.

Greg's expression became harried. "Three? Three cats? Our house is going to be so busy. We're not a wildlife refuge."

But maybe we are—at least a little bit. I reminded him that Ari was savage in her own way when we brought her home. Saying as much was a colossal rhetorical misstep, and we both knew it as soon as I finished speaking.

"Exactly," concluded my dear husband with the panache of a Roman orator. "And aren't we still trying to resolve that?"

By this point in the conversation, Ari was barking fiercely at a moth on the porch. When it didn't respond, she pawed at the window. Sometimes, I swear these two are in a complicitous conspiracy against me. Either that, or Ari just has very bad timing.

Still—and despite the fact that my wild dog had just proven my practical husband somewhat correct—he did the unexpected and relented. He took my hand and said he wants me to be happy; if adopting a cat (he was clear in his use of a singular noun here) will do so, then he's on board. I hugged him and grabbed the car keys.

That was an hour ago. Since then, we have driven across the countryside in a nervous silence, wondering what we will think when we meet this feral litter. In that time, much of Greg's resolve has returned.

"Only one," he reminds me as we ring the doorbell. "We only have room for one more animal." I pretend to agree.

After a brief introduction, Cheshire leads us to feral cat land. As we walk up the stairs, she warns us that, although they have learned to trust her, the cats will not transfer that trust to other humans. At least not at first.

"These kitten-cats were born wild, and they lived on their own outdoors for five months. That's about as long as you can go and still hope for domestication," she says.

We count back the months since they were rescued and brought to Cheshire.

"The cats were born last September?" I ask.

Cheshire nods.

"So they spent the winter outside in the wild?"

She nods again.

"How on earth did they survive?"

"I have no idea. But these are tough little animals."

Not that you'd know it at first meeting. The four kittens launch an elaborate crisis drill as soon as we enter the room. Each flies off her perch and scatters about the room, as if moving toward her appointed place of cover. The three humans move their heads back and forth quickly, trying to keep track of the lightning speed and precision movement.

"Well," Cheshire finally says with a deep breath. "Here they are."

We are introduced to the litter. Even though she is terrified, Mouse looks even more the clown in person than she did in her picture. I'm captivated. But what about her three sisters? What will become of them?

Before I can say anything, Greg turns to Cheshire.

"I really think they ought to at least stay in pairs, don't you?"

She smiles in agreement. I blink, looking for the husband who accompanied me to this house.

Greg continues. "I mean, I think it's the right thing to do. For the cats. I wouldn't want to separate Mouse from the only family she has."

I remain dumbstruck. And pleased.

Cheshire quietly steps away from the room, leaving us to get acquainted with four terrified cats. I sit down on an overturned chair.

"Two cats?" I smile.

Greg looks sheepish. "They seem so scared," he says. "I think they need one another."

I would leap up and hug him if it wouldn't further scare these little cats. Instead, I just tell him this is one of the reasons why I love him.

But how do we choose Mouse's companion? Each is so charming in her own way. We can't make this decision for them. I go downstairs and find Cheshire engrossed in a book.

"We need your help," I say. "Who would be the best choice to go home with Mouse?"

Cheshire comes upstairs and surveys the room. "They're all great," she says. "But at night when I hear scampering up here, I think it's coming from Mouse and Leila Tov. I can't confirm it, but I think they're playmates." She pauses. "I'm not going to lie to you, though. Leila Tov has come the least far in terms of socialization. I don't know that she's ever going to become really domesticated."

That doesn't bother me too much. Leila Tov is a photographic negative of her sister: lean and black and mysterious in her reticence. I like the contrast. And hopefully we'll have Mouse to cuddle someday. I also like the idea of helping a cat who really needs it.

"Do you think Leila Tov will be hard to place with another family?"

"I do," says Chesire. "I've had the most inquiries about Cora, and a few people have visited Mavis and Mouse. But none so far for Leila Tov."

That settles it for me. I look to Greg. "Can she be the one?"

He agrees.

Getting the two cats into a carrier is a comedy of errors for the five of us. Cheshire tries to extricate Mouse from her perch on the windowsill, but Mouse has laid root. Patiently, Cheshire tries to remove each of Mouse's barbed claws from the screen. Her paws are enormous, with an extra thumb on each hand. She looks like Mickey Mouse with his big white gloves. Or, even better, like a two-handed catcher for the White Sox.

Leila Tov, who is much more graceful and lacks the extra digits, is an even greater challenge. Each time we pour one cat into the carrier, the other escapes. By the time both are stowed, the three humans are exhausted.

We shake Cheshire's hand and promise to stay in touch. She follows us to the car with reminders about helping the cats get adjusted to their new house.

"And don't worry if they don't eat or use the litter box. It could take days. When their brother was adopted, he didn't eat or pee for over a week."

This does not sound promising.

Greg and I drive home in anxious silence. We have once again made a mostly impetuous decision, and one for which we have little experience or qualification. As for the juvenile dog waiting anxiously at home, we can only hope she associates our new cargo with Cam and not the lurking feral cats in our driveway. Cheshire's constant reminders that we can return the kitten-cats provides just enough comfort to persuade us to keep driving.

Once home, we lug the carrier into my back office, where we set up food and water, a litter box, and what we hope will be an appealing cat nest of flannel sheets and thick towels. The setup looks very much like it did for Cam's final hours. Maybe this will help chase away some of those residual ghosts, too.

The sister cats have stuffed themselves into the back corner of the carrier, intertwined in fear. Their tiny dark faces point outward, revealing only four wide green eyes. We open the carrier door and peer in. They try—unsuccessfully—to wedge themselves farther back in the carrier. This is going to take a while.

Greg and I leave them alone in the room and shut the door behind us. We take Ari for a very long walk, hoping the quiet house will give the kitten-cats time to adjust. When we return an hour or two later, the cats have disappeared from the carrier. As Greg distracts the pup with dinner, I hunt for the new inmates, beginning under the futon. No cats. I peek behind the bookcase. No cats. Chair, desk, end table. No cats. Are they Houdinis? Can they, Harry Potter-like, dissipate into thin air? I love this idea, despite its obvious unlikeliness. And I have to admit that I'm a little disappointed when I find the two very un-wizardly-looking sisters crouched in the microscopic space created behind our TV armoire. I peer through the small wedge between furniture and wall. The two dark faces turn in my direction, eyes still wide. I coo and cluck. They do not respond.

This courtship continues for the next day or two, as Greg and I alternately pop into the room every few hours to check on the lack of progress made by the cats. On the third day, I contact Cheshire to see if she has any advice.

"You have to minimize their hiding places," she counsels. "Make it harder for them to seek refuge completely away from you. But don't be aggressive in approaching them, either. They should still be able to dictate the terms."

Greg and I puzzle out how to make this work. Eventually, we decide to pull out the armoire from the corner, thereby creating a bigger space—one that, eventually, could accommodate a human appendage. We do this with quick bursts into the room—just long enough for us to remind the cats that we share this new house with them, but not long enough for Ari to realize something's up.

Miraculously, this plan works—at least as far as Ari is concerned. The cats, meanwhile, become distraught that their place of residence has been compromised and somehow manage to beam themselves to the area behind the futon, where they remain for the next thirty-six hours.

On the fourth day of their new residency, I see a flash of black tail as I open the door. At least they've begun wandering in our absence. A little food seems to be missing, too. Around midnight on the fifth night, we hear a mad soccer match taking place downstairs. The rumbling of pouncing cats stirs Ari, who trots over to Greg's office where she can stand, directly over the ceiling of the back room, with one ear cocked and her eyes as wide as the cats'. *Something's down there!* she seems to say. She paws at the carpet and looks at us more intently. *Hey, guys. Something's down there!!*

We tell her she has new friends but that it will be a while before they are formally introduced. This clearly infuriates the caninaturalist, who spends the remainder of the soccer match lying sphinx-like, following the sound with her wolfie ears and pouncing on the floor from time to time. Apparently no one will sleep tonight. Each time we make bleary-eyed eye contact, Ari gives us a dirty look and corrective bark: *Why on earth are we up here, when something's playing down there?!?!* Her expression suggests something between contempt and pity. Humans clearly don't get it, and she reminds us as much throughout the night. Each time she does, we groan and search unsuccessfully for sleep. Maybe the caninaturalist is right.

The next day, Greg and I decide that our presence isn't going to make a great deal of difference in the back room. And, to be honest, we've begun to miss our TV. We take the pup with us: The three animals are going to have to get to know one another eventually. In the meantime, we humans intend to watch a movie. For the first hour we're all together, Ari seems to have forgotten that we have company in the room. Gradually, though, she puts two and two together as she paces around the small space: *Litter box and exotic food, yes that's very interesting. Humans unnaturally interested in the wall behind the futon. Most peculiar. And what is that? That faint odor . . . it seems almost familiar to me . . . vaguely feline, I daresay. Wait. I think I've got it. We have new cats!*

At the risk of yet another cliché, I swear I can see a tiny compact fluorescent illuminate somewhere just above Ari's skull. I turn to Greg and state the obvious.

"I think she's figured it out." This is both a confirmation and a warning.

A moment later, we watch with trepidation as Ari trots to the side of the futon and inserts her long snout, breathing deeply. Sure enough, that's a cat smell. She jostles and dances, trying to get a good look. Greg and I forget about our movie and turn to the back of the couch, peering down. The two dark faces turn from us to the pup, who is now whining softly, desperate to get their attention. We've gone too far to turn back—the cats are going to have to meet this canine gadfly.

Forty minutes pass with the five of us in this awkward configuration. Still, Ari is no closer to wooing the cats. Tired from her vocalization and constant tap dance, she retreats to her dog bed and lies down, sighing heavily. We all wait. And then, a few minutes later, a clownish little face emerges from behind the futon. Mouse looks around once or twice, then wiggles out into plain view. She steps gingerly in the direction of Ari. They both sniff the air. Ari looks restless. I say her name in a long, slow tone of warning. But it's needless. She's riveted to the floor, waiting to see what Mouse will do next. Mouse responds by taking a quick lap around the room, staying low and nervous on her haunches. Ari lets her explore, craning her neck owl-like to keep this new cat in view. Mouse completes the circle and returns near Ari. The two sniff the air again, then Mouse retreats underneath the futon, presumably to report back to her more reticent sister. Ari yips a salutation, and Greg and I sit in quiet amazement.

Over the next week, we try mimicking Ari's call to Mouse with no success. Ari, on the other hand, continues to prompt brief encounters with the cats, who both emerge from behind the futon at the urging of this very social dog.

The caninaturalist has once again become our ambassador, this time an emissary representing both the human and feral world. Without her, we make little progress communicating our benevolence to these frightened, feral sisters. Somehow, though, she's able to convey something positive about our character—and probably much more. Given how difficult it is to acclimate feral cats to a new social environment, I'm both impressed and intrigued by Ari's success. Is it her communion with the natural world? Her transcendentalism? The fact that she was once semi-feral herself?

Of course, that last designation is mine, and I doubt many wildlife biologists would share it. When they use the word *feral,* they generally refer to those animals who have returned to a wild state after once being domestic. Does this include Ari? Probably not. Her unsupervised life in the shelter bore more similarity to Peter Pan's Island of the Lost Boys than it did Mouse's half year in the wilderness. Still, I pose this theory to a small group of my science colleagues. They look skeptical. I ask how closely they guard their definitions.

My colleague Jim Chacko, an expert in fisheries and aquaculture, admits to a certain capriciousness in scientific identification.

"We are not good at definition." He says this low and quietly, as if he might be excommunicated for his admission. "I cannot say why, but people in my field have started calling all wild fish 'feral,'" he adds.

I tell him this conjures images of rogue salmon wearing punk clothing or little goldfish throwing satchels over their shoulders and hitting the open road.

"Goldfish don't have shoulders," he corrects. He doesn't deign to comment on the idea of fishy couture. "And I mean fish *already* in the wild."

"So what do you call fish that were once domestic and are now wild?"

"Escapees."

You have to hand it to ichthyologists. They're efficient with their language, if nothing else.

They also happen to be pretty accurate when you consider the existence of most truly feral animals. When it comes right down to it, these animals—or their close ancestors—all flew the coop (so to speak). And once they did, far more than their lifestyle changed. Texas, for instance, boasts feral species ranging from the mundane non-native to the bizarrely inappropriate: elk and boar, oryx and yaks, wildebeests and giraffes. A clever writer for *Texas Parks and Wildlife* magazine even coined the term *texotic* to describe the animal contingent. And it is no small contingent: At last count, the state estimated that at least 275,000 exotic animals, representing over seventy-five species, call the Lone Star State home. That's more than any other state in the Union. Hunting these animals is big business, even by Texas standards: Last year, it brought more than three hundred million dollars in revenue.

One place not clamoring to laud Texas is Australia, where they have plenty of their own feral game animals to deal with, thank you very much. Not to mention the rabbits, cane toads, yellow crazy ants, and half a million feral camels that call the continent home. The destruction caused by these foreign animals has been immense, and Australia is often cited as a worst-case example of what happens when meddling colonialists decide to change an ecosystem for their benefit. Just recently, biologists discovered a feral population of bumblebees on the island of Tazmania. Commercial beekeepers are currently lobbying to allow for the introduction of this species on mainland Australia. In their application, they insist that "little ecological harm" will come from the introduction of one more invasive species.

This seems like famous last words to me. Still, having just introduced two new feral creatures into my own habitat, I can't help but empathize with the beekeepers: The introduction of such animals is impossibly alluring, particularly when it happens in my TV room. But do I, like these same beekeepers, run the risk of creating ecological harm? Introducing my lost child puppy certainly compromised Cam's habitat—and her psyche. I ask my science colleagues the question none can answer: Can these cats do something similar? They do not know—or they won't say.

Back at the house, all five of us are obsessed with what it means to be a semi-wild invasive species. Each evening, Greg and I join the pup in my office for a few hours of cat-watching—hoping against hope we might find a sense of connection with these two mysterious creatures. During the day, I comb books and articles for information on what a feral life might look and feel like. I have my own fantasies, of course. Growing up, one of my favorite films was *The Jungle Book,* based on the stories of Rudyard Kipling. My profound love for the film arose at least in part because it constituted my first drive-in movie experience: I was astounded to learn that I could actually watch a movie in the car while wearing my PJs and eating a big Tupperware bowl of my mom's special popcorn. Singing along to songs like "I Wanna Be Just Like You" and "The Bare Necessities" made it close to perfect. But even under different viewing circumstances, I would have been taken by the film. The idea that a human child could be raised by a singing bear and then befriended by panthers, monkeys, wolves, and an orangutan (all in one little biome!) delighted me. My only real confusion was why a kid who obviously had it so good could be wooed out of the forest by a pretty girl.

What I didn't know at the time is that the cartoon Mowgli wasn't so far off from the dozens of feral children raised by animals over the past several hundred years. Sure, they don't belt out duets with Louis Prima or walk around in well-placed diapers, but real feral children have been raised by animals including wolves, leopards, goats, bears, wild pigs, chimpanzees, sheep, ostriches, and dogs—to name a few. All of these children share a few key characteristics with the animated version of the feral Mowgli: seemingly preternatural physical abilities (particularly running and climbing), heightened senses, great tolerance for heat and cold, and hirsuteness (bodies covered with a great deal of hair).[2]

The relationship between these children and the natural world seems particularly relevant to my current project of caninaturalism. Here were humans who really did let animals dictate their approach to nature. But when it came to resocializing them, that orientation proved problematic for doctors and researchers. Most feral children so internalize the behaviors of other creatures, they no longer identify with human preferences. They don't do all that well once brought back to society, either: Of the fifty-some feral children found in the modern era, the overwhelming majority have been imprisoned in asylums and died well before the average human life expectancy.

This is not to say that there aren't plenty of reasons to want to bring a feral child back to civilization. Jean-Jacques Rosseau probably wasn't so far off the mark when he suggested that the natural existence can be brutish and short—especially if you're a wild child. Few have access to proper diet, clothing, or hygiene. This isn't just a matter of social appropriateness: It's also a biological hindrance when it comes to the perpetuation of the species. Feral children are also usually found suffering with a whole host of parasites, including tapeworms longer than they are tall. But of even greater concern to most contemporary thinkers is the feral children's lack of communion with other members of their species. Like dogs, humans are predisposed—both genetically and dispositionally—to be a part of an intraspecies community. Our well-being depends upon being part

[2] So profound are these characteristics that our good friend Carolus Linnaeus even devised a separate species for what he called "wild man" (*Homo ferus*) after a series of children and young adults were found roaming the European countryside. Although scientists have criticized Linnaeus's subspecies categorization, they do acknowledge profound differences between feral and domestic children—particularly when it comes to cognition.

of a group. People in social networks are happier, and they live longer, too. In this regard, we're not so different from our canine companions or other group animals, all of whom need companions to survive and thrive.

But couldn't we argue that feral children have a community? All of their stories share one crucial thread: The children survived in the wild because they were adopted and raised by a group of animals. And if we want to say that such adoptions don't count because they do not constitute a human community and thus are insufficient, what do we want to say about the millions of pets living as the sole representative of their species in our homes? Aren't we also depriving them of community? Isn't that a feral existence of a different kind?

These are the questions consuming me this month as our caninaturalist project turns inward and toward the artificial ecosystem created in my home. And I'm not alone. Although it may be coincidental, Ari has begun shortening our afternoon walks—tugging me back to the house as soon as she's taken care of business. Once there, she bypasses her food dish and canters into the back room, first pawing at the door, as if to say *Knock, knock! Don't worry, just another uncivilized quadruped here.* Before entering, I get a reprimanding look from this blue-eyed dog: *I've worked hard at this. Don't blow it.*

I promise to do my best. And I mean it. Never before have I been so aware that I am a student sitting at the knee of this furry guru. I wait just inside the door, sitting cross-legged and making myself look as innocuous as possible. Meanwhile, Ari works her magic again and again. She and Mouse have settled on a process that almost seems routine: Ari pads over to the futon and inserts her snout, then retreats half a dozen steps. Mouse tumbles out from behind the couch. They both take a few sniffs of the air, as if to confirm they are who they think they are. Then there is more intimate sniffing. Sometimes, there is even a nose nudge or two. And on a very rare occasion, when both are feeling exceptionally patient, I can ease my way on hand and knee over to Mouse, who will sniff my hand, too. On the rarest of rare jackpot days, she lets me touch her fur. But that is only after checking in with the caninaturalist, who appears to agree to monitor the situation and step in should I attempt to overstay my welcome.

Ari takes this new role very seriously, and she's not about to let me do something stupid. I know this—as clearly as I know my own name. And I find it undeniably intriguing.

So, too, do many animal behaviorists.

Scholars know that young mammals tend to form social kinships with individuals familiar to them. Most immediately, this includes their mother and any littermates. But baby animals will insert themselves into other groups, just like feral children do. Wild kittens, for instance, often nurse from female cats other than their mothers. Domestic kittens raised in close kin-proximity to an animal such as a rat or guinea pig will not consider these species as prey later in life. The same is true for domestic dogs. Both species, in fact, have sophisticated their sense of the familiar to such a degree that they will refrain only from killing the particular breed of small mammal or rodent with which they were raised. Thus, while a dog or cat may show no qualms about killing a mouse, squirrel, or rabbit, it wouldn't dare harm a rat—wild or domestic—if one happened to live in the same house with them growing up.

Animal trainers often use this to their advantage. As previously noted, many shepherding dogs are placed from a young age with the herd of sheep they will one day be protecting. Not only do they come to recognize every member of the herd as part of their family, but they also begin to identify with the sheep and even take on some of their behaviors. In general ethologists—and a good percentage of the general public—have celebrated this assimilative ability. They have also rejected the claims by some animal rights groups that such employment is both confusing and abusive to the dogs. Have we given these objections their due? Is there a moral or existential problem for imprinted dogs? And what about the many foster parent stories of people raising coyotes, goats fostering rhinos, raccoons rearing kittens, and dogs suckling rats? Are all of these animals suffering from a collective identity crisis?

I pose these questions to Deborah Wells, an animal behaviorist specializing in rescue dogs and the environmental enrichment of captive animals. Wells spends a lot of her time considering the psychology of animals living in shelters or other enclosed settings. As a result, she has had plenty of opportunity to observe all sorts of human-arranged interminglings of animals not generally seen in the wild. The whole matter of identity for these and other animals, she says, comes down to the basic crux of nature versus nurture.

"It is true that you can train young animals not to show specific behaviors—or, alternatively, to exhibit specific behaviors—if they are introduced to these behaviors at specific points in their development. But," she adds, "an animal's internally motivated behaviors will eventually come to the fore."

I ask if this is another way of talking about an animal's instincts.

"Exactly."

However, Wells says, there is at least one identifiable difference in animals raised with other species. All animals have mechanisms for showing approach anxiety when they're faced with something—or someone—unfamiliar. And these responses can vary wildly depending upon an animal's upbringing—especially if that upbringing includes other animals (or a lack of them).

"Feral animals show fear reactions to humans or other foreign species," says Wells. "If they don't encounter humans or dogs or cats during that sensitive period of development from three to twelve weeks, they will later react to those species as if they were completely alien. An animal raised in close proximity to these foreign species, on the other hand, identify them as familiar."

I ask if the latter creates a need for species self-help manuals.

"Not that we know of," she says. "In fact, sometimes animals need that kind of interaction to remind them to think like animals."

In Northern Ireland, where Wells teaches at Queen's University, the Belfast Zoo recently resorted to one such surrogate system after the birth of a Barbary lion. Extinct in the wild since the 1920s, the lions are among the rarest cats in the world. So when the zoo successfully bred a cub in captivity only to have her mother reject her, they took great pains to make sure the baby would survive to adulthood. That included hand-rearing the cub (whose name is Lily) by keepers, a technique that results in greater viability for cubs but also a little too much human interaction. To combat the socializing effects of all this people time, zookeepers used an Akita puppy named Keepa as a surrogate caretaker.

"Really, though, Keepa's more of a surrogate buddy than a caretaker," says Wells. "The puppy is big enough to endure Lily's rough-and-tumble, and Lily gets a chance to act like a lion."

I ask why Lily doesn't act like an Akita. Or why Keepa doesn't think she's a lion.

"That's an important question. The main reason the Akita puppy won't act like a lion is that genetically she is a dog. Thus, much of her behavior is instinctively driven," says Wells. "Were we to deny the pup complete access to other dogs, then we might start to see a few problems or even aggression toward other dogs. However, in the case of Lily and Keepa, this didn't occur, since the puppy went back to its mum (and was in contact with other dogs) at the end of each 'working' day."

Now that Lily is sturdier and understands some basic animal behaviors, she, too, is spending some time with her mom, which Wells says will ensure that Lily develops liony behaviors as Keepa maintains her recreational life as a dog.

That reintroduction is a crucial moment when it comes to collective identities. For most group or herd animals, seeking out our own is a crucial part of our survival. That's somewhat complicated for dogs since, as Don Hanson explained back in April, we've so interfered with their biology that they depend upon us as much as other members of their species. And maybe that's the sticking point with feral children, too: They've come to depend on other animals at least as much as, if not more than, they depend upon humans. In fact, the biggest problem for those psychologists working with recovered feral children was the fact that the children showed utter indifference and occasionally even hostility toward other human beings. Feral creatures call into question our notions of self and other. In some very real ways, they reveal that notions of human and animal are probably best considered as a continuum, rather than two tidy categories. And as much as we'd like to believe that opposites attract, we tend to seek out—and even love—that with which we are most familiar.

In our house, Ari seems to be filling that role of the familiar for Mouse and Leila Tov. Something about her overtures is safe—or at least invitingly familiar: Like the cats, she sniffs as a way of identifying; she knows when to make and avoid eye contact; she uses her ears and tail to help communicate. It's doubtful the cats think this pup is a giant, clumsy cat, but she must at least seem more closely related to them than Greg and I are. Plus, they share some of the same vernacular. That's bound to be comforting in a strange house filled with new things and scary people. In this regard, the pup really is a kind of intermediary between human and feral feline. And because she is capable of befriending us both, I suspect Ari can eventually bring us together as long as the two cats and pair of humans let her lead the way.

For her part, Ari continues to find delight in this role. She has forgotten about the feral cats—and even the red squirrels—lurking outside our house. These aloof wanderers can't possibly compete with two new creatures willing to engage her. So instead of sitting on the back of the living room couch, Ari now takes up permanent residence outside my office door, her nose pressed to the crack near the floor. And on those glorious evenings when we enter this portal into the world of feral cats, Ari continues to trot deliberately to the back of the futon, where she waits patiently until the cats emerge. When they do, she moves from us to them, making sure everyone is aware of one another and glad to be together. This, then, makes her glad, too, which she tries to tell all of us with big sloppy kisses and pounding tail thumps. *Hey team,* her smile seems to say. *Look at us. Here. Together. We're a pack. Isn't that just the best thing ever?* Leila Tov still isn't sure. But Mouse is learning to appreciate the appeal of camaraderie, even if it is a strange, interspecies kind. I have to believe that is at least in part because she—like Greg and me—finds this social young dog impossibly lovable. And if gleeful communication is any indication, Ari clearly loves that she is being loved.

Food for Thought

[november]

November is Greg's least favorite month. He claims it's an uncomfortable meteorological limbo—too late for fall foliage; too early for good snow. Normally, I take issue with this. I really like November: the starkness of the barren trees, the thick gray skies, and the creeping chill of winter. I also appreciate the way this month shifts our energies homeward, toward fleshing out nests, stocking up, hunkering down. Often, these are largely ceremonial gestures—vestiges, perhaps, of our pioneer forbears and primordial rhythms. Here in New England, though, they come out of real necessity as well. By this time each year, we've usually received our first of several snowfalls, and the temperature regularly hovers below freezing. That, too, creates a significant shift in the way of the world—and a beautiful one at that.

But not this year. Instead of sharp, starlit nights and the powdery brightness of a snowy morning, we've experienced thick, soupy skies and perennial dampness. As a result, human and animal alike are suffering from the bone-chilling rain and lack of sunlight. At harvest dinners and the last of the farmers' markets, our friends and neighbors admit they are depressed: not certain about whether they ought to be unpacking winter gear or hanging on to the accoutrements of fall. We share their sentiment and, for the first time, I have to agree with Greg: This really is an unfortunate in-between time.

As for the dogs in our lives, they seem to be encountering their own difficulties with the month. Maybe it's the lack of sunlight and the constant dampness. Perhaps it's the hustle and bustle of humans preparing for the holidays. Then again, there could be a more instinctual cause—one at which we fully domesticated creatures can only guess. Whatever the reason, this month dogs experience their own brand of limbo, and they stumble more than usual along that invisible line between the wild and the domestic. Doing so, as we all soon will learn, can be downright dangerous—even deadly.

We can't know that at the beginning of the month, of course. Still, Greg's grim characterization seems unusually prescient. The three of us lie in bed one gray Saturday morning, musing on this strange time of year. Ari, uncharacteristically still in the early morning, has curled herself in the crook between my arm and hip. It's that predawn time when she's allowed to join us on the bed, and rather than her normal routine of pouncing on my feet, she's decided to use the morning as an opportunity to nestle in close.

Meanwhile, I can tell from Greg's movements that he is awake. It's only six o'clock; still, I suspect he's been up for an hour or two, contemplating his courses and writing deadlines. I roll over to see. Sure enough, he looks wide-eyed and quietly thoughtful. I smile. It's a rare day that finds us both lingering in bed, and I want to savor each minute of it before we leap back into our daily routine. Greg strokes my cheek—I can tell he agrees. We interweave our hands and talk about the month. I ask him to explain why he does not like this time of year.

"It's the most somber time of the calendar," says Greg. His voice has that endearing, early-morning softness to it. I snuggle closer as he continues. "People get so down in November. I think there are chemical effects to the loss of daylight and color," he speculates.

I agree that there might be something to this. I know of at least two close friends who feel the very real effects of seasonal affective disorder every year. "But," I say, playing devil's advocate, "why November? Why not December? That's when things can get *really* bleak."

Greg shakes his head. "That's the return to spring. By the time we hit the winter solstice, we're turning back around again. It's more hopeful. Think about the holidays in December—they're about light, not darkness."

"Yes," I say, "but why?"

"Physiology, I think." He pauses. "That and social pressures. Either way, people get more short-tempered and nostalgic this time of year. I think we're all less communicative and have less energy to give to relationships."

In the past, this has certainly been true for the two of us. Our biggest arguments have traditionally been this time of year, when we're short on time and patience—a difficult combination for any couple. In the years before we were married, November became a perennial time to reconsider our relationship and wonder where it would eventually lead us. We'd trot out the ghosts of frustrations past; we'd challenge each other to say the wrong thing or, even worse, to question the advisability of the relationship altogether. After we were wed, we thankfully abandoned the impulse. Still, we struggled to avoid bickering over holiday travel plans and household chores and who suffers the most from being overworked.

This year, however, feels different—more quiet and peaceful, with less of the strained peace, the frenetic appointment-hopping, the pressure to be somewhere or something in particular. We've relaxed. We've let some of our work go, and we've stopped believing that we must leave home to have a good time. I can't help but wonder how much of that difference is the result of our life with Ari. Even now, during our busiest time of year, we continue our weekly walks in the woods: the pup tethered to me by her now worn canvas leash; Greg and I connected by our gloved hands. We make an interesting and clumsy chain, the three of us. Ari is still a dreadfully rude walker on leash, pulling this way and that or stopping directly in front of us to investigate a rock or candy wrapper. I suspect she thinks the same of us, pausing as we do to worship the vivid sunsets—the streaks of tangerine and plum sweeping across the dusky horizon. This has become our Thanksgiving, and we celebrate it often.

As we do, we wonder if any of this makes sense to Ari. We ask her again and again if she understands beauty, if she can feel the soaring effects of aesthetics. Her perplexed expression tells us the answer is probably no. This makes us wistful—sad, even. We want her to see the natural world in our light, too.

According to Greg, our regret is utterly appropriate for this time of year.

"There's no way around it," he concludes. "November is a melancholy time."

I ask if he has chosen this word deliberately. *Melancholy* comes from the ancient Hippocratic belief that the body is regulated by four bodily humors. Too much or too little of any one of these humors was believed to create both physiological and mental distress. For centuries, melancholia was considered an excess of black bile, which in turn was believed to be secreted by the spleen and responsible both for depression and anger. It was also most closely associated with the classic elements of autumn: cold and dry air, the feel of sterile earth, the tendency for downed fruit to ferment. I ask if this is what Greg means when he thinks of November.

"Definitely," he agrees. "That's exactly what I'm talking about."

As dawn stretches out its tentative light, the pup grows impatient for her morning walk. She begins hopping on and off the bed, as if to remind us how it's done. I can tell by Greg's expression that it's time for him to get to work, too. We leave the conversation—for now—and agree to begin our day.

After Ari's walk, I sit down and look for other cultural precedents that might support Greg's grave monthly forecast. There are plenty. The Finnish word for November is *Marraskuu*, which translates literally as "the month of the dead." The Celtic calendar has similar markers. Ancient Celts celebrated the dark season with Samhain—the precursor to our contemporary Halloween—by illuminating gourds and building enormous bonfires believed to direct the dead. Their harvest feasts often included places set for the deceased, who were thought to join them in need of some cheer. A merrier but no less poignant holiday is celebrated in Latin cultures with Day of the Dead. During the first two weeks of November, celebrants invite deceased friends and relatives into their home by telling stories and serving rich food. It's a complicated time: half celebration, half bittersweet remembrance and what some people call open fatalism.

I'm particularly interested in this connection between the somber and the celebratory, between feast and grief. Food and death—two inescapably interesting topics for most humans. And I have to agree with Greg on at least one count—the two coalesce in some meaningful ways this time of year. In the cultivated landscape of North America, this is the time of slaughter: Since precolonial times, farmers have found it too difficult to keep livestock such as pigs and sheep alive during the winter. Better to kill them now when the cool temperatures will help to preserve their meat, and then breed a new generation in the spring, when nature takes care of the feeding pressures.

Thanksgiving, the month's biggest secular holiday, is also based on that weird mix between death and life. Since the epic first meal in Plymouth, Americans have gone "a-fowling" to celebrate the richness of the harvest and to get ready for a long, lean time. Writing about the first Thanksgiving, Pilgrim Edward Winslow related with great pride how the men "exercised our arms" and "in one day killed as much fowl as, with a little help besides, served the company almost a week."

Celebrating a good crop by killing every bird you see strikes me as a cultural anachronism. So, too, do the more quiet symbols of the month. The reigning astrological symbol for the month is the Scorpio, which simultaneously symbolizes water, intercourse, and death. The official flower of November—the chrysanthemum—has long been associated with death and funerary decorations across the globe, and yet it is a favorite edible blossom among chefs and amateur salad makers alike.

Food and death—how can they fit together so naturally? What can they mean?

We get our first clue a few days later.

Despite our commitment to time outside with Ari, Greg and I cannot deny that we're in the real meat of the semester now and starting to show signs of fatigue. This newfound quietness around the house appeals to our latest pack additions, who now have full run of the place. Mouse surprises us all by trying out life as a lap cat now and again. Leila Tov, still far more reserved, remains scared to death of close contact. Still, she begins appearing in our bedroom at a much greater frequency—usually sitting on a dresser and eyeing Mouse with something like wary envy.

The same stillness that the cats find so attractive is anything but for my energetic young dog. The caninaturalist project has been abbreviated as we all try to make do with a few short excursions into the woods around our house. These mini walks are all Greg and I can muster right now, and yet they don't even come close to placating the pup. One Thursday evening, the two humans return home to slump over a meal and offer the pup a few halfhearted pats. Clearly bored, she races around the house and tries her hardest to leap upon every prohibited surface: the couch, the coffee table, a desk chair—anyplace we are sure to scold her and, thus, initiate a game of will. When we do not notice that she is standing on our bed, Ari amps up her assault, systematically removing the comforter, the blankets, the sheets, and the mattress pad. We find her poised and growling on the flung pile of bedding. This is a restless dog no longer content with sunset gazing and bedroom chatter.

To make it up to her, I offer her a narrow, doughnut-shaped bone while Greg and I collapse on our newly made bed. She seems content with the compromise and takes the bone into Greg's office, where she dedicates herself to sucking the marrow with a deliberation Thoreau himself would surely admire. But a few minutes later, she's up again, racing into the room with the bone in her mouth. She leaps on the bed, and I tell her to get off. She hops up again, and I repeat the command with more force. Ari loves to share her toys with us—an impulse we adore in theory and tolerate in its slobbery actuality. Even so, I don't want this bone, nor do I want a dog flaunting wanton rule breaking.

Ari gets the hint, but instead of slinking off into Greg's office, she stands next to my side of the bed, hanging her head despondently. We look down and find the source of this misery: Somehow, the pup has managed to lodge the bone up and over her bottom fangs, trapping her tongue and the underside of her chin in soft little accordions of mashed flesh. She looks miserable, and hangs her head as if in colonial stocks. We try desperately to remove the bone, failing each time. But despite our rude intrusions into her mouth, Ari doesn't retreat. Instead, she stays close, keeping at least one paw or flank in contact with my leg at all times. Her expression is one of pure defeat. It's heartbreaking.

Greg and I increase our attempts to remove the bone. But after fifteen minutes, we have to admit our own defeat. There's just no way to get the bone off Ari's jaw without cracking a tooth or tearing her skin in the process. For the life of us, we can't figure out how she managed to wedge the bone on this tightly. It is stuck; and so are we. I call the vet's office and am connected to Dr. Jeremy Bither, who listens patiently as I try to explain our current situation. It's nine at night, but he doesn't hesitate: "I'll meet you at the office as soon as you can get here."

When we arrive forty-five minutes later, Dr. Bither sedates Ari and removes the bone, but not before first taking half a dozen digital photographs. "You don't mind, do you?" he asks after the first few images. The pup's body lies limply on the table, her eyes rolled back and her chin still smashed inside the bone. She looks horrible. But that's precisely what appeals to him.

"We get quite a few of these cases each year," he says. "It'd be good to show our other clients the dangers of inappropriate toys." *And the foibles of careless pet owners?* I wonder to myself.

"Sort of," he admits, as if reading my mind.

A very groggy dog and I return home two hours later. Ari, still barely conscious, does not stir as I turn off the car and open the door. A storm working its way into the region has blanked out all the stars. I can see nothing, nor can my comatose dog, whose unblinking eyes do not focus on me or anything else around her. I gather her in my arms (no easy task—this is a long, forty-five-pound dog now) and carry her up the front steps of the porch.

Inside, we find Greg sitting before the season's first fire. Mouse and Leila Tov perch on a wooden beam near the woodstove, appraisingly us calmly. It's a heartening scene. I fold the pup into her bed and join Greg on the couch. We sit quietly, watching the flames and feeling the calming effects of dry heat. The cats do the same, intrigued by what is probably their first experience with a fire. After nearly an hour, Ari stirs just long enough to drag herself closer to the cats and the stove, and then falls back into her deep and dreamless sleep.

The next morning, before I can worry about Ari's condition, she crashes onto the bed, pulling the covers off my face and nipping at my nose. When I do not respond immediately, she leaps off, gives a hearty play-growl, and catapults back up with even more enthusiasm. She shows little evidence of last night's the trauma and the ensuing anesthesia. As for the rest of the suspect bones, she seems to have forgotten about them as well. Greg and I smile at each other superciliously. While Ari slept, we spent part of the night burying each and every one of these bones with the icy care of murder suspects. It will take more than the capricious interest of a juvenile dog to find them.

Two days later, Ari and I visit the vet's office for our follow-up appointment. She looks alert and cheerful as we once again make the forty-five-minute drive into town, and I see no evidence that she associates the trip with the misery of a marrow bone lodged over her jaw. Instead, she seems delighted by the view. As I drive, she studies the landscape, barking at the flocks of wild turkeys and herds of beef cattle converging on the now barren cornfields. As best I can tell, Ari does not distinguish between the two groups of animals. The turkeys, with their prehistoric wildness and impulse for flight, and the cows, with their soft eyes and well-tended coats, are equally exotic to the pup. Her bark is one of neither alarm nor clear friendship, but more of an acknowledgment of difference. I wonder aloud if she associates these animals with potential food or if their distance and current status—alive and intact—obfuscates such associations. She answers with a wide-mouth pant and equally wide eyes: *Who cares? They're just interesting. Give your questions a rest and check out these giant animals!*

I insist we can do both. She pretends not to hear.

When we arrive at the vet's office for our post-procedural checkout, even I have to admit this isn't the place for big, theoretical musings. Walking to the front door, we pass a man standing heavily on the front lawn. His back is to us; still, I can see that he holds a dog who is either dead or sedated. I pull in the slack of the leash and hold Ari close, both because I am reminded of her mortality and because I do not want to flaunt her vibrant puppy life in front of someone who might be grieving.

Inside, we're soon distracted by a young boy of about five, who approaches while we wait at the counter. He tells me matter-of-factly that his name is Jack, and then introduces us to his two new kittens. Ari and I are delighted to make their acquaintance. Jack's mother, on the other hand, seems both amused and mildly concerned by her child's assertive sociability. He nevertheless insists that we peer inside the carrier, and so all four of us crouch down and stare at two minuscule cats. They can't be more than two months old, and they are absolutely delightful with their thick stripes and square little kitten faces.

"I named them Oscar and Maple," Jack tells me proudly. "For my two favorite things."

I guess at what they might be. "*Sesame Street* and autumn leaves?"

"Nooooo," he says, dragging out the syllable with feigned exasperation. "Hot dogs and pancakes."

I laugh, congratulating him on his choices. "I really like pancakes with maple syrup. Especially this time of year."

This makes perfect sense to him.

I look down at the kittens. "Do Oscar and Maple eat hotdogs and pancakes?"

Jack gazes at me in disbelief. How can an adult be so foolish? "No, silly, they're cats," he corrects. "Cats eat cat food."

I cannot argue with this reasoning.

Meanwhile, Ari's name is called. Our appointment is over in an instant. One of the vet techs comes out to the waiting room and takes a quick look at Ari's chin. The swelling has gone down; the abrasion is healing. She opens the pup's mouth. No sign of laceration or infection. We receive a clean bill of health, and the vet tech takes a picture of the smiling, healthy dog to complement the troubling images taken in the ER.

As I wait to pay our bill, I notice that the man from outside has returned. It is my friend Chris, though it takes me a few seconds to realize as much. He appears haggard and ten years older than I have ever seen him. Andrea soon exits one of the exam rooms, trying her best to maintain a gracious smile for the staff as she joins Chris at the counter. The façade doesn't work very well. She, too, seems sallow and weary.

"Bentley?" I ask.

Andrea nods. Before she can elaborate, Dr. Bither steps into the waiting room, bringing catheter pads, anti-seizure medication, and the very special extra-emergency pager number, should they need to contact him in a crisis. Andrea turns to me. "Baker's chocolate," she says by way of explanation. "We don't know how much he ate."

Dr. Bither's expression conveys the seriousness of the situation. It is no exaggeration.

If there is an Achilles' heel to domesticated dogs, what they eat is surely a part of it, particularly if what they eat has any cocoa in it. The sense of taste is a surprisingly complex—and compelling—motivation in dogs. Along with touch, it is the only sense baby puppies possess when leaving the womb. And although their sense of taste is far less sophisticated than ours (we have about nine thousand taste buds; dogs have just over seventeen hundred), when reorchestrated in their brains along with memories of past dietary pleasures and the instinctual needs to procreate, taste becomes a serious motivator for all dogs. The problem is that this sense is anything but refined.

In fact, when it comes right down to it, there isn't much a canine won't eat. While domestic cats like Oscar and Maple may stick to a narrowly defined diet of animal protein, Ari and Bentley are not nearly so choosy. Like other members of the Canidae family, dogs can scavenge for refuse or eat freshly killed prey, and their palates appreciate broad samplings of animal, vegetable, or mineral. In this regard, they are at least as diverse as we in our food choices. Probably even more so.

Ask any vet or longtime dog owner, and you'll hear an unbelievable litany of what dogs consider dinner. In Pennsylvania, our elderly neighbor cooked French toast and sausage every afternoon for his daughter's pug. Joel, our instructor at Green Acres, swears his hound would walk to the end of the earth for a piece of raw broccoli. Kinch lived for baked earthworms, made crispy by several days broiling on asphalt.

The list of utterly inedible edibles is no less impressive. Animal hospitals report finding heirloom jewelry, entire stuffed animals, and infinite forms of molded plastic all in the guts of dogs. It just goes to prove, I suppose, that taste really is subjective—and sometimes downright absurd.

To further complicate matters, scientific research suggests that domestic dogs are also motivated by what *we* like to eat. A recent study at Cornell University reveals that generations of life with us really has changed food preferences for dogs: They have come to prefer cooked meat to raw; they also prefer processed meat (think bologna and Spam) to the newly dead variety. Individual lifestyles also affect these preferences. If a dog sleeps in the same room as her human companions, her food preferences will more closely align with theirs; if her owner regularly eats a heavily processed diet in her presence, the dog will come to crave that, too. Research also indicates that interactions with humans will compel dogs to develop preferences for foods not instinctually desired: things like sugar or alcohol or even chlorinated water. Some of these choices—such as clean drinking water or vitamin-laden dog food—are at least partially responsible for the amazing health of dogs as a species. Others—like potato chips or beer—have undoubtedly compromised their biological success.

For dogs, then, being omnivores really is what contemporary environmental journalist Michael Pollan deems a "dilemma." Pollan explains that being an equal-opportunity eater requires a lot of brain power in order to safely navigate the seemingly endless choices. With so many possible things to ingest out there, there are bound to be some pitfalls—like hallucinogenic plants, or pork rinds. When faced with these options over generations, evolution often steps in and provides sensory cognition to help us make better choices. Most omnivores are in tune with the bitter taste of a poison or the pungency of rotting food, and they know to avoid such tastes.

It seems, though, as if Mother Nature didn't quite trust a dog's ability to make good on this skill. As a result, she gave canines an unusually short digestive tract. It takes a healthy human anywhere between twenty-four and seventy-two hours to digest a meal. The same food usually makes its way through a dog in about six hours, which leaves less time for problems to occur. Add to that a diverse assortment of pancreatic enzymes (including melancholic bile), and even long-dead deer legs will go down the gut of a dog remarkably smoothly.

That's not the case, however, with chocolate. All cocoa products contain theobromine, a mild stimulant prized for its ability to gently raise a human's mood and lower blood pressure. This may be why the alkaloid won its lofty name (it translates from the Greek, quite literally, as "food of the gods"). However, when assigning the moniker, no one considered its effects on canines. Unlike humans, who can process theobromine in about eight hours, canines are unable to convert it quickly or efficiently. As a result, the alkaloid remains in a dog's body, compromising his cardiovascular and nervous system, which can cause severe seizures and cardiac events. If a dog survives these effects, he still has to contend with often fatal damage to his kidneys and other life-threatening ailments. The darker the chocolate, the higher the level of theobromine. The higher the level of theobromine, the more dangerous to the dog.

This explains the long faces of my friends. When Andrea awoke at 3 AM, she found Bentley ensconced on the living room couch, happily making his way through a canister of baker's cocoa. Andrea had no way of knowing how Bentley found the cocoa or how much he had consumed, but his powdery snout and paws clearly indicated he thought he was having a great time. She rushed him to the veterinarian's office, where they administered large quantities of activated charcoal, which binds with the cocoa and prevents absorption. They also sedated him, flushed his body with intravenous saline, and installed a catheter in his paw so that Chris and Andrea can administer anti-seizure medication directly into his veins, if and when he begins to seize.

Dr. Bither minces few words in explaining the situation to us. Theobromine is a stimulant to the central nervous system. Over the next few hours, Bentley will experience an elevated blood pressure, nervousness and trembling, and a feeling of tremendous thirst. Depending upon how much chocolate he consumed, he may also experience those seizures, along with a stroke, heart attack, or total renal collapse. Any of the last scenarios will probably be fatal.

This is grim news indeed.

"So now," concludes Chris without a hint of humor, "I suppose we're on a death watch." Dr. Bither nods in agreement. He places a consoling hand on Andrea's arm and returns inside. Meanwhile, I am still holding Ari's leash, and she's becoming impatient. She is too young to interpret the wide range of human emotion, and she doesn't understand the severity of the situation. Instead, she mugs for attention, rolling on her back and chortling. This is not the time for such displays, and so I help Ari into our car and then join my friends.

We walk out to their Range Rover, where a very groggy Bentley looks up at us. He's wearing an Elizabethan collar (which somehow always makes a dog look pathetic), and he slouches on the backseat, unable to hold up his head. He seems both miserable and confused, and he tries unsuccessfully to focus on us with his big brown eyes. They are, I note to myself ironically, a rich shade of chocolate brown. Chris, Andrea, and I huddle close, looking down at this dog and wondering if he will make it. It's a terrible thought to ponder—if a creature lying before you will live or die, particularly when the situation was caused by domestic life.

The three humans pull away from the car window. I give Chris and Andrea a hug, and they promise to call with an update the next evening: According to Dr. Bither, they'll know for certain after twenty-four hours if Bentley will survive. I offer Bentley my best smile and tell him to be strong, knowing perfectly well that he can't understand me but hoping his will to live will fight the deleterious effects of the next several hours. Besides, it can't hurt.

I'm eager to leave this place. I love this veterinary clinic and its staff; however, it's hard to separate from it the sadness associated with a sick or dying pet. I wonder how veterinarians do it—how they deal with so much animal pain and human sadness over and over again. As I do, young Jack steps out with Oscar, Maple, and his mom. He gives me a big wave, his mother jokingly rolls her eyes, and they put the very healthy little kittens back into their car. That, I suppose, is how vets do it. They remember that life goes on.

And so must our lives. I continue with my errands, though I am still more concerned about Bentley and his family than I am the tedium of a Saturday morning.

We pull into the parking lot of the big supermarket down the street. I remove Ari's harness so there's nothing that will tangle her while she is in the car, and then tell her I'll be right back. As I wander up and down the aisles of the grocery store, I find it difficult not to think about Bentley, since every aisle has some cocoa product in it: energy drinks and granola bars; yogurts and enchilada sauces; even the produce aisle offers chocolate fondue for strawberries and apples. What was once a relatively exotic ingredient imported from Africa and South America is now a near necessity in most homes. We humans love chocolate—and most of us think we have to have it. Forget about eating for your body shape or blood type; forget about eating local or sustainable: whether we're sipping coffee, eating a sandwich on pumpernickel bread, or even dining out on braised short ribs, we're often ingesting some version of the cocoa bean.

It's understandable: Not only does chocolate taste good, but the theobromine exerts a pleasant physiological and mood-altering effect. Even so, we usually prefer the full-fat, full-sugar version, which actually has less theobromine than its more austere cousin, pure dark chocolate. There's a reason for that, too. Like many omnivores, humans deem fat and sugar as high-value ingredients, and we seek them out whenever possible. They're what got my early ancestors from Europe to New England, and then from New England to the Great Plains—metabolism-sustaining, energy-inducing, edible supplies. That same high-cal fuel gets Ari's Arctic kin across the tundra in even the worst winter conditions.

It makes sense to me that we humans—and our canine companions for that matter—would want fat and sugar in our diets. Our cells need both, and they provide what chefs call good mouth feel. That might be why chocolate is ranked as Americans' favorite food. If there's truth to the idea that a dog's food preference is defined by ours, then Bentley and other dogs must be hooked. He lives in a culture that celebrates love with Hershey's kisses and converted the Celtic holiday Samhain into Halloween, when kids go from door to door demanding individually wrapped chocolates. Even if we didn't have a biological need for such treats, we've all certainly been socialized to appreciate them.

But Bentley didn't seek out leftover Halloween candy; instead he went straight for the nonsweetened, defatted, and arguably unpalatable cocoa. Why would a dog be attracted to something so clearly harmful and, frankly, gastronomically unappealing?

According to psychologist and canine behaviorist Stanley Coren, there's no easy answer. Coren explains that the sense of taste is one of the most difficult to study in canines—largely because it is so difficult to translate their tastes to ours. We know that, in general, foods that are useful and digestible in animals became associated with a "good" taste; harmful food tends to taste "bad." But, Dr. Coren warns, these values do not transcend species: What tastes great to Ari and Bentley might be utterly repugnant to me. That explains their penchant for what I would consider unmentionables—fox scat, squirrel fur, rotten snakes. We can't know why these things taste good to dogs—we just know they do.

Although I can't really fathom it, I appreciate—at least on an intellectual level—why something like scat or rotting carcasses would appeal to dogs. But how can baker's chocolate or any other toxin actually taste *good* to them? Aren't our biological aversions to dangerous food supposed to override our curiosity? Yes and no, says Coren. He reminds me that dogs have a sweet tooth—or at least a preference for a chemical called furaneol, which occurs in natural sugars.

That would explain why Bentley might want Halloween candy; but the chocolate he ate was unsweetened. So what gives?

The answer, says Coren, rests in another instinctual trait held by most dogs: to wolf down their food as quickly as possible.

"Dogs dislike bitter *if* they taste it," he elaborates. "However, dogs often gulp and swallow without tasting much at all except for the traces left in their mouths after they have swallowed. This will usually dissuade them from eating that substance the next time, especially if the bitter taste is associated with a distinctive odor. However, it obviously won't help on that first encounter—which can be fatal in cases like chocolate."

Studies of wolf behavior indicate that most canines do not experience hunger like we do. Instead, they accustom themselves to an all-or-nothing existence in which they either gorge themselves on up to one fifth of their body weight in a single sitting (that's the equivalent of twenty-eight pounds of meat for a 140-pound human). Despite evolutionary differences between wolves and domestic dogs, the latter have retained many of these feasting tendencies. As a result, many dogs tend not to taste their food until it's too late.

I know for a fact that Ari is a gulper: She can swallow whole a piece of pizza or smashed vole. And judging by Bentley's portly appearance, he's done his fair share of rapid eating, too. That might be fine in a true wilderness environment, where the ratio of appealingly edible objects to lethal ones is in the dog's favor. But Ari and Bentley aren't in the wild—at least, not really. And that creates a real conflict. Instinct tells dogs to eat everything—and quickly. Domestic life, however, offers them food choices that are deadly if consumed in this fashion. No wonder dogs sometimes seem confused and become poisoning victims. And should we be surprised that 30 percent of all dogs are obese? That's about the same as the obesity rate among the humans who oversee their mealtimes. Both overweight dogs and humans suffer from nearly identical life-threatening ailments like diabetes and heart disease.

Make no bones about it, food can be a threat for all sorts of reasons. And if ever there were proof of this maxim, it lies on the couch in the form of our poor suffering friend Bentley.

Once we return home from the grocery store, I give Ari a biscuit and then set to work reconsidering our house and its potential dietary dangers. Ari's food is well secured in a wicker chest, so she's not likely to gorge. There's also no way she can reach the cocoa, stashed as it is on the top shelf of one of our kitchen cabinets. But what other poison might she ingest? I make note of the obvious threats in our house: cleaners, certain houseplants, and of course anything with theobromine. But what really surprises me is the list of potential poisons Ari might encounter *outside:* stinging nettles, bufo toads, newt salamanders, holly, oleander, and common hops. Then there are the gothically moribund mushrooms, with names like death cap, death angel, and the more innocuous-sounding but no less dangerous fool's mushroom. The effects of these toxins vary considerably, from a swollen mouth and diarrhea to complete liver or cardiac failure.

Coren says most adult dogs know better than to gorge on such things, but what about curious adolescents who wolf down their food? I consider our alternatives: Wiring shut Ari's jaw? Never allowing her to leave my sight? These are clearly not viable options. So instead, the two of us slouch by the dining room window, staring with disbelief at the potential dangers outside.

When Greg returns home an hour or so later, he finds us in this position of awkward repose. By way of explanation, I rise from the floor and tell him about our morning. His immediate response is ironic laughter: We had, after all, been joking about dogs and Halloween candy with Chris and Andrea only a week earlier. But one look at the expression on my face causes him to reassess his own. This is serious. Bentley could die.

"Poor Bentley," says Greg, sitting down across from me at the dining room table and shaking his head with real empathy. The news means more cause for melancholy, which neither of us needs. Greg places his hand atop mine. "Poor Bentley," he repeats. "That poor guy."

The next twenty-four hours feel awkward to us as we take Ari on her walks and play with her around the house. Even after undergoing her emergency procedure earlier in the week, Ari is robust and very, very hale. Despite the dreary weather, she urges us on long walks and games of chase in the yard. It feels wrong to play and laugh with her, when dear friends may be mourning just across the river. Throughout the day, we pause often and wonder aloud how Chris and Andrea are doing, then make constantly shifting predictions when we haven't heard from them. Do they have any news to report? Perhaps Bentley is fine and they've left for the day? Maybe the family is too upset over his death to call? I worry about Andrea's three daughters and wonder how they are taking the news. And still, I puzzle over the dangers of eating.

By seven on Sunday night, we still haven't heard from Chris and Andrea. Ari and I take our last walk out in the moonlight. After we return, she settles in by the fire while I pick up the phone. I now fear the worst, and I want to let my friends know I care.

Chris answers on the second ring, and immediately shouts to Andrea. "It's *Kate*!" He sounds his usual, gregarious self. A stage actor, Chris has a voice that is both melodic and capable of great tone. Currently, that tone is one of friendly exuberance. "We *forgot* to tell *Kate* about *Bentley*!"

"Oh, no," sings back Andrea with cheerful regret. "We forgot to call. We're awful!"

Their voices sound reassuring, and so I ask for the prognosis.

"Bentley is *fine,*" assures Chris, accenting each word deliberately and with great emphasis. "Bentley's okay!" Andrea echoes loudly again from somewhere else in the room. "We're so sorry we didn't call!"

Chris recounts the past twenty-four hours. As he talks, I'm delighted to hear his usual merriment has returned, along with his sharp wit.

"So in the end," he says, "Bentley just had a bad stomachache to show for his efforts. He's going to be just fine." Chris pauses. I can feel his smirk across the phone lines. "Besides, Bentley eats like a goat. All the bras and paperclips and plastic spoons lodged in his gut probably prevented it from actually absorbing much of the chocolate."

Bentley was lucky—he beat the biological odds. Still, eating is undeniably complicated—and growing more so all the time. Try as we might to avoid it, the game of naturalistic consumption is played out by all of us every day. And despite the differences in our gut lengths and sense of taste, humans and dogs are quite similar when it comes to dietary needs. We each require roughly the same ratios of protein, carbohydrates, and fat. Moreover, the best sources for these nutrients are almost interchangeable between the two species.

Like most dog trainers, Don Hanson at Green Acres recommends that domestic dogs eat foods that include whole fresh meats, unprocessed grains (like brown rice), and plenty of vegetables. He urges pet owners to find sources that are free of pesticides, herbicides, and preservatives. He warns against excess sugar and fat. He even recommends considering a multivitamin or other supplement. These days, you'd be hard pressed to find an MD who wouldn't make similar recommendations to his or her human patients. And an increasing number of us are beginning to pay attention. Organizations such as Slow Food International and organic societies have shown rapid increases in recent years, in part because consumers are beginning to agree that all food should be "good, clean, and fair." These groups seek to undo two hundred years of so-called modernization of food by returning to a more unadulterated form of eating. They forage for wild asparagus; they cast elaborate flies for Pacific salmon; they buy small batches of artisanal, local cheeses.

I'm a firm believer that Ari's diet should reflect these philosophies as well. So we buy expensive kibble loaded with duck and beets and flaxseed oil, and I pretend not to see my husband's disbelief when he notes our checking account balance. Food is life, after all.

Food is also death. There's no escaping it. And after rubbing up against death with Bentley, I'm more prepared than ever to understand that connection. The simple truth, of course, is that a lot of organisms die so that we can eat—a fact particularly understood by those people who hunt for their own food.

Hunters fascinate me: Not only do they embrace the ideals of slow food, but they also assume the role of predator; they come face-to-face with the life—and death—of what they consume. It's tempting to align human hunters with animals like wolves, who also employ elaborate strategies to bring down prey. But the analogy only goes so far. Human hunters are ecological visitors—sometimes participants who venture in long enough to take part in a biological cycle, only to step out again.

This, I decide, does align them nicely with canine naturalists. So, too, does the long history of hunting dogs. For centuries, Afghan hounds have assisted in hunts for everything from leopards to hares in their native land; in Korea, Ari's kin the jindo hunts everything from rabbits to badgers and wild boars. That's just the beginning of the dog–hunting relationship. In fact, keepers of dog breed standards list eighty-eight breeds still used regularly for hunting: Danish Kooikerhondjes are legendary for their ability to hunt water fowl; Mountain View Curs have been used to hunt lions; the Perdiguero de Burgos love stalking deer. The human–hunting dog relationship is such a strong one, "gun dogs" is now one of the most popular categories both in dog shows and breed catalogs. *Gun Dog Magazine,* founded in 1981, has a circulation of more than forty-one thousand readers in the United States.

Still, it's not always a blissful union among human, canine, and firearm. Recently, an Iowa man made national headlines when he was shot in the leg by his hunting dog. The man had set down his gun and climbed a fence in order to retrieve a pheasant. His dog stayed behind and somehow managed to accidentally pull the trigger, releasing more than a dozen shot pellets into the man's calf. Media outlets ate up this new riff on man-bites-dog journalism: The story was covered by dozens of newspapers and TV news shows, ranging as far afield as Seattle's NBC affiliate, Vancover's CBC, and even the BBC in Europe.

I doubt Ari will pull a trigger anytime soon, but that doesn't make our excursions into the woods all that safe right now, either.

Beginning this week, thousands of armed men, women, and children will disperse across Maine. Most have spent the past several months practicing (1) how to be invisible and (2) how to shoot at moving targets. Last year, 873 deer were shot, killed, and tagged in our little corner of the state alone. Considering that the general equation for legal hunting in Maine is one hunter = one deer, that means at least eight hundred armed hunters will probably begin sharing our woods tomorrow. The odds are not in favor of a tawny dog and a woman who wears earth tones.

Ari and I decide we need more information about this culture and its practices if we're ever going to find a way to be outside for the next month. In keeping with my nubby food-death equation, I eventually settle on the perfect opportunity.

Each year, the deer season begins with gluttonous, predawn meals across the state. Called hunters' breakfasts, they are as much a staple of the season as camouflage and pickup trucks. In the wee hours, hunters and nonhunters alike roll out of bed beginning at 3 AM to wolf down ambitious plates of home-cooked food. Nearly every town in New England has one of these meals, and they are usually advertised on big banners sponsored by Miller Lite, or on homemade paper flyers tacked to convenience store bulletin boards.

Until now, Greg and I have never done much more than acknowledge the signs with idle curiosity. *Breakfast at 3 AM?* In our college days, we might have considered predawn diner visits a reasonable nightcap after a long pub crawl; but these events are something different entirely. Hunters' breakfasts *start* a long day—they don't end one. Add to the mix that they are, of course, intended for people about to embark upon a long day of sitting alone in a tree with only a rifle for company, and we've always assumed that we are not the target audience for such events.

This year, however, I tell Greg and Ari we *must* attend. Both look at me with momentary disbelief. This is the expression I was expecting, and so I've come prepared. I quickly explain that the trip is necessary research: Hunting is an undeniable fact of our natural world, and we cannot be naturalists without acknowledging it. Besides, these breakfasts represent a key moment in local culture, and we owe it to ourselves to understand that.

"We can play cultural anthropologists," I tell them. "It's like we're in Bali."

I expect Greg to object: This seems like a pretty harebrained idea; plus, we're exhausted. The last thing either of us needs to do is wake up in the middle of the night and eat waffles. I begin planning my next rebuttal. But he surprises me by agreeing after only a moment's hesitation.

"Sure," he says cavalierly. "Let's go."

Now it's my turn to look with disbelief. *Did he really just agree? With so little persuading?*

I ask him again. "So you'll go? Seriously?"

He seems disappointed by my surprise. And that's when it hits me: We really have changed over the past several months. We are canine naturalists. We are ready for anything. I give him an enthusiastic hug. "Thank you," I tell him. "And really, this is going to be great."

The next morning, we rise in the dark and the chill. The two cats are perplexed by our movement—this is usually their time to run about the house undisturbed. Mouse scampers onto the kitchen counter where she is safe from the playful jabs of a puppy's muzzle; Leila Tov beats a hasty retreat to the tiny spot underneath the living room coffee table. For once, however, Ari pays them little mind. She's too curious about what *we're* doing awake so early in the morning.

Trying our best to play participant observers, Greg and I don thick work-pants and fleece pullovers. No one in their right minds would mistake us for local hunters; still, we won't stick out *too* much in Carhartt pants and bright stocking caps. Hunters are required to wear at least two articles of safety-orange clothing. Although the deer can't see the fluorescent shade, other humans can. It's kind of like hanging a sign around your neck that says, DON'T SHOOT ME—I'M NOT AN UNGULATE. With that in mind, I tie a blaze-orange bandanna around the groggy pup—just in case. We stop in the yard long enough for her to pee, and then the three of us are off, driving down dark, windswept roads littered with oak leaves.

Half an hour later, we arrive at the neighboring town's Knights of Columbus Hall, which is lit up like a party on an otherwise dark street. The parking lot is crowded with pickup trucks and mud-splattered jeeps. Greg laughs at my diminutive Honda with its bike rack and WAGE PEACE bumper sticker. We decide we should park somewhere inconspicuous.

No dogs are allowed inside the hall, so I tell Ari that she'll have to wait in the car while we eat, and I promise her a piece of bacon in return for her patience. She is still confused by this change in our routine, but she settles into the driver's seat and looks like she's prepared to hold down the fort. As she does, Greg and I make our way to the hall, passing a group of about ten hunters who loiter outside the building, gnawing on toothpicks to hide their excitement. They're not allowed to take their first shot until the official sunrise, and it's clear that a year's worth of anticipation and a few early morning cups of coffee have left them irrepressibly impatient. They stand in loose formation, shifting their weight often and laughing nervously. These are people who have spent months studying the movements and patterns of deer; they have built stands in trees and taken countless practice shots. Every second of this day has been mapped and plotted—except for the agonizing hour before the sun breaks the horizon.

I want to ask them what all of this means—and what they know—but I don't have the nerve. The men seem too imposing in their expectancy, and I worry they will respond to my questions with distrust. So instead, I drop my head and pass by silently. They look at us curiously as we cut through the middle of them to get to the front door. One tips his hat to us, as if glad we're sharing in the day with him. I smile nervously in return but say nothing. This is his territory—not mine.

Inside the hall, cheerful women offer us plates of baked beans, biscuits and gravy, scrambled eggs, pancakes, French toast, doughnuts, bacon, sausage, and canned peaches. Giant carafes of hot chocolate, cider, and coffee stand at the ready nearby. The woman serving us seems amused that I only want a small spoonful of eggs and one piece of bacon. I promptly wrap the latter in a napkin. The woman looks on with a perplexed smile and whispers to Greg that he can come back for more as way of compensation for my lack of appetite. Her voice says we are welcome here, and I appreciate her consideration.

A handful of eaters sit spread out around the dining area, which is still garishly decorated for Halloween. Greg and I take our seats at a table underneath a picture of Pope John Paul II and a sesquicentennial poster honoring Columbus. On our table are two pumpkins: one featuring a spaceman tableau, the other made up to look like Rudolph the Red-Nosed Reindeer.

We take inventory of the room. Unable to rise much before four, we have missed the first wave of serious hunters. Instead, we've arrived at the changing of the guard—thick men in safety orange and camouflage are being replaced by senior citizens eager to have an event with which to fill their morning. Still, the table next to us offers a classic New England scene: a father, son, and grandfather, dressed in muted wool and lingering over apple cider before making their way out. The grandfather looks as if this may be his last year hunting, which might explain the lingering.

The conversations around us center on the logistical problems of deer harvests. How do you get a 150-pound stag home once you've shot and killed him? Do experts prefer field dressing or disemboweling back home? These are conundrums neither Greg nor I have ever considered. But everyone else in the room has. I eavesdrop as the men weigh the merits of heavy lifting and dragging a carcass behind a four-wheeler. Both appear to have serious drawbacks. They speculate about better alternatives involving winches, ropes, and (if possible) army helicopters. They decide such resources are unlikely and return to the merits of dragging.

Wild canids, of course, don't worry about such things: They simply eat their fill at the point of execution and leave the rest to scavengers. They also don't worry about whether they did the executing or were simply the first to stumble upon the recently deceased. This rankles the men. One of them laments that coyotes dragged off his trophy last year before he could return to it with his four-wheeler. He's had a bounty on the heads of coyotes ever since. "Damn pests," he concludes. I try to hide my concern.

The conversation soon shifts toward local gossip, and the last of the hunters exchange seats with the elderly crowd. We will learn no more this morning, and so decide we'll depart as well. Back out in the car, I give the surprised pup my piece of bacon. It's about as far from hunted game as you can get, but at least it's not chocolate. She is overjoyed by the grease and salt, and proves the Cornell scientists right: Processed meat is definitely where it's at.

Back home, we set out for our morning walk. The weatherman has predicted another day of blustery wind and rain, so there is no noticeable sunrise to speak of. Still, before we leave our driveway, we begin to hear the reverberation of rifles echoing off the hills. I count five shots during our ten-minute walk, and I'm relieved when Ari has relieved herself and we can go back inside. This is no time to linger anywhere in the woods.

As the week wears on, I find myself inescapably torn between tolerance and resentment. The overwhelming majority of hunters, of course, are conscientious and very, very safe. By and large, they are respectful, conservation-minded individuals securing food for their families. Most follow state guidelines and ensconce themselves deep in the woods or on private property. They wear safety orange and take great pains to make only the cleanest of shots. Still, accidents happen. Local lore contains tons of stories about hunters mistaking pets, livestock, and even lawn furniture for deer. There's some truth to these myths. Each year, farmers and horsepeople take great pains to identify their animals as *not*-deer: Dairy farmers spray-paint their cows either with words like COW or just with geometric patterns of safety orange. Our neighbor has woven yards of fluorescent surveyor's ribbon through her horses' manes and tails. She also insists that each wear a permanent bright orange blanket. The horses look like they are dressed in old-fashioned life preservers. At some level, I suppose they are.

Even so, horses, cows, alpacas, and goats are accidentally killed every hunting season. Earlier this year, our neighbor's wolfhound, who stood tethered to a lead connected to their garage, received a flank of shot in his hind leg. He lost the limb but survived. Not everyone is so lucky. Recently, a novice hunter mistook a Saint Bernard for a deer and dealt it a fatal shot before realizing what had happened. There are human casualties as well. Despite the requisite orange, reports of hunters mistaking one another for deer begin making the nightly news. Most sustain treatable injuries. Still, every hunting season includes a human death toll. Often, these are heart-wrenching stories of fathers accidentally killing sons or friends shooting friends. This season, a seventeen-year-old girl in her backyard was mistaken for a deer by a hunter trying to get one last shot at dusk. She died en route to the hospital.

The challenge for all of us, then, is this: How can we coexist outside? The entire ecosystem has changed for this month, complicating every possible relationship of predator and prey. We must all redefine what it is to be in nature. This is no longer just a question of ecology. It's about personal safety—for everyone.

This is especially true for Ari. Her tawny coat and white blaze mimic the markings of a deer, even if she is only half its size. What's worse, her wolfie nature has put her at particular risk. The anti-coyote sentiment expressed by the man at the hunters' breakfast is shared by most hunters, who see wild dogs as competition for deer and game birds. Already we have found three coyote carcasses in the forest. With their pointed ears and long, elegant snouts, they look hauntingly like my dog.

It's too risky to be in the woods these days, so Ari and I rethink our outdoor routine. It's relatively easy for me: I can run on the treadmill at the gym, or stay at home and grade papers. As for the naturalism, I'm sure there's a way to do it from afar. If not, I'm willing to take a hiatus in the interest of safety. Ari, however, is far less adaptable. She is a high-energy yearling dog accustomed to big-mileage walks and runs. Truncated walks equal excess energy which, in turn, equals destructive behaviors in the house. That's the thing about primitive dog breeds—you can take them out of the wolf pack, but you can never really take all the wolf out of them.

I struggle over possible solutions. We can walk in town, where there are no hunters, but that necessitates daily car rides, and it will most certainly compromise our naturalism. We could walk at night, but that presents challenges as well.

Instead, we try abbreviated walks during low-peak hunting times. Like canids, deer are most active around dawn and dusk, so many hunters take a midday break to get warm and have a meal. We capitalize on this siesta by trying early-afternoon strolls. Shrouded in orange and sticking to well-traveled roads, we make a ridiculous pair. Ari is clearly dissatisfied with the compromise. And she wants us to know.

Greg and I begin keeping a list of new household casualties. In just two weeks, the pup has eaten a couch pillow and gnawed through a chair leg. Today, she shredded our new down comforter. It was a wildly extravagant purchase by our standards, and I had been fantasizing about long nights under its lofted warmth. When I climb the stairs late in the afternoon, however, I discover drifts of fowl snow throughout our room. I refuse to look at the caninaturalist for the rest of the day. When Greg's stepmother calls later in the evening, I tell her about the destroyed comforter. She concludes that Ari was probably just looking for the duck. I find little consolation in this observation and, instead, look scornfully at the bits of white feather poking out the sides of the pup's mouth. She doesn't care the slightest bit that hunting waterfowl is out of fashion—not to mention out of season.

Deer season ends the last Saturday of November. I, for one, am very thankful.

The next morning, we rise with the sun, eager to reclaim the woods. I owe Ari a long run—a chance to explore and be in nature on her terms, not mine. Greg's prescience about November gloom has already proven far too correct, and we're eager to lay the month to rest. We don warm running clothes and trail shoes, then harness the pup and make the short trek to the start of the town forest. The three of us are ecstatic: We are back in nature.

Once we cross the stream, Ari waits impatiently to be let free of her leash. I unclip her without a second thought. We are far from roads, and there are no hunters around. I am certain we are safe. As she bolts ahead, Greg and I start our own easy jog. It is a gorgeous morning. After a month of soupy rain and uncharacteristically mild weather, the crystalline sharpness of November has finally arrived. Intricate frost has etched itself on the wild grass, writ large and obscenely brilliant in the early-morning light. Between puffs of breath, I gloat.

"See," I say to Greg, "November can be beautiful."

He nods indulgently, perhaps swallowing the urge to point out that, technically, November is over and December is less than twenty-four hours away. He doesn't say anything, though; he just smiles at me. Today is too lovely in its cold austerity for technicalities.

Besides, we need to become reacquainted with the forest. The woods feel empty to us this morning, and they have assumed a mussed appearance. The main trail, having been well trammeled by hunters for three weeks, is thick and textured with ruts. The foliage alongside is trampled and tattered. What we notice most of all, however, is the quiet. No birdcalls. No rustle of startled animals. Just vacant silence. Nature has retreated deep within herself, waiting out the temporary human onslaught.

We continue running, eventually reaching a fork in the trail, just past the old cemetery. Our big decision for the day: Should we go straight, toward the brook, or head right and loop out past the cedar grove? It feels good to have nothing but topography on our minds. I call to Ari, to show her that we've voted for the stream.

Nothing.

I stop and call her name. No answer. I try again, elongating it into two full syllables:

"Aaarrr-eeeeeee."

Still nothing. Not even the telltale sound of her tags or the rustle of a lanky dog bounding through brush.

My heart sinks. I'm not yet terrified—just perceptibly concerned. Greg and I both stop, cupping our hands over our brows as if that might somehow give us superhuman perception.

It doesn't. We listen again.

Silence.

We look at each other.

"Arrriiii."

It is now a question. *Where are you? Why aren't you coming?*

Still nothing. The questions become more rapid, more grave.

Please answer me, puppy. Are you okay? Can you hear me? Where have you gone? How can I get you back?

"Ari?" Greg tries this time, his voice clear and bold. It doesn't work.

We pace back and forth, hoping she will reappear. It's been more than ten minutes. Hardly a moment, really, but plenty of time to become frightened. This is the longest Ari has been missing. She always returns on the trail: It's the one place we can depend on her. I am now truly scared. I look at Greg. He's obviously concerned as well. We both stand in one place, rotating in sloppy circles as we scan the forest around us. Still nothing. This isn't working, and we both know that she may be getting farther away—or if she has been hurt, our chances of saving her are decreasing.

Ten minutes become thirty.

We decide to split up: Greg will take the trail to the east, I will remain at this intersection. As Greg trots away, I can hear his deep voice call the pup's name. He sounds assured. Firm but friendly. I am certain she will respond. But as the minutes continue to pass, both Greg and Ari remain absent. I am alone, lost at this intersection and drowning in the silence.

As I trot up and down the trail first in one direction and then the other, I think back to that night last February when I saw my relationship with Ari at a metaphoric crossroads. The fact that I even considered giving her up makes me nauseated. I can't imagine not wanting her by my side.

I am overcome with adrenaline and endorphins and countless other hormones, all pouring into my bloodstream. My body recognizes the increasing severity of the crisis, and it is responding the only way it knows how. I jog back and forth and back again, hoping I will see the familiar blur of a racing dog. I listen for the muted tinkle of her tags. Nothing. In this silent forest, there is suddenly—inexplicably—too much ambient noise. I can hear my own breathing, the sound of my running shoes on frozen ground, the wind, the leaves, the slow traffic on the highway several miles away.

The sound of the traffic—remote as it is—terrifies. I imagine finding Ari's body on the side of the road, lying limp and broken. This is too much for me to bear. I begin to sob. Earlier, I worried she would be lost or stolen. I wanted her back with me. Now I just want her alive. I make deals with multiple deities: It's okay if another family finds her or she becomes her full coyote self, forever wild and feral. It's okay if I never see her again, so long as she is allowed to live. Do I believe this? I'm not sure. Still, I make every possible promise.

I can no longer control my thoughts or emotions. Even Cam's death did not feel as frightening as this. This is true terror in all of its complicated, consuming manifestation. Shame, concern, fear. Perhaps it is more akin to hysteria.

Greg returns. He has been gone a long time. I look up, hoping against all logic that the pup will be trailing behind him. She is not. He shakes his head, looking both sorry and concerned. When he sees my condition, he accelerates from a jog to a run. Pack hierarchy takes over: His wife, his mate, is in trouble. For a moment, Ari is forgotten. He hugs me, pulling me close. This makes me feel worse. Ari is the one who needs comfort and attention, not me—the person who might have gotten her hurt or killed. I try to explain this to Greg, in between rasping, jagged, weeping breaths.

"She's . . . gone." I begin with the obvious. "It's . . . my fault."

What follows is a torrent of would'ves and should'ves and everything in between. I have spent exactly ten months in the company of this dog. She is barely a year old. It is too soon.

It's always too soon, of course. That was the irony I felt with Kinch's death nearly two years ago. That was the grief I encountered with Cam's passing in August. And it's undoubtedly what our friends felt earlier this month when Bentley risked his life for a cocoa fix. For the time being, none of that matters. All I want is some assurance that Ari is—or will be—okay. And that's exactly what I can't have when she is gone.

Missing. I don't know if she is alive or dead; I don't know if she's a hundred yards or a hundred miles from me right now. I know nothing at all—and in a way, I think, that's almost worse than knowing for certain.

Greg and I are both chilled to the bone. We dressed for a brisk run, not a stuttering search. Plus, we are two miles away from our telephone. If someone found Ari—or accidentally hurt her—we would have no way of knowing. Greg and I look at each other. We don't know what to do in this situation.

Kinch always returned. As a hound, he was a tracker through and through: When he was done chasing a deer or a fox, he'd just retrace his steps and follow his nose to wherever we were. The night before Greg's dissertation defense, Kinch went missing at a large state park. Greg spent the entire night in the dark, looking for and calling out to Kinch. The next morning, ten minutes before Greg's big meeting, a man called us: He had found the beagle waiting patiently by the first parking space in the state park's lot—precisely where we'd left the vehicle the previous night. Once, when we were hiking the Appalachian Trail, Kinch raced off in pursuit of a deer. We called and waited for nearly an hour, then Greg proposed we continue on our way. The idea seemed mad to me at the time, but we had only been dating a short while and I didn't know either Greg or Kinch well enough to object. So I agreed. Just as Greg predicted, Kinch found us a few hours later—he had followed us to the place where we were going to camp.

As a beagle, Kinch's instincts included a desire to track us. All dogs are particularly adept at smelling and distinguishing human sweat or, more precisely, the butyric acid it contains. In fact, studies demonstrate that dogs can pick up the scent when a single gram of it has been dispersed over 135 square miles. A beagle's ability to do so is even more pronounced. Everything about Kinch's personal biology was bred not only to enhance this ability but to make sense of it in a meaningful way.

Even with all this skill and prowess, the take-home lesson from Kinch and even Ari's behavior over the summer should have been, *Keep dogs on leashes*. But it wasn't. We believed—we continue to believe—that they need space and time to roam and run and pursue those instincts, wolf or not, that continue to course through their veins. The moral to Kinch's stories was always: He'll come back. He always comes back.

Ari, of course, is not Kinch. Shc lacks his street smarts, his time on the lam, his breed's proclivity for tracking. We do not know how she responds in a situation such as this—whether, in a panic or sheer ecstasy, she will continue to run farther and farther away. Whether she will know to come look for us and, if she does, if she will retrace our steps to the place where we separated, or if she'll keep going to where she assumes we might now be. Factor in her gadfly tendencies, and it's just as likely that she'll hop into a car on its way to God-knows-where as it is that she'll come home.

Greg and I continue our pathetic little loop back and forth. We're shivering in the cold; our nerves are overstimulated and wavering between crisis and exhaustion. I begin to propose that he return home—to get warmer clothes, to check messages. But he shakes his head. He is worried about me; he will not leave me alone. We will stay together. Normally, I would find tremendous comfort in this solidarity. But right now, I can feel nothing but panic and leaden dread.

Ari is gone. That is all I know.

Lost Dog Reward

[december]

Each year, more than ten million dogs are lost or stolen. That's one-sixth of the population of pet dogs. Every year. Of these hapless canines, just under half will eventually find their way home again. The others face a variety of fates ranging from a new life with a new family to death by any number of means. Others will meet new humans well versed in dog-reassignment projects.

Indeed, dognapping is a rising concern throughout the world. Here in the United States, the top three dog breeds most likely to be stolen are the pit bull, Labrador retriever, and Chihuahua. Part of this trend might be sheer demographics: Labs have held the most popular (and abundant) breed status for years; the Chihuahua comes in at number eleven. Other reasons for the trend might be the social value of dogs and a breed's cultural prominence at any given time. That may be one reason why, when Paris Hilton's beloved sidekick Tinkerbell went missing, the Hilton family publicists gave the Chihuahua the false moniker first of "lost dog" and then of "Napoleon" in their posters advertising a thousand-dollar reward. When asked why she lied about her dog's identity, Hilton told the magazine *In Touch,* "If they find out Tinkerbell is my dog, they'll hold it for ransom. Everyone knows I'm rich, so they'll want millions." To her way of thinking, popular dog breed plus popular hotel heiress equals expensive dog recovery. She's probably right.

Pit bulls, on the other hand, are nowhere to be seen on the list of popular breeds. And they aren't owned by many prominent socialites, either. They are, however, notorious for aggressiveness when abused or trained as fighting dogs. Dogfights are rapidly increasing in popularity in the United States, and participants in the illegal pastime need a constant stream of new fighting dogs to replace those who are injured or killed for poor performance. The cheapest way to find replacement dogs is to steal them. The Humane Society estimates that dogfighting may be one of the leading causes of other missing dogs as well: When training pit bulls and rottweilers as fighting dogs, their so-called handlers will often use what they call bait dogs—Labs, beagles, and mixed-breeds—so that the fighting dogs can learn killing techniques without risking injury. The dogs too docile to serve even as bait sometimes wind up in medical research labs, where scientists test how much vegetable wax can safely be ingested or hair spray can be sprayed into an eye without permanent damage. Because these stolen dogs have been so socialized to interact with people, they are often willing participants in experiments—even wagging their tails to greet their experimenters each day. This amiability motivates scientists to request domestic dogs over cats, rats, and other lab animals. As a result, some dog brokers deal exclusively with the stolen-dog scientific laboratory market.

Regardless of why a dog was stolen, he has only a 10 percent chance of ever seeing his owner again. That's a best-guess estimate and one of the only ones out there. The data is equally fuzzy for dogs simply lost or missing. Since the majority of lost dogs are never seen again, it's hard to track statistics for what becomes of them. In fact, as I write this chapter, only one scholarly article on lost dogs exists in the major academic journal databases. Published in January 2007 in the *Journal of the American Veterinary Medicine Association,* this study traced the recovery of a sample group of lost or stolen dogs in Montgomery County, Ohio. What researchers discovered was both important and probably a little obvious: Most of the dogs who reunited with their owners were able to do so not because the dogs returned home, but rather because they sought out other humans.[1]

The most important finding of the lost dog study, however, was what researchers *didn't* find: namely, pet owners and veterinarians well versed in dog search and rescue techniques. Most dog owners in the study had no idea how to go about a successful dog recovery. Most vets and dog wardens didn't really know, either. This is a national phenomenon.

In Los Angeles, for instance, the city's highly regarded Animal Services Department (LAASD) took in 25,608 lost or abandoned dogs during 2007 alone. Of these, a mere 3,970 were returned to their owners. Another 10,212 were adopted by new families. A total of 13,787 of the dogs were euthanized. Nineteen escaped custody.

According to Linda Barth, assistant general manager for the LAASD, the problem of locating lost dogs often comes down to human ecology, or the relationship between human cultures and the natural landscape. "Every culture has its own response to domestic animals," she told me during a recent phone interview. "That's true when these pets are lost, too. In Los Angeles, for instance, we have widely disparate pockets with different immigrant populations. They're like micro-cities. We might see a few patterns, like more multiple animals in one area or another, but in general the response to missing animals is reflective of the nature of the people who live in a given area. That varies widely."

Barth says a lost or stray dog who appears in a suburban or closely knit community is much more likely to arouse notice than one who wanders on the fringes of different biomes, in relatively uninhabited areas, or in places that have a lot of transient dwellers. Those dogs that stick to areas of relative wil-

[1] Of those dogs eventually found, 35 percent were located because the owner called or visited county animal shelters. Another 18 percent were found because of their license tag (a dog warden, for instance, was able to reunite dog and human), and 15 percent were found thanks to lost dog signs. Only 1.5 percent of the dogs were recovered because of microchip technology. Then again, only 8 percent of the dogs even had microchips.

derness can be impossible to spot or recover. And avoiding human settlement is surprisingly easy to do, even in a bustling metropolis like Los Angeles.

"Los Angeles is absolutely riddled with natural areas," says Barth. "The city is filled with flood-control channels, which serve as freeways for domestic and wildlife animals. They intertwine like veins throughout the city. An astute dog will figure out quickly how they work and can move around undetected."

The City of Angels is also a city of surprisingly plentiful green space: Los Angeles boasts hundreds of square miles of parks and protected land, including the four-thousand-acre Griffith Park, which is perhaps most famous as the site of the iconic white HOLLYWOOD sign. Barth says she has a feeling more than just a few lost pets are currently residing there.

How many?

"We just can't know how many missing pets or domestic animals might be in these areas," says Barth. "But it's probably substantial."

If an inquiring caninaturalist were to doggedly keep asking about the issue, Barth—who is too helpful and friendly to say *get lost*—would eventually estimate that Animal Services probably finds missing animals about a third of the time. That means the other two-thirds (which could easily be more than fifty thousand pets annually) probably continue to wander about the city and its natural spaces.

But that, Barth stresses again, is just a rough estimate. And what becomes of these dogs on the lam, she admits, is often anyone's guess.

The fact remains that no one really knows what becomes of dogs not reunited with their owners—or how many dogs and owners are never reunited. In fact, while many cities and organizations keep ample information about annual dog bites or barking dog complaints, they do not keep similar statistics for lost dog and runaways.

LAASD is trying to change that, says Barth. The city's dead-animal collectors now regularly carry microchip scanners with them on their routes. When they come across a dead dog, they scan the corpse for microchips and/or retain the dog's tags. Animal Services employees then try to match this information with records maintained by the county and microchip providers.

"It at least gives pet owners a little closure," says Barth.

Other cities have their own version of record keeping for dogs who die while lost or missing. Atlanta's received national attention several years ago when *New Yorker* writer Susan Orleans published an essay about one family's quest to find their missing dog in the Southern city. In Atlanta, writes Orleans, city workers are required to keep daily tallies of roadkill for every fiscal year. When I called the city to ask about these statistics, the solid-waste engineer I spoke with seemed reluctant to talk about it. He also seemed irritated that his switchboard operator had patched me through to his office. But he, like Barth, was also too polite to hang up on me, although he did ask that he not be quoted directly or identified in this book. When entreated, he estimated that each day the city receives anywhere between three and twelve calls reporting roadkill involving both wild and domestic animals. This, he thinks, represents about a quarter of the roadkill instances in the city. If that's true, it means the city of Atlanta deals with more than ten thousand dead animals on its roads each year.

Here in the far-less-populated Maine, we have learned firsthand (and on multiple occasions) that roadkill is handled more organically. As a result, statistics on the number of pets who are killed on the roads isn't available. According to Brian Burne, a maintenance engineer for the Maine Department of Transportation, DOT workers, game wardens, and state police are instructed to dispose of dead animals in the woods within the highway right-of-way. If that is not a viable option, the animals are buried as close to the area where they were killed as possible. The state does not keep a record of the types or numbers of animals. And, given the relatively large geographic size but small population density of Maine, the state animal undertaker service is restricted to those animals who die in what Burne calls "travel lanes." In other words, if the carcass is on the shoulder or in a ditch, nature—and the six stages of decay—takes its course. Even with this restricted collection provision, however, Burne estimates that the state spends more than a hundred thousand dollars per year on roadkill disposals.

Although that figure may seem high, it's paltry compared with what people spend trying to locate their missing dogs. Pet microchip implantation, for instance, is a million-dollar industry whose success has been based largely on the assurance it provides dog owners that, if lost, their pets will be relocated and found. A corollary industry has also grown rapidly in recent years: pet detectives. These individuals charge anywhere from seventy-five to two hundred dollars an hour for phone consultations and tracking to find missing pets.

If pet owners aren't willing to shell out such exorbitant fees, they can rely on what little information is known about missing dogs and how to find them. The much-visited website of Sherlock Bones, one of the largest pet detective agencies, reports that the overwhelming majority of recovered dogs—83 percent, to be exact—are found anywhere between twelve and forty miles from home. And it usually takes owners several days—if not weeks—to locate them.

The reason for this delay, says our behaviorist contact in Northern Ireland, Deborah Wells, relates again to a dog's fear mechanism. Once a dog realizes he is lost, he also realizes that he is vulnerable: away from his home range, open to predation or aggression. As a result, many lost dogs tend to hunker down in secret hiding places, where they hope to escape detection by potential aggressors. Many also deliberately avoid direct interaction with people or other animals. The trick, then, is to approximate the new home range established by a missing dog and focus a search there.

But how do you go about this? And how can you know if a dog is really lost?

This is no academic question. Ari is still missing. *Really* missing.

Based on what we know about lost dogs—particularly potentially timid ones like Ari—the question for me and Greg comes down to this: How long will it take Ari to discover that she's lost? And how much ground will she have traveled in the meantime? Jindos are known for their amazing speed. Although huskies are celebrated more for their endurance than their pace, the International Siberian Husky Club nevertheless reports that sled dogs covering twenty miles or more often do so at speeds of twelve miles an hour or faster—and that's with a full sled and thick snow. Ari is not encumbered by either. And given that we don't really know in which direction this spry dog was heading, we are dealing with a possible range of better than seventy miles. That's far too much ground to cover.

Frankly, even an acre is too much to cover when it's scrubby woodland, which is where we last saw the pup. The town forest is a working landscape. Since it was first cleared to make pastureland in the 1800s, it has been logged multiple times. The results are clear from the amount of underbrush on the forest floor: Fallen logs, brambles, and raspberry bushes all compete with seedling poplars and more mature maples, oaks, and conifers. This creates a fierce battle for sunlight and root space, which also restricts maneuverability when trying to bushwhack through the mess—especially without any of the usual bushwhacking implements. Factor in the abandoned foundations and rock walls that cover the forest floor, and you soon have a seemingly infinite number of hiding places where a dog Ari's size can take shelter.

In other words, Ari could literally be right under our nose. And since we lack the sophistication of hers, we would never realize it. We now know all too well that vulnerable animals go out of their way to make themselves invisible. Most of them are pretty adept at this and are found only when they want to be. That may be why, in wilderness settings, more dogs find their owners than owners their dogs.

That fact is small comfort to most humans, particularly those who feel a burning maternal impulse to locate their missing pets. But in our particular case, it turns out to be a very happy happenstance indeed.

I can't say precisely how long Greg and I paced up and down the town forest trail, hoping to find our missing dog. Plenty long, certainly, for me to think about the dogfighting industry, animal detectives, and roadkill policies. And after I had thought about all those things and more—after we had cried and shouted and waded through brambles and briars and acres of underbrush—the familiar tinkling of three dog tags (bone-shaped ID, rabies vaccination, and state license) tolled from somewhere down the trail. A moment later, a familiar white blaze and blue eyes appeared. With them came a self-satisfied expression: *Hey slugabeds, good to see you! But why are you still standing right where I left you? You wouldn't believe what you've missed out there. You really need to get off the beaten path now and again!*

Greg and I look at each other, bone-weary, exultant, and fighting the urge to race toward Ari in greeting. Doing so, we fear, may prompt her to flee again. Nevertheless, we want her back on her leash. Now. But she's in no hurry to cooperate. Instead, she approaches with a devil-may-care, jauntily cavalier cadence in her step that seems to suggest, as far as she is concerned, this dog was never actually lost; she was just exploring. We call her, careful to avoid direct eye contact or anything else that might make her reluctant to come near. We just want her back with us, we say. *Please?*

This approach seems to work. The pup continues to trot up the path and toward us. My heart rate begins to lower—but only momentarily. If my biggest fear was that Ari would wind up lost or dead, my second fear is certainly that she would return seriously injured. This may in fact be the case.

As Ari nears, we see blood on her snout and front paws. She slows to a walk. I reconsider her approach: What if what I thought was lackadaisicalness was actually the result of injury? Greg and I look at Ari, then each other, then once again at the bloodstained dog. That's all it takes. We race toward her, forgetting that such a display is an obvious sign of aggression. She flattens her ears in response and steps away from us. We recant, crouching down and cooing.

Ari remains wary. However, after a few more attempts and a lot of treats, she allows us to leash her. I try to get a cursory assessment of what's causing the bleeding, but she doesn't want me messing with her nose and paws, and I'm afraid she'll race off again if she's given half a chance. So instead, we walk quickly back to the car, trying to evaluate her gait as we do. Miraculously, Greg and I are trauma-center calm in our demeanors and approach.

Back home, Mouse and Leila Tov scamper away as soon as our triage unit arrives. I take Ari to the bathroom, where I can clean her and get a sense of her injuries. Another trip to the vet's office is probably in order, but it's hard to tell with all this fur. I dab at her snout and paws, wiping away the blood and looking for its cause. I can't find any. I dab harder, combing through individual hairs and trying to get a good look at her skin. It's fine, and perfectly intact. I can't account for it. Greg comes in and studies her, too. It seems as if there's not a mark on her. He says as much.

"So why on earth is she bleeding?" I ask.

Greg looks at her nose and front feet again. "Maybe she's not."

I do my best to scrutinize him calmly. Mildly myopic and not currently wearing his glasses, my husband may very well miss some of the finer visual cues at a moment like this. But a dog red in tooth and claw? Please. I give him a look that says, *How can you possibly be so blind?*

Unblinking, he matches my scrutiny with his own. I'm supposed to be the logician in the family, so why am I missing what—at least to him—is obvious? He waits patiently, but I still don't get it.

"Maybe it's not her blood," he finally offers.

"I beg your pardon?"

"Blood on her snout and paws? No cuts? Sounds to me like she's not injured—she did the injuring."

Impossible.

But of course it's not. As we learned in July, domestic dogs aren't outrageously effective predators. Still, they're certainly not pacifists, either. When I told a well-known editor friend of mine about our caninaturalist project, he joked that canine naturalism in his house consists primarily of finding all the squirrel and woodchuck parts after his black Lab dismembers them—not the sort of thing most readers would want to see in print.

His is certainly not the only dog who approaches nature in this way. So why, then, am I so certain my dog does not possess the skills or disposition to kill another animal? Maybe it's because, to this day, the only animal she has ever so much as injured is the unfortunate vole king, and she seemed sincerely regretful that she had. Maybe it's because she truly is the kindest creature I have ever met—not to mention one of the most engaging and, if the situation calls for it, submissive dogs I've encountered. There's a fair amount of blood on her. I admit it's not hers; I just don't buy she did the injuring necessary to cause it.

Still, I'm curious about its origins. Really curious. For the next few days, I look for clues in Ari's behavior toward the squirrels and birds we see on our walk, but she shows little more than her same wide-eyed curiosity and overtures toward play. At home, she continues to either ignore or romp with the adopted cats. She even allows the boxy and brazen Mouse to snuggle close with her in front of the woodstove. They are the model of docile tranquility. Or at least they would be if they didn't keep casting looks at me that clearly say, *Stop staring at us!* They're right, I know. But I can't help it. Something mysterious and primal happened in the woods. I need to know what it was. Try as I might, though, I cannot find a single speck of evidence that would explain Ari's departure and bloodletting.

At the end of the week, I take the caninaturalist—on a very thick leash this time—to the town forest. We retrace our steps, and I watch her closely for a sign. What sent her disappearing into the underbrush? Did she fight with another animal? Has she really turned predator? The cavorting pup trotting by my side gives no clue to these mysteries—unless pouncing on maple leaves counts. We continue our way down the trail, enjoying a pleasant romp but still no closer to understanding what happened that fateful morning.

A few minutes later, the trail crossing and site of Ari's disappearance rises into view. Ari remembers the spot as distinctly as I do, and we're both eager to get there. The pup hops on her back feet, straining to angle us just off the left of the trail, where I thought I saw her soar into the brambles when she went missing. She clearly wants to go back.

I have to make a decision: Should we keep walking, tethered to each other in a way that will keep us together and safe but will not answer our latest mystery? Should we, also still tethered, scrounge in the acres of underbrush and forest, hoping we might find answers about what sent her racing away and momentarily out of my life? Or finally, should I let her off leash and trust her keen senses to lead me to the place where she went missing?

The safe choice is the first one. An acceptable alternative would be number two. A real caninaturalist would choose number three; however, it is certainly not the responsible decision. The raw desperation when Ari disappeared has not tempered with the passage of a few days. I certainly don't need to repeat that experience. Ever. Then again, we committed to a year of natural inquiry, and this moment more than qualifies.

What to do?

I think back to the plans and commitments I made in February. I don't have to abide by them—and certainly not if I am going to jeopardize the life of myself or my dog. I know this. But I also know how far we've come and how much we've both gained through seemingly capricious decisions such as these. The reasonable pet owner would keep on walking. The caninaturalist would remove this dog from her leash and prepare to race off in pursuit. So who are we? I look down at Ari. It's clear she's answered this question—at least for herself. Can I let her make the decision for both us? She meets my gaze and holds it, grinning as she does. *Come on,* she seems to say. *Let's go!* I take comfort in the *let's* and interpret it to mean we will run off together. The fact that I am hinging my decision not only on an imaginary conversation between me and my dog, but also on that dog's mastery of formal grammar, doesn't strike me as irrational. Who has time for the finer points of reality when there's exploration to be had?

I take a deep breath and prepare myself for the ontological and ethical baggage that might accompany my consent. *Okay,* I say to Ari—her cue that she's about to be released. But not until I'm absolutely prepared to sprint in pursuit. She watches me carefully: *Okay, friend, are you ready?* Not really. *Set?* Hardly. *Let's go!* If you say so.

As soon as Ari is free from the leash, she makes a beeline for an overgrown side trail. She porpoises through the feral raspberries and ferns, then arcs her body up and over larger seedlings taking root. Pure liquid motion. It is astounding to watch. I follow clumsily behind, catching the toe of my boots on unseen rocks and tangling my hair in naked branches. Still, I refuse to let her out of my sight. At least for very long.

The pup soon disappears up ahead. But I'm prepared this time, and close enough behind her to follow the sound of her tags. I've insisted that she wear her safety-orange cravat as well, so I get a glimpse of color now and again in the bare patches of forest. This proves invaluable as soon as the jangling of her tags falls silent. Adrenaline and good old-fashioned determination have suddenly endowed me with sniper-sharp vision. I will not let my eyes off that bright orange bandanna—or the dog to whom it is attached.

Ari, meanwhile, has developed an equally singular focus—though not on me. About thirty yards ahead, she stops and stands with her back toward me, her head buried deeply in something. This is no dog—this is a truffle-rooting boar. She doesn't even notice as I stumble my way through the thicket separating us. I soon see why.

The pup is crouched, coyote-like, over the entrails of a deer field-dressed by a hunter during the recent season. Her nose and front paws are once again a familiar shade of crimson, and she is working diligently at unwinding the small intestine once belonging to a large buck or doe. She is in ecstasy: Forget fox scat, frozen breakfast pizza, or even rotten deer legs: This pile of guts is a gastronomical jackpot. So much so that Ari ignores my breathy approach. No wonder she didn't come when called last week. Even though this pile is just a hundred yards or so off the trail—and clearly in earshot—all of Ari's attention is dedicated to these festering innards.

We've been here before. Not this particular spot or this particular part of a corpse, of course, but the same situation nonetheless. I don't know how I feel about the fact that a two-month-old dog with a deer leg behaves exactly like a twelve-month-old dog with a pile of guts. Was I expecting her to grow out of this phase, like a child with a doll or toy truck? Maybe. Was I thinking that the bond between the two of us had grown so profound that the joy of walking by my side would always eclipse other stimulation? Probably. Neither, of course, is ever going to be true. I'm certain there's at least one caninaturalist lesson to be learned here. But first I need to collect my dog.

When I get just within arm's reach, the pup lifts her head but retains her coiled stance. I step closer, and she scuttles a few steps away. Her face is pure, calculated determination. I can just about read her thoughts as she weighs her options: *If I stay with the pile of organs, the human will have a better chance of catching me; if I move too far out of reach, that same human might swoop in and steal a spleen or other delicacy. Hoard and be caught; relinquish and be free. What to do?!* She's in agony over the decision.

I edge closer to the pile, walking a slow circle around it and the barbarian dog. True to past form, Ari dances around the cache, thinking strategy. She has created a hierarchy of value out of this heap of guts. If I can figure it out, we might be able to reach a compromise. But what is most important to her within this pile? I have no idea. To be honest, I don't even really know what we are looking at.

Hunters and wildlife biologists claim that most deer organs, aside from the bulky ruminant stomach, are surprisingly similar to human organs, and thus easy to identify. That's not a great deal of help to me, since I don't really know anything about my innards, either. Ari probably doesn't know much more about the comparison than I do, with one major exception: Some of these bits are a lot more enticing to her than others. Once she's back on the leash, I let her nose around the pile. I want to know what most attracts her to this remnant of the hunting season: Is it the squishy green bit, or the mottled red one? And why?

The captured dog isn't saying much, and it's near impossible to tell simply by observing her unwind long-dead organs like string or a child's plaything. We need further research—something scientifically accurate.

Back home, I call our neighbor Risto and ask if he knows where I might find some fresh deer organs. To his credit, Risto pretends that this is a routine neighbor-to-neighbor request. He tells me he shot his deer on the last day of the season and still has all the parts. This delights me more than I would have thought possible. He does not balk at my enthusiasm but, instead, offers to pack the guts for safekeeping until I can collect them.

After work that evening, Ari and I make the short drive over to Risto's property, where he and his golden retriever puppy, Miko, are awaiting our arrival. Both stand next to a bulging burlap sack emblazoned with a happy sunflower. I doubt this current use is what the birdseed company envisioned when they designed the bag.

Miko seems oblivious to the bag's contents. But Ari is alert and even a little alarmed. The organs are so fresh they've barely entered the first stage of decay. To her, they still represent death and not food. She raises her hackles and sniffs warily at the ground around the bag. When Miko invites her to play in a different part of the yard, she looks relieved. Meanwhile, Risto and I heave the sunflower bag into the back of Greg's truck. Then he takes me over to examine his newly gutted deer carcass.

I am artificially exuberant by this experience, which is so far beyond my normal comfort zone it makes me heady. I'm also anxious to embrace my grisly examination, so at the risk of being rude, I cut short my appreciation of Risto's hanging deer and retrieve my dog. Once back in Greg's truck, I remain a flutter of excitement. "Look at me," I say to Ari and anyone else who might be listening. "I'm a naturalist. I have a bag of animal organs!" Does this make sense? No. Not even to my dog. But I don't care. I'm getting down and dirty with my natural world.

That enthusiasm fades, though, when Ari and I return home and I feel the full weight of the bag in my hands. I haven't eaten red meat since I was thirteen. Even as a kid, I was repelled by it. On more than one occasion, my mom had to persuade me that what looked like blood on my plate was actually a mysterious ingredient called "meat juice": This was often the only way she could get me to eat a steak or hamburger. Gullible as I am, I believed her. Nevertheless, I still balled up most of it and hid it in my napkin.

This is all a long way of saying that I don't really know what to do with most meat or meat by-products. I certainly have never handled a sack of gutted organs still adhering to one another with connective tissue. What on earth was I thinking?

For a full day, the organs sit in the shade next to my car, while I think of excuses not to deal with them. Midway through the second morning, I tell myself these are not the sort of things that improve with age and lug the bag to the backyard. There, I set up a makeshift MASH unit and begin separating the organs from their connective tissues, identifying them as best as I can with the help of a field-dressing manual I found on the Internet. As I match sketched spleen and kidney to the actual organs, I am pleased at how reasonably I behave. I decide that I may be learning how to be a detached scientist after all.

Ari, on the other hand, is utterly attached to the matter at hand: She watches from my office window with pointed interest as I cut organ from organ. I gently wash the deer's heart, lungs, and liver, then photograph them next to one of Greg's tape measures. Her face is stern and corrective, and she yips a sharp bark now and again to get my attention. When I come inside, I bring with me the smell of deer blood. Ari is first wary and then very, very interested. She licks my jeans as if they were a denim Popsicle and doesn't mind that they taste more like detergent than ruminant.

Later in the day, I shift my focus from simple identification to interspecies comparison. Are these deer guts really like my own? The idea intrigues me, particularly since my dog wants very much to eat them. If mine are similar, will she try for a bite of my liver one night while I sleep? In my blood-streaked state of exuberance, I persuade myself that these are questions crucially important to answer. I email our organ photos to my brother, a physician. When I haven't heard back from him in a few hours, I call his cell phone and discover he is visiting his in-laws. I ask if they have high-speed Internet. He responds with the habitual sigh of family members on the phone with me. Nevertheless, five minutes later he calls back from their computer room, where he sits examining three vivid photographs.

"What are these?" he asks.

I gently explain that they are a liver, heart, and lungs. I suggest that a doctor who does not recognize them may want to consider another profession.

He sighs more loudly. "No, I mean *what are these from*?"

I tell him, somewhat for science and mostly just to be a smart aleck, that they are human.

"Oh," he says. He does not ask why they are photographed in my yard next to Greg's tape measure. Either he isn't really listening to me or he has become so anesthetized to blood and gore in his profession, he no longer thinks it odd that his writer-sister would be in possession of human organs.

I sit quietly, hoping one of these explanations will occur to him. It doesn't.

"So how'd you get them?" he eventually asks. His voice is mildly curious—no more, no less.

I tell him they came from my neighbor, who is a hunter. This also does not strike him as strange or potentially troubling.

I decide it's no longer entertaining to mess around with him—not if I'm not going to get at least some kind of reaction. I relent and tell him they are deer.

"But," I add hopefully, "they could be human, right?"

"Oh, yeah," he says. "Definitely."

I hope this doesn't mean he is a bad doctor.

We both call up website images of human organs, then talk about size and weight. It turns out that my deer liver, which weighs two and a half pounds, is almost identical to an average human's. The deer's heart weighs just a tad more; its lungs a tad less. They are the color and dimension of their human equivalent. I recant about my brother being a bad doctor and wonder aloud if my dog would ever consider eating my organs. He sighs a third time and tells me he has to get back to the family supper.

Ari and I, meanwhile, get back to her pile of seasoned organs out in the woods, where I'm hoping we can apply the information garnered during our recent anatomy lesson. These organs, though, have been outside for well over a week by now, so little that is identifiable remains. Mostly, they are just a tangled pile of half-eaten tissue. I can only speculate that the leathery pouch of dried organ is what was once the sophisticated system of papillae and honeycomb chambers that make up a ruminant stomach. Ditto for the little squishy bits, which may have once been a bladder or spleen. In fact, only the intestines are clearly identifiable—mostly because my industrious dog, perhaps with the help of some of her woodland compatriots, has unraveled a good portion of their sixty-five-foot length.

Despite their time outside, these guts are outrageously vivid. If a child were to draw deer intestine, he or she would select crayons with names like olive and bittersweet, asparagus and dandelion. This would probably lead the child to believe that deer intestines left to fester in the woods are a pleasant and delightful sight. That child would be wrong—unless that child has the mind of a twelve-month-old dog.

Or possibly a fourteenth-century cook. In fact, while few people have ever admitted to being crazy for deer guts, historically they have nevertheless been considered not altogether repugnant by some people and a good square meal by others.

Taken in sum, the digestive organs of a deer are known as its umble. When spoken with a thick cockney accent *umble* sounds exactly like *humble*, which is why we've conflated the two when talking about pies. This conflation has resulted in what Frances Phipps, onetime antiques columnist for the *New York Times,* aptly called "the longest-running pun in the English language." Phipps explains that, for centuries, eating has been a communal activity. And even in the strict hierarchies of medieval feudalism, that often meant a single slain animal would feed all members of a household—servants included. When dining on the slain deer, the most esteemed guests or household members sat near the head of the table, where the salt (another esteemed guest) was located. If you were lucky enough to land a spot at this part of the table, you were definitely worth your salt. Lesser guests sat below the salt, a reminder of their own paltry worth. Least guests and servants didn't even get to sit at the same table as the salt. This distinction wasn't just about sodium: It also dictated your right to a particular cut of meat. While landowners and hosts would dine upon roasted and salted venison loin, reluctantly invited guests and servants got the scraps, which were further tempered by wrapping them in the relatively cheap filler of piecrust. This was perhaps the earliest form of Hamburger Helper known to Western civilization. And people then weren't too much more enthusiastic about this thrifty meal than contemporary Americans are today. If you had to dine on humble pie, you also had to swallow your pride.

As happy as I am to eat my shirt or even some crow, I'm not about to try Ari's umbles—even in the name of caninaturalist discovery. But the voyeur in me is awfully curious about whether other people are filling up on innard pies. Back home, I log onto the Web in search of modern incarnations of the dish. There, I find tripe.com, the official site of "tripe, tripe, glorious tripe." I also find a disturbing number of elementary school lesson plans for recreating a medieval Christmas feast in "merrie olde Englande," which seems to be an education exclusively about cholesterol and unsanitary eating. A culinary list-serv includes a posting asking if anyone has a palatable recipe for humble pie. An earnest member of the discussion group responds to the query with, "Mix a little humility with a large dash of apology, stir in some grovelling to taste, and serve whilst bowing and scraping, and wearing a hair coat." Very funny, these digital foodies. When I type "umble" into the search engine of my own favorite recipe database, it comes up with what—in most social circles—might be a reasonable retort: "Didn't you mean blue cheese canapés with pecans and grapes?" I wish.

Ari sure doesn't. As out of fashion as umble may be in the twenty-first-century culinary blogosphere, it continues to captivate this pup's palate. Each of our woodland walks—even those that occur strictly on leash—become a tortured dance to get near the pile of deer guts. Ari is in love with this pile of rotting organs, and no amount of cajoling or bribing will force her to forget about them. Each time we get anywhere near the pile, she leaps and wiggles her way over. She laughs when I try to lure her away with a biscuit—as if barley flour and a little chicken fat could possibly compete with festering colon and bladder. When off leash, she becomes all coyote and continues her crouched scuttling by marking time between her cherished pile and the human in pursuit. I try to reason with her. To trick her. And when that doesn't work, I resort to old-fashioned bribery. Meanwhile, the caninaturalist continues to guffaw at my desperate naïveté.

We have reached the limits of positive reinforcement training. This practice depends upon the strength of the reward: specifically, that said reward is both worth whatever behavior a trainer has requested and better than whatever reward the trainee can come up with on his or her own. All animals—including humans—are adept at self-treating. That can be a tough act to beat if you're a trainer offering measly bits of biscuit (even if the biscuit was handmade with love a few nights earlier) in the face of rotting organs.

The reasons for this conflict go back to what Deborah Wells calls "internally motivated behaviors." All animals—from houseflies to humans—possess instinctual desires and responses. We can try to redirect or extinguish these impulses through a variety of training techniques: clicker training, shock collars, being grounded without supper, handing out treats, or putting a little gold star on a homework assignment. But to do so, we have to be persuaded that this external reward or punishment is greater than what we gain from following our instincts.

Overriding this internal desire is far more difficult than it sounds. The outside layer of mammalian brains is known as the cerebral cortex (which means "tree bark" in Latin). It controls sensory perception and discrimination; it also controls what we might think of as id behaviors: the impulse to follow scents, eat junk food, and so on. Working in concert (and often conflict) with the cerebral cortex is the hippocampus—a semicircular part of the inner brain so named because early scientists believed it resembled a sea horse in shape. This part of the brain controls memory, what we might call emotion, and learned behavior; it also decides what a mammal will or will not retain in memory.

When it comes to most domestic mammals, the trick is to train them to favor their hippocampus over their cortex: to reinforce the knowledge of a treat or potential punishment as justification for overriding the urge to hunt or scavenge. This is not so different from the human mind, of course. Our brains are remarkably similar to dogs', save the development of the frontal lobe, which allows for what we like to think of as the high-functioning skills such as language and critical thinking. But all of us still experience that tension between the information gathered by the cortex and the evaluation of the hippocampus. Ask any human who decided he wanted that second piece of pie or fourth martini or really expensive pair of skis even though he lives in Nebraska, and you'll see this tension at work. We know we might feel bloated or hungover the next morning; we know we may be pouring money down the drain on needless stuff; nevertheless, our hippocampus, through conditioning, switches off that knowledge and allows us to embrace our perceived wants, rather than our knowledge of their effects.

This same tension informs any direct interaction we have with wildlife. It's why some people can train squirrels to eat out of their hand or why hunters know a bear is likely to approach a baited trap, even if it smells humans in the vicinity. Desire is a powerful thing—and the singers of doo-wop ballads were right: It can turn us all into fools. That's why ten months of maturation and hundreds of dollars of dog classes don't really matter much to Ari right now. Her hippocampus is no match for deeper, instinctual behaviors. So much so, in fact, that in a situation like this she is clearly willing to risk separation from me or even an inadvertent risk to her own safety, all because she's too focused on the id and its desire for deer guts to give anything else a second thought.

Foolish as they may be, I have my own desires right now. Initially, mine come more from my hippocampus than my cortex: I want a walk in the forest that does not include a gallery tour of rotten umble. I want a dog that understands this want. Badly. In fact, I come to want these things so much that I forget to consider things like a canine's version of the Great Chain of Being or the difference between human and dog values or what is reasonable to expect of a dog who has been a mediocre student in a few introductory behavioral classes. In short, I have become one staggering cortex. And what does this contemporary Neanderthal do with her fully actualized internal releasing mechanisms? Certainly nothing that could be considered reasonable or worthy of her frontal lobe. Oh, no. Instead, she growls like a savage, then pulls down her thoroughly modern, boot-cut jeans and pees on the entrails while her juvenile dog looks on with horror and disappointment.

Never in my life have I ever considered such an action. When and where else would urination be an acceptable means of claiming ownership? Filene's basement? A Columbus Day white sale? The corner bakery? Certainly not. Even on camping trips, I'm a reluctant user of the back forty when it comes to relieving myself. None of this matters right now, though. Without thinking, I instantly intuit it is the right thing to do. And surprisingly enough, I'm right—at least as far as canine interaction is concerned. The minute I've marked these congealed, mottled innards as mine, Ari relents. *Okay, boss—you want these organs? Fair is fair. Could I get you some horseradish? Maybe a nice Viognier? While you enjoy these, I'll just wander off and see if I can find another pile. . . .*

"Hold it right there," I say. Enough is enough—for both of us.

I don't like exercising pack hierarchy any more than I have to. Ari is still a timid dog, and she remains quick to roll into a submissive pose when faced with another dog or most humans. I know she knows that, should a particular situation warrant it, I can claim dominance. But that's not what our relationship is supposed to be about—certainly not after all that we've been through in the past year. We've helped each other through tough situations; we've seen the beauty and mystery of the world together. Our interaction, then, ought to be, as much as is possible in an interspecies friendship, about reciprocity and mutual respect. There must be a more equitable way of dealing with these rare moments of disagreement. Besides, I can't possibly spend my days yanking down my pants and urinating on every carcass I see. Eventually, people are going to start to talk.

In My Backyard

[january]

The scene has become a familiar one over the past month or so. Greg and I sit on the couch, sipping tea and listening to Saturday-morning radio. Plate in lap, he is polishing off the giant stack of pancakes he made and I could not finish. It's a good system, and one that often results in two empty plates and a bemused waiter or waitress when we go out to eat. It also beats the former system, which usually found him wantonly pirating food off my plate and leaving me to wonder if I would ever get a full meal. When we were married four years ago, we wrote wedding vows for each other: I was made to promise that I would dull my use of sarcasm; Greg pledged to leave me half of any dessert. We're still working on living up to both promises. It's a good thing the marriage hinges on other vows, too.

As Greg cuts mouthfuls of breakfast this morning, Leila Tov sits on the back of the couch in Ari's favorite command post. We've relented and placed a wool blanket there, acknowledging that (whether we like it or not) this spot will always be prime pet real estate. For Leila Tov, it also offers easy egress, should the closeness of this scene prove too much and a quick getaway become imperative. It hasn't yet. Instead, she looks on with something like bemusement as Mouse jockeys for a second breakfast. Each time Greg raises his fork, the brazen cat pushes her speckled pink nose onto the plate, hoping she can at least get a mouthful of syrup before he notices. She's not that quick. As Mouse reaches out, Greg sighs and then attempts to guard the plate with his free hand. Frustrated but undeterred, Mouse slips her boxy head between his arm and the plate. Greg resists again, and then tries unsuccessfully to reason with her. Meanwhile, I join Leila Tov in looking on and very much appreciating Greg's reversal of fortune: The food thief has become the thieved. This makes me laugh. LT looks like she might do the same. Greg, on the other hand, grimaces at all of us and moves his blocking arm closer to the plate as he tries to finish the breakfast.

Like Greg, Ari is not nearly so amused by this scene. Mouse's delinquency is one of the only things that can rouse the lazing caninaturalist on a morning like this, when she is otherwise occupied communing with the woodstove. This time it is Ari who sighs heavily as Mouse tries once again to filch pancakes. Her eyes seem to say it all: *Hey. Hey! Heyheyheyhey!! Those pancakes belong to the human. And if not to him, then surely to me. I don't remember YOU begging in the kitchen back when he was cracking eggs and sifting flour.*

Mouse ignores the warning. This perturbs Ari. The caninaturalist rises, shakes her tags, and comes over to butt Mouse with her full-grown snout. *Hey, I said! Get in line, feline. How many times do I have to tell you?*

More than twice—that's for sure. Ari tries a third reprimand, but I intercede and explain her monitoring services won't be needed right now. She sighs again and drapes herself across my feet, still giving Mouse a steely eye and no doubt wondering why I am allowing this breach of protocol to persist.

At times like these, we call Ari a hall monitor and Mouse a pest. We don't really mean either. Mostly, we're just glad to be here together. At home, and immersed in our own household ecology.

I pick this term deliberately and with great appreciation for its etymology. Scientists don't always have a reputation as wordsmiths, but Ernst Haeckel certainly was one. He coined the term *ecology* in 1866 and defined it as a series of complex relationships comprising any animal and "its inorganic and organic environment; including its friendly and inimical relations with those animals and plants with which it comes into contact." Haeckel's choice of words plays on the Greek *oikos* which means "home" in the sense of household, the basic system of relationships defining agrarian antiquity. In its original sense, *oikos* included the house itself, the extended family, the servants and slaves, the farmlands, and even the familial dog—all of which interacted with one another and defined their collective destiny. For the ancient Greeks, *oikos* was about knowing your place—in every sense of the world.

Modern ecology takes this notion to heart. So, too, do most environmentalists, or anyone interested in arriving at a personal sense of place. What they all agree upon is this: Understanding anything—including ecological systems—begins with the familiar. And the familial. Without this knowledge, even the most aesthetically and biologically diverse landscape can just seem like space. When that happens, you can forget all about the advantages of having your own sense of place—and the benefits it brings. That's a loss not to be taken lightly. Place matters a lot, whether you are human or canine.

Even those domestic dogs left to wander unrestricted tend to create home ranges less than half a square mile in area, preferring a small place they can know intimately over one with more biodiversity. Once they establish this territory, they'll cling to it as their own, even if they are forcefully relocated.

As for me and Greg, place has also been something we always admired but only recently began to really understand. We moved to Maine seven years ago. A few summers prior, we had fallen in love with the rugged coast, the hardscrabble farms, the working inland forests, and the stark granite mountains. We loved the smell of balsam and the look of a northern New England sky, especially when a high-pressure system rolls in. We admired the independent perseverance of locals still tied to ancestral acreage, and the earnest pluck of back-to-the-landers who sold everything to move here in the 1970s for an experiment in sustainable, communal living. This was the kind of place where we wanted to make our home.

That's saying a lot for us. We were both raised in families that moved from bioregion to bioregion every few years. As a result, neither one of us really felt like we were from much of anywhere. In fact, we've both lived in Maine as long as either one of us has lived anywhere else. We'd like to believe we will spend the rest of our lives here. Our guts tell us we probably will. The wanderlust of earlier years has subsided and we find comfort in the notion of settling. Besides, this landscape just feels right.

It can take a lifetime to get to know any one place, and few people are lucky enough to sustain the kind of study necessary to become truly intimate with a landscape. We know this. But we also know we've made more progress in the past eleven months than we have in the other six years combined. We owe much of this newfound familiarity to Ari and her insistence that we get to know nature as well. How else could I talk about salamander sex and cedar roots with any authority whatsoever?

Of course, getting to know a landscape also means getting to know its people, and that I think is our biggest omission to date as naturalists. The truth of the matter is that, for all we know about amphibian reproduction and indigenous flora, we know precious little about how the majority of humans in our environment interact with these wild residents. It's not that we don't make small talk with other townspeople or read the newspaper or attend town meetings on a regular basis. We aren't really hermits or misanthropes, either. Nevertheless, if asked we would have to admit we don't have the slightest idea about what's really going on in our community.

Some of the reasons for this omission may be cultural. Here in New England, the penchant for what folks call Yankee reserve can be legendary, if not notorious. Mainers are particularly taciturn. They are also serious about place—and who can claim it. Unless you come from a family that has spent generations here, you are from away—no matter how long you've called the state home. This is true even for people who were born here. A favorite piece of local folk wisdom says it all: *Just because a cat has kittens in an old stove doesn't mean they're biscuits.*

We have lived here for less than a decade, so we're not even close to a biscuit by those standards. Still, blaming our obliviousness on stove analogies seems a little half baked. We know that, if we are ever to really know this place, we must find a way to become a part of the lived culture of it as well. There are all sorts of ways we could go about this process. But this month, we'll discover that sometimes it can take a loquacious dog or the threat of a foreign intrusion to make inroads. We'll also learn that, on a few occasions, it can be good to have both. First, an update on that loquacious dog.

Now just over a year old, Ari is about as mature as the average human high school student. She has another year before she'll achieve her full twentysomething self, which anthropologists and ethologists agree is the new age of maturity for the twenty-first century. Along with this coming-of-age may also arrive the stereotypical apathy and disaffected sense of the world that pop media would have us believe define the era. In the meantime, though, she's not unlike most seventeen-year-olds I know: eager to spend time with her peer group, a little resentful of parental control, but still willing to make reconciliatory overtures to preserve familiar relationships. In short, she is growing up. Along the way, she is also discovering the potential benefits of reason and proportion—at least on occasion. And although still prone to dramatic shifts in mood, much of her personality has formed and will now remain fairly constant for the rest of her life.

This is not to say she is done learning, of course. We can keep working on all sorts of new behaviors throughout her life, and even when she is an old dog she'll still be willing to learn new tricks. Nevertheless, much of who Ari is has now been settled. What remains is my need to come to terms with it—particularly after the last two months.

I'm not a huge fan of pop psychology, but I understand enough about the five stages of emotional processing to know where we stand when it comes to our relationships with one another and with the natural world. I know, for instance, that Ari is always going to be just enough of a wild child in the wilderness that no reasonable amount of schooling will ensure I can get her back to me every time I need to. I spent a good long time denying this was true. I even tried my hand at bargaining and, on a few days, attempted a little resentment thrown in for good measure. I'm ready to try acceptance. That means the only truly safe way for me and Ari to be out in nature is to do so on a leash or in a backyard.

The fact of the matter is that, at least in our house, a certain amount of instinct is always going to trump enforcement. It has taken a long time and multiple animal scenarios for me to accept this. It took dozens of slain mice, killed and then eviscerated by Cam, for me to understand that a lap cat is still a predator. Tripping over a fleeing Leila Tov has taught me that direct eye contact will always be a threat to a feral animal. Rotten snakes and koi fish, deer legs and guts have taught me some valuable lessons about the inner Ari, too. If I have learned anything this year, it is that Ari may be a domestic dog, but that doesn't always mean what I would like it to.

Frankly, I think most of us have forgotten what *domestic* really means. The word actually comes from the Latin *domus* which, like *oikos,* means "house." Unlike the Greek incarnation of the term, however, the Roman notion of *domus* focused on the structure of the house and those who dwelled directly within it. That limited definition makes it, I think, a particularly rich root for our modern word *domestic*, particularly as it applies to animals. When this use of the word *domestic* entered early-modern parlance around the sixteen century, people were fairly specific about what it meant: living *near or around* human habitations. That's a whole lot different from being a willing supplicant to the rules of said habitation. Ask most pet owners, and they'll agree: Just because members of a species agree to move out of a natural habitat into a human-made one doesn't necessarily mean those animals agree to all the provisions on the lease.

As Ari's student, I have learned time and time again that the distinction between wild and domestic is often not a very meaningful one. That's not for lack of trying on the part of my species, however. In fact, Western culture has tried to maintain this dichotomy for as long as the terminology has existed. Consider Alfred Lord Tennyson's phrase "red in tooth and claw," which Greg applied to the blood-streaked caninaturalist last month. When Tennyson first coined the phrase, he used it as a way of distinguishing between the godly order of civilization on the one hand and a Hobbesian idea of nature as brutish and mean on the other. Just in case any domesticated species might balk at joining the former camp, Tennyson reminds us that its members are the embodiment of love—what he calls "Creation's final law." Nature, under his definition, offers a shrieking, ungodly existence, along with bloody snout and paws. Better to avoid that kind of life at all costs—unless the idea of damnation appeals to you.

Humanity's view of nature tends to be far more secular these days, but we still maintain the wild-domestic distinction whenever possible. This is one reason why urinating on a pair of boots I see at Lord & Taylor may claim them for me as my own, but will also certainly get me kicked out of the store before I can pay for them. It may also be why so many media depictions of nature emphasize the red in tooth and claw. Take a look at any of the nature programming on television, and you'll see countless ads for shows emphasizing the dangerous side of wildlife. On the very day when I write this paragraph, for instance, Animal Planet is promoting a series of shows including "Killer Ants," "Killer Bees," "Killer Elephants," "Killer Crocs of Costa Rica," and "The Snake That Killed Cleopatra." Factor in specials like *When Animals Attack* on the somewhat sensational Fox Network or *Dangerous Encounters* and *Planet Carnivore* on the otherwise abstemious National Geographic Channel, and you begin to think Tennyson is right.

The same is true when you look at our preferred depictions of domesticated animals, which also tend to support Tennyson's idea about dichotomies. There, we go out of our way to emphasize lovability—and we've been doing so proudly since Tennyson's own Victorian age. That impulse only grew when Walt Disney introduced the world to a highly neotonized mouse named Mickey and his pet dog, Pluto, around 1930. Since then, we have favored a strange blend of infantilization and anthropomorphism in our views of domestic animals. Along the way, we began to insist that domesticated animals maintained not only nuclear families, but care bonds with other species as well. In this new world order, dogs court by sharing plates of spaghetti, spiders become literate to save pigs, and cats in hats agree to clean up the house before Mom gets home.

There are problems with such depictions, at least as far as what they do to our home lives. In 1996, for instance, the release of Disney's live-action *101 Dalmatians* prompted tens of thousands of families to adopt spotted puppies. Within a year, thousands of these pups were kicked to the curb. The lucky ones made their way to Dalmatian rescue groups, who saw an exponential rise in dogs needing foster care. Others were given to a wide variety of animal shelters or simply abandoned. Not surprisingly, then, when the film company announced plans for a sequel in 2000, it met with heavy opposition from the Humane Society, which worried that the film would create another canine crisis. The two organizations butted heads publicly for several months, until they reached a compromise: Disney would run a public service statement in the film's credits announcing, *If you are adopting a pet, be sure that you are ready for a lifetime commitment and research your choice carefully.* Disney's producers thought this was a perfectly responsible solution; the Humane Society was considerably less satisfied.

To make matters worse, the war between Disney and the Humane Society was far from over. A year later, the debate between the two groups again erupted—this time over the suitability of huskies as America's favorite pet. Disney's *Snow Dogs* (2002) and *Eight Below* (2006) both starred sled dogs—mostly Siberian huskies and Alaskan malamutes, although native Greenlandic sled dogs did most of the heavy pulling and stunts in the latter film. Suddenly, people across the globe were absolutely infatuated with these primitive cold-weather dogs. And once again, the Humane Society objected. In an official press release, spokesperson Brian Sodergren articulated HSUS's position on the films: "People need to be honest with themselves. While Siberian huskies are wonderful dogs, they are not the right animal companion for everyone. They are intelligent, high-energy dogs that can become bored and destructive if they don't receive adequate exercise, training, and attention. They like to dig and roam, can be very vocal, and require significant grooming."

Sodergren didn't say anything about their penchant for eating or rolling in decaying animals, but his message rings true nonetheless—at least in our house. Greg and I don't mind the fur or the creative vocalizations. We know more about roaming than we would ever care to. As for the destruction? Let's just say that under the veneer of this very lovely dog—the one so demurely draped across my feet and so insistent on making sure that her feral friends uphold house polices—lies a potentially questionable companion: one more than capable of disemboweling a couch or completely emptying a kitchen in two minutes flat. Knowing that a good part of this behavior is a combination of our lax training skills and Ari's DNA, we humans thought it best to consider a compensatory widening of our own *domus,* namely by fencing in our yard for the caninaturalist and her undomestic tendencies. We even went so far as to visit friends with different fencing designs to see how Ari would respond. Here's what we learned from that little experiment: When Sodergren says huskies like to dig, what he means is that they can excavate a trench capable of housing most of the Western Front. Said foxhole is certainly more than adequate space for a wriggling dog to escape. Descriptions like *high-energy* are code for Olympic-caliber decathlon skills, with a particular emphasis placed on hurdles and the high jump. Unless we import the Loki Clan Refuge's ten-feet perimeter shields, there isn't much this rowdy athlete can't leap over.

So what to do?

After a few weeks of searching, we find the answer right where Ernest Haeckel promised we would: in the familiar. We join a new agility club in the area, which challenges both of us physically and mentally—at least once a week. Meanwhile, we walk. And walk some more.

Under this new system, each morning we leash up and create a well-worn path down our road and over to our neighbor's disused apple orchard. There, we mark the dawn with the known world. We cross the wide expanse of Judy's meadow, making our way up and over a small rise before dipping into the edge of forest. We cross the dry streambed, circle the stand of cattails molting in the thick bog, head through the new-growth forest, and then return to the stand of apple trees far older than me and the caninaturalist combined. Along the way, we count stones and trees and abandoned junk from farms long ago. We monitor the cattails and deer tracks, noting how they are either dwindling or growing from day to day. There is much to see in this minutiae. Maybe too much to see.

It is January in one of the coldest states in the Union. We ought to be clambering over snowdrifts by now, or gliding along Risto's cross-country trails in a tangle of ski poles and dog harnesses. But we're not doing either. This year, the winter season has been marked by far more fog and rain than it has snow. As a result, what should be a monolithic expanse of white is, instead, a weathered extension of late fall. At least initially, we don't recognize this landscape. The autumn leaves, now long-since fallen, have sorted themselves out into compacted piles pushed against rock walls and tree stumps. Most of our other foliage gave up the ghost long ago, too. Giant sunflowers have buckled and now drape their half-eaten heads on the earth. Ferns lie in broken tangles of bright orange nearby, along with the now-hollow reeds of lily and orchid stalks. In fact, the only plant audacious enough to embrace this unexpected warmth is the grass, which grows golf-course green in the meadow.

Inside the orchard proper, the tight web of brush holds on to more than its fair share of autumn leaves, and our morning walks are punctuated by their muted sound underfoot, along with the residual smell of fermenting apples lying at the base of trees. Sometimes, we happen upon a flock of finches resting in the branches. Other times, we spy a family of deer or fox breakfasting there. When we do, the caninaturalist and I stop soundlessly, both of us transfixed on this world happening just outside our door.

Scenes like these are evidence that our own agreeable compromise is working. Pastoral and lovely in its overgrown state, the orchard acts as home to flora and fauna of all kinds, even now in the dead of winter. Together, Ari and I can find an entire ecosystem functioning within these few acres. As a result, we both agree that we can keep busy—and controlled—on our walks here, just a few steps from home.

We enjoy a week of stillness and then another. A dozen meditations on this particular place. Our walks in the orchard begin to feel routine in the best possible sense of the word. And then, one morning, Ari seems unusually anxious as we enter the meadow. She pulls hard on her leash, chuffing like the infant dog who first walked with me nearly a year ago. When that fails to increase our pace, she arches up onto her hind legs, hopping like a gawky kangaroo over the rise. Out of nowhere, a blur whizzes past us both before I can indentify it. The caninaturalist knows what it is, though. She springs from her two-footed position and launches into the air, spins a half circle, and lands in the direction of the moving streak. She chortles her biggest greeting. Loudly. Her dog-laugh causes the blur to stop, turn, and face us in all of its canine beauty: long brown locks, feathery oversized paws, golden eyes, and chiseled features. This is an absolute Adonis of a dog. Before Ari and I can swoon with delight, though, another dog—smaller, shorter hair—joins us.

Who are these gorgeous creatures?

No one answers my question—at least not in human language. Instead, they concentrate on their own canine introductions: a few sniffs of the air, followed by playbows and spins. It doesn't take more than a moment for Ari to make friends. It's just one of her enviable traits. Her new companions seem to get that. The two mystery dogs dance around Ari, barking high up into the sky. *Hey, great to meet you! Hey, glad we found you!*

The sound of their voices floats over the meadow, delivering their location to a still-unseen person who answers with her own:

"Mesquite? Sparks?"

The dogs answer with a simultaneous cock of their heads. They know their names. Now, so do we. A moment later, our neighbor Elizabeth makes her own way over the rise, looking a little harried and concerned. I wave and shout a greeting over the din of play-growls. We haven't seen her since we found the dead kitten several months ago. It's nice to meet during a less somber time.

"I'm sorry," says Elizabeth as she continues to make her way across the frosty meadow. "They must have heard you and your dog—they bolted up the trail before I could catch them. I didn't know that anyone else was walking back here."

I tell her there is absolutely no reason to be sorry—that Ari couldn't be happier to make new acquaintances, and I'm embarrassed to admit that I didn't even know Elizabeth had pet dogs. I tell her meeting like this is long overdue. She looks relieved and points out her morning walking loop, a shorter version of our circumambulatory route around the orchard. We agree to join them.

Ari is more than delighted to truncate her usual walk now that she has her first real dog pack to romp with. The three of them become a single organism, shuddering its way around apple trees, into the bog, and around piles of stripped and drying wood. Elizabeth looks on, trying to characterize this canine mass.

"They look like a big dog blob," she finally concludes.

I agree: They have taken on a new identity, one bigger than any individual. I try to pick out Ari's tawny coat as it courses along in the new multi-dog organism. She looks delighted. Her gait assumes the bobbing arches I have come to associate with her sense of joy, her mouth parts in an excited grin, and she stops only to put a paw on the shoulder of one of the other two dogs, as if to say, *Hey, buddy, this is great, huh?*

The other two dogs are used to being a pack. Still, they seem excited about the new addition, and they race off after the caninaturalist, showing her some of their favorite spots, most of which are murky puddles and patches of bog. Ari hasn't been swimming in months, having apparently decided (just as Greg and I have) that it is far too cold for a dip. Today, however, she leaps into every liquid body with great abandon, following her two friends into the slime, everyone soon bursting back onto terra firma with a collective shake.

As the dogs squish their way down the trail, Elizabeth tells me stories about our area and its inhabitants, giving name and identity to what lies behind the sparsely placed gravel driveways making up our little community. I learn about the country singer who released another album earlier in the month, the couple who left their jobs at the NYPD and brought their kids to Maine just after September 11, the retired schoolteacher, and the boatbuilder who writes books about wooden vessels. We have all traveled the same dusky paths in the town forest, perhaps serpentining our way past one another unseen. We have waved from our cars or maybe even stood in line next to one another at the general store, waiting to pay for our gas and homemade fudge. Really, though, that is mostly all. They know little about me, and I know less about them—despite the fact that we have occupied the same basic space for several years. I ask Elizabeth if she thinks that lack of contact is wrong—or at least unusual.

"I don't think so," she says after a few moments of contemplation. "People come here to get away from everything. A lot of people like their privacy. Besides, it's hard to keep a homestead running here. There's wood to chop and canning to do and animals to feed. That doesn't always leave a lot of time to socialize."

I relate a story one of my colleagues told me just after I was hired at the college. He had been playing softball with the same group of men for several summers, and he invited them over to his house for a cookout one night after practice. There was an awkward silence. Eventually, one of the men explained. "We have to build up to that kind of thing," he said. "We've only know each other for five years. Be patient."

At the time, I assumed this was an amusing anecdote told to break the ice and commiserate over legends of local culture. But I'm learning there's more than just a bit of truth to it as well. Relationships take a lot of time to build around here. Unless, of course, you are an affable dog or, by extension, her sometimes-recluse of an owner. Every dog owner I've met has stories to tell, and even quiet New Englanders want to swap canine tales. Elizabeth and I are no different. A few of these anecdotes, and the rest of the conversation just seems to grow from there. We tell each other about our jobs, our hobbies, our thoughts on this unusual season.

As the two humans continue to talk, the three dogs bound ahead, crashing through naked brambles and sending up puffs of dried leaves, or spinning out on the slippery surface. In perfect symphony, they sniff the same rotting pine logs; they mark the same corners of the trail. Theirs is a shared sensory experience in every possible sense.

Reluctantly, the five of us reach the edge of the orchard and the end of our walk. As we do, Elizabeth calls out to the dogs. All three make their way over, their breath forming warm clouds of white that insinuates itself into their chin hairs and freezes there, creating little gray dog beards. This makes them look wise as they jostle for treats and attention. Mesquite, the chow mix, sits on command, and the other two follow suit. We sort out leashes and biscuits, then try to persuade the new friends that it really is time to go back to their respective houses. Sparks flops on the ground in front of Ari, pawing at her feet. Ari gurgles hopefully in return. Both give us a dirty look: *How could you possibly separate us now? We're just getting to know one another.* We are empathetic. Elizabeth offers to meet us back in the same location next Thursday.

"My dogs haven't seemed this young in ages," she tells me. "It's good for them."

I tell her it's good for us, too.

On our walk the following week, the dogs reunite as their enthusiastic organism and slip between trees and trail. They look as if they have never been anything except this hydra of a sensory machine. As they pulse forward, Elizabeth offers some disturbing news: A development company is looking to subdivide the wooded land encompassing the town forest. What's worse, they've been in touch with a local cell phone tower contractor who wants to erect a two-hundred-foot communications tower somewhere in our neighborhood. That contractor has been approaching homeowners on our road. One seems particularly interested. If the tower goes up there, it'll be in close proximity to our land—and will take out a good part of the natural buffer between residences.

A couple down the road has decided to call a neighborhood meeting so that we can strategize about ways to fight this proposal. "It's frightening," says Elizabeth. "This landscape could quickly be changing."

I feel a sharp sense of propriety probably not warranted by my few years living in the neighborhood. I'm not from here. I have barely arrived and, were it not for Ari, I'd know little about this place. Still, Greg and I have made it our home, and we take that decision seriously. We feel a real responsibility toward this landscape and have vowed to preserve it as best we can. Cell phone towers and razed forests aren't part of that pact. I tell Elizabeth we want very much to attend the potluck. She gives me the telephone number for Jayne and John, the hosts, and tells me I should call.

A few days later, we arrive at the neighborhood potluck in the dark of early evening. John takes our coats and kidnaps Greg for preseason baseball talk. Ari and I make our way into the spacious kitchen, where half a dozen people are sipping wine and talking about the unusual weather. They look up as we enter.

"Oh, look!" says Loren, a spry middle-aged woman with white hair and a kayaking sweatshirt. "It's that blue-eyed dog."

"Ari," says Risto, grinning at us. "Her name is Ari."

Cami, Risto's wife, smiles and introduces herself. "Hello," she says in her warm Finnish accent. "We have seen you walking to the orchard lately."

"We have, too," says Lucy, the woman who owns the horses down the street. "Every single day."

I nod, blushing. "We decided it's best to stick closer to home these days."

"You're so good," says Jayne. "You never miss a day. I should come walk with you."

"We all should," says Deb. "It could be a neighborhood thing. We'll all walk Ari."

I beam at this camaraderie. Acres separate our homes. Other than the annual town meeting, no organized infrastructure brings us together. Nevertheless, these women know something I did not: Even with barriers of pine and disused rock walls, our little area constitutes a community. Over the years, they have watched this same landscape undergo changes both subtle and profound. Along the way, they've helped pull a car out of a snowdrift or quietly left a quart of maple syrup on someone's front porch. And without my knowing it, they have folded me and my blue-eyed dog into their fabric, too. There is no grand pronouncement or handshake to go along with this inclusion—just a stated awareness and the casual kitchen talk that makes up many a neighborhood gathering. I listen in, hoping to catch up on just a little of their lived history.

Talk of walking, though, soon returns us to the unavoidable topic of our missing season. Everyone agrees: No one ought be able to walk much of anywhere right now, at least not without big snowshoes and ski poles. We are all troubled and say as much.

"It's too warm out," says Jayne, placing a tray of vegetables and hummus on the counter.

Lucy agrees. "It's not natural. Something's wrong."

No one debates this assertion. That in itself is worth commenting upon. Over the past year, something remarkable has happened in the United States: Our collective consciousness has accepted that global warming is real. This is no mean change. In 1989, Bill McKibben published his now legendary book *The End of Nature,* which foretold the consequences of climate change. Few people other than hard-core environmentalists listened. Most of us were placated by climatological charts suggesting normal temperature ebbs and flows that might support the notion our climate would turn back on its own. Not many people assume as much anymore—not after rapidly reduced polar ice caps and perennial droughts in places once lush.

Here in the Northeast, it's unlikely that our missing winter is purely the result of global warming: After all, the strange season is too dramatic and isolated for the kind of long-term effects associated with climate change. Nevertheless, it is a powerful reminder that global warming is real—and can be severe.

People across New England are beginning to notice. Just recently, the much-esteemed environmental writer and activist Janisse Ray, along with three of her friends, decided to take action. On New Year's Day, they draped a huge banner asking WHERE'S WINTER? from a covered bridge near their town in Vermont. Then they donned wet suits and formed a flotilla of inner tubes that floated down the river and eventually under the covered bridge. Their point was both simple and severe: people should not be able to float down a Vermont river in January. They shouldn't be able to leave the house in just a wet suit, and their water shouldn't still be in liquid form. To emphasize this point, one member of their crew wore a sign that said I'D RATHER BE SNOWSHOEING. We all would. Especially, I suspect, the animals built to do so.

I tell my neighbors what I know about dogs and climate change research. Up near the Hudson Bay, researchers are using scat-detection dogs to chart behavioral changes in polar bears. What they've learned is troubling: polar bear reproduction is on the decline, and mature animals are both smaller and thinner. This doesn't bode well for the species. The opposite is true for Ari's totem animal, the coyote. Throughout North America, they seem to be growing both in size and pack population, presumably because they are facing less competition from animals like the polar bear.

As I relate this last detail, Ari cocks her head and gnashes her teeth, as if she understands—and is rooting for—the coyotes. This makes the women in the kitchen laugh and fawn at the play-fierce caninaturalist, who in turn ups her antics for the new audience.

At the sound of our laughter, Jayne's six-year-old-daughter Reilly appears. She looks like a woodland sprite with her blond curls, pixie face, and velvet green dress.

"Aaarrrr-rrriiii!" she cries, running over to hug my dog. Ari takes Reilly's hand in her mouth and leads her in circles around the table. Reilly looks ecstatic. Unbeknownst to me, this effervescent kindergartner has become Ari's number one fan. Jayne tells me that Reilly looks for us each morning on their way to school and keeps a catalog of my rogue dog's movements. She's amazed at how many details Reilly can keep straight—especially from the backseat window of a moving mini van.

"Reilly really loves Ari," Jayne says. She looks over at the two, now dancing in a close embrace. "Really, really loves Ari," she adds for emphasis. The women in the kitchen laugh.

The six-year-old sprite and one-year-old dog head for the upstairs.

"Wait a minute," corrects Jayne. "You need to ask permission first."

"Can I take Ari up to my room?" Reilly asks me.

"She will probably try to dress up Ari in holiday clothes," warns Jayne.

"That's okay," I say. "She might like it."

It's time for dinner. Greg and I take the lid off of our wild rice casserole and set it next to the roasted squash, the homemade bread, the cranberry salad, and the chocolate pudding cake. John arrives with the main course: a platter of grilled moose meat. He and his son, also named John, went on their first multigenerational moose hunt earlier in the season. The younger John shot and killed a moose weighing more than eight hundred pounds. The diners are dutifully impressed by this fact—and delighted that the Johns are sharing their prized meat.

"Really," says the elder John, moving dishes around to accommodate his Brobdingnagian platter. "Eat up. You're doing us a favor. We've run out of freezer space."

As John heaves the enormous platter onto the table, I quickly take stock of where Greg and I are sitting. I can't help myself—at least, not after last month. I lean over and whisper a question only my husband can hear: *Will we merit moose loin or umble pie?*

He looks at me suspiciously. "You don't eat red meat."

I tell him I know that. I just want to know where we stand as far as traditional meat allocation is concerned. Are we worth our salt? Do we rule the roost? I want the right to loin, even if I have no intention of eating it. I eye the platter and the salt again, wondering if medieval notions of class and game still have a place in our culture.

John observes me examining the platter. I smile.

"Do you also serve umble?" I ask.

Greg's grip becomes tighter on my knee. *Careful,* it says. *We're trying to make new friends here.* I try to ignore him.

John looks confused. "Umble?"

I tell him the story of the longest-running pun. He smiles politely, but doesn't seem to find it as entertaining as I do.

"Oh," he says. "You mean the guts."

I nod.

John wrinkles his nose. "Unh-unh," he says. "Never liked them. I tried deer liver once. It was okay—mostly because it didn't taste like liver."

I ask him if they saved the moose organs.

"No way," he says.

"Why?"

"Well, for starters the moose liver was like this big." He extends his arms as far as they will go, suggesting the liver was about four feet long. I like that he shares my penchant for exaggeration.

"It was massive," he says, then pauses. "We also found a worm in there about this big." His hands are now about two feet apart.

I tell him that sounds equally as monumental.

"Yeah," he agrees. "And there were a bunch of spots on the liver, too. That's a bad sign. We left it all out in the woods."

I thank him on behalf of medieval servants everywhere. Greg's grip becomes more intense. I start to ask another question, but Greg coughs loudly and takes a sip of wine. Luckily for him, any further conversation about the moose is preempted by Reilly, who reappears with Ari in tow. The caninaturalist is wearing a large red bow around her neck. She does not look at all pleased with this new accessory. Neither does Reilly, all things considered.

"She wouldn't wear the dress," says Reilly with chagrin. "I even said please."

Jayne gives Greg and me a sympathetic smile. I wink in return and tell Reilly I'm sorry—that Ari has always been something of a tomboy. She accepts this, but still seems disappointed.

Meanwhile, neighbors at the other end of the table have begun talking about the planning permits for the subdivision and cell phone tower. The conversation quickly filters down to our end as well. This new topic does not interest Reilly or Ari, so the two scamper into another room to let the grown-ups talk in peace.

Everyone at the table has a story about our place. Many of them moved to our area in the 1970s to try out communal living and piecemeal farming. Lucy and Jim met at one such farm, which they now own. They remember when it was the only house on Stagecoach Road. The next to arrive were John and Jayne, who built the first part of their house—then just a one-room camp, really—while they were pregnant with their oldest child. Jayne had to walk nearly half a mile to get to their car when she finally went into labor.

Most of the people at the table have lived here long enough to see this little patch of upland forest change dramatically already. They can also remember when our house was built twenty-five years ago. A small log cabin set back in a pine grove, even it seemed like an intrusion to them. Still, they are realists when it comes to the life of our community. Towns are not so different from the human body: Parts of them are always stretching, wrinkling, caving in, or spreading. It's organic. It's about natural growth.

At least sometimes.

The plan to build a new subdivision or a massive tower on our road seems like something different entirely. We talk about what the latter will do to the ecosystem—to migrating birds and salamanders, to the health of kids like Reilly. Our wilderness has never been all that wild, but it's just unsettled enough for most of us. We have come to love the scrappy forest and its inhabitants. Blinking lights and hundreds of feet of steel and concrete aren't likely to add much in the way of embellishment—aesthetic or otherwise. We want to take action and begin to discuss how.

Eventually, Greg raises what many of us are thinking. "Are we just being selfish in not wanting this tower? Is this just a matter of 'Not in My Backyard'?"

His question silences us. Most of the people at the table have read about wind-farm battles on Cape Cod, where card-carrying environmentalists suddenly oppose turbines only when they block a coveted view of the sea. We don't want to be that problem. Jim and Greg agree to review the town ordinance and other possible sites for the tower. They'll ask what other people in the town think, too. If the town really wants a tower, and this is the best site, we'll acquiesce. John and Norma offer to contact the state municipal association and a few neighboring towns to see if they have any advice for us. Meanwhile, Deb and I volunteer to write letters to the local newspapers, explaining our concerns. We'll all attend the next town planning meeting to find out if permits have been filed. Jayne offers to send the request asking that we be placed on the meeting agenda. That way, we'll at least have the chance to tell the selectmen how we feel. Jim warns that the cell phone tower contractor will be there, too. Since the contractor doesn't live in our town, he's not allowed to speak unless acknowledged by the meeting moderator. He probably will be, though, so we construct what we hope are thoughtful counterarguments to his application.

This is local democracy in its best form. We smile at one another: We're proud of our solutions—even if they are just theoretical ones right now.

It's nearly ten o'clock. We're all a little worn out. We pack up our empty dishes and dirty utensils, along with notebooks and calendars. We'll meet again in two weeks—regardless of whether there are permits to consider. The camaraderie is reason enough.

I go in search of my dog and find her curled up with Reilly on the living room floor. Both are snoring softly, and the red ribbon is nowhere to be found. Ari hears me in the doorway and rises quietly, as if not wanting to disturb her new buddy. She gives a yawn and stretch, then pads over quietly on her big dog feet. We rejoin the parting guests, and the ten of us shuffle toward the door, collecting mittens and saying our good-byes. I tell my new friends that it was nice to meet them. We all agree it took too long. We won't make that mistake again.

"We're having a cookie swap next weekend," says Norma on our way to the cars. "You should come."

I tell her I'd love to. And I mean it. I really can't wait to see them again.

The next day, Ari and I participate in the Audubon Annual Bird Count. The count is part of a citizen science initiative, which allows average Joes like us to help scientists collect much-needed data on bird conservation. We've been assigned a ten-square-mile territory mostly surrounding our house; our task consists of cataloging every bird we observe over a twenty-four-hour period. This is my fourth bird count and Ari's first. Even though I have several years of experience on her, Ari is clearly the leader of our expedition. She has been counting birds for almost a full year now. There's nothing different about today as far as she is concerned, except that the human seems to be allowing for more stops than usual and is carrying paper and a pen. This pleases Ari, who sometimes feels hurried by my pacing of our strolls. Today, she makes sure to stop for any movement in the bare trees. When she does, I follow the hypotenuse made by her snout to get a bead on whatever creature has won her attention. Her timing is perfect, and never once do her caninaturalist senses fail to uncover a bird otherwise hidden in the canopy.

As our census list grows, I'm delighted to notice that, for the first time ever, I'm not only able to identify more than a dozen avian species, but I also know where to look for them. All I have to do is think like my dog. With that in mind, we pause in the hollows just before the town forest, where I intuit we will meet a band of chickadees. And we do. When we haven't been startled by a grouse, we walk over to the stand of pine where I remember seeing two of them nest. Ari and I both jump when they flush from their hideaway; as much, I think from the delight of knowing the location of their home as from surprise at the eruption of wings. We continue for hours like this, barely noticing the damp cold or the shifting light.

Back at home for a cup of tea and a chance to get warm, we discover that the elusive Leila Tov has surfaced for the day as well. She rests on the back of the couch, where she has a front-row seat to the grosbeaks congregating in our apple tree. I sit down beside her and, uncharacteristically, she agrees to remain. Ari, sufficiently wearied by the walk, feels no compulsion to chase the reclusive cat. Instead, she joins Leila Tov on the back of the couch. Together, they make two furry pods with very alert eyes. The three of us rest in quiet harmony for a good part of the afternoon, counting the birds that alight on our feeders and making room for Mouse when she, too, decides to join us. Greg calls during his lunch hour for a report on our tallies. I am as eager to tell him about our new feline participants as I am about the cardinal in our pine tree.

Wintertime dusk arrives early this far north. By three o'clock, the sky is preparing for its finale of color and fading light. Ari jumps from the couch and shakes her tags: *Whaddya say? Time for one more trip outside?*

"Absolutely," I tell her.

I don my winter coat, and we return for the last census of the day. This time, we stick to the civilized and visit the feeders of our new friends. Over at Elizabeth's, we find a group of goldfinches dining on thistle. Sparks and Mesquite watch us from the window and give Ari a hopeful paw or two at the glass. She responds with a bark of greetings: *Great to see you, too. Love to stay and chat, but we're watching birds right now.* They look like they understand.

Across the street, Cami asks if I have heard anything new about the tower application. I tell her I haven't, and we both agree that this is good news. She inquires about our bird tally and listens as I tick off the species we've found today.

"I usually have a titmouse down at my backyard feeder," she offers. "Why don't you go see?"

We do and are not disappointed. On our way back past the house, Cami waves us over. She hands me a loaf of bread, wrapped in aluminum foil and bright ribbon. "*Pulla,*" she explains. "It is the celebratory bread from my country. We make it with cardamom and sugar, then braid it for unity." I take the loaf and hold it tight against my coat. I have nothing with me to offer in return. I pat my jacket pocket just in case, hoping I might find a forgotten piece of sea glass or a pinecone. Maybe even the stub of a pencil—any token something to reciprocate. I find nothing and so must depend upon words.

"Thank you," I say. "It means so much. We will savor it."

We return home on a path Risto built through the woods separating our two houses. We pass the pond where Ari found the koi fish last summer. There is no sign of it now, but I'm pretty sure she gives the scene a thorough once-over as we pass by.

Back inside, we dole out her dinner, then leave the bread and a note for Greg. Once everyone is settled, I drive into town to attend the pizza dinner for the bird count participants. About twenty of us are present: a few elderly women who monitored their home feeders throughout the day; a rugged group of young farmers and loggers who took the day off to patrol the nearby lake; naturalists and ornithologists from the college, including our friend and the event organizer, Dave Potter. Talk around the table begins, not surprisingly, with birds. It was an uneventful day for most count participants. Because of the lack of snow cover, the birds have little cause to congregate around feeders or running water: There's just too much open space, too many exposed seeds and nuts to warrant that sort of thing. Still, everyone has something interesting on their list to brag about. Two college students report a black-backed woodpecker sighting on campus; other birders recorded kinglets and a sharp-shinned hawk. The eagle whom Ari and I met in September stood up to be counted, as did the three loons on the lake. I add our tally to the communal list. In total, our group saw more than two thousand birds representing forty-four different species. Not bad for a day's work. We are proud, and kick back over our homemade pizza.

As the evening winds down, the conversation shifts to dogs. Most of the people sitting at the table have at least one in their lives, and those who don't have fond memories of sharing a home with a canine at one time or another. Stories about these past and present animals soon replace tales of snow buntings and mergansers. We can't help ourselves: It's as if the absence of our canine companions makes it all the more essential that we speak of them. Or maybe it's because we can't possibly talk about nature without mentioning the dogs who join us out there. They are integral parts of our ecology—in all of their incorrigible lovableness. We swap stories about their penchant for nature. These are compelling, but not nearly as much as the tales of what happens inside our homes. Jennifer, who directs a local land trust, reports that her new hound dog can open refrigerators with his paw. She's taken to bringing a child-lock with her whenever they visit friends or family. Christie's two terrier mixes decided to replant their blueberry bushes earlier this week: Apparently, they thought the plants might overwinter better inside their kitchen. Brett reports that his dog brings him his slippers when he returns—but only if Shiloh has chewed off the sole earlier in the day.

I laugh—but not with pure empathy. *Ari could never do such a thing,* I try saying to myself, but that only makes me laugh harder. *Of course she could.* All is fair in love and war and dog ecology. Everything in a home—from who gets what portion of dessert to whether baths are required after dog swamp parties—is about compromise. It's about being wildly domestic, or domestically wild, or any other combination of the two. That means we humans have to give a little—maybe even more than we'd like. But in return, we get a relationship more complexly rewarding than any ancient Greek or Roman could have imagined. Like the others sitting here tonight, I love my dog. It's a love more profound that neotonized attraction or imprinted biology or transferred maternalism. And with that love comes the best caninaturalist lesson of all: the necessity of compromise.

I'm beginning to understand that the same is true for human ecology as well. This is what my neighbors have known all along. We are as much a part of the landscape as anything else. That means we, too, must make room for what we can and claim territorial rights against the rest. *Oikos* is not just about home and hearth. It is those things, of course, but it's also so much more. Sometimes, it just takes a canine's sense of *domus* for us to believe as much.

Final Exam

[february]

The end of our year as canine naturalists is near. Just this week, we celebrated Ari's first anniversary as part of our family. And how else but with a walk in the woods followed by a friendly cat chase inside? No black ties or balloons or cake, but I think the whole family had a good time nevertheless.

Anniversary celebrations aside, this is not the same clan Ari entered twelve months ago. Most noticeably, of course, is the loss of Cam and the arrival of Mouse and Leila Tov. But there are other differences as well. Ari now has an extended family of sorts in our neighbors and their dog pals. As a result, our once quiet days are now marked by social engagements both planned and spontaneous: Reilly stops by on her way to dance lessons; we arrange meeting times with Elizabeth,

Mesquite, and Sparks; we happen upon Risto and Miko when exploring the boundary line separating our property. On any given day, I can just about count on the fact that Ari's decision to turn us in one direction or another during our walk is really her attempt to make sure our stroll intersects that of one of our new friends. It usually does, since Ari has a keen ability to remember where they all live—and when they're likely to be outdoors.

Inside our house, life has changed as well. Despite four walls and a roof, this little cabin is now defined by the natural world. We no longer set alarm clocks, knowing perfectly well that the sun will rouse us. If for any reason it doesn't, a furry face eager to step outside most certainly will. Once we all rise, our day will be marked by quiet communion—and maybe a rowdy wrestling match or two.

We are a peculiar little family, the five of us, but I'd like to believe we're a tight-knit and respectful one at that. Ari has taught us so much since last February, but the biggest lesson of all has been to value the connections we form within our own ecology. I've been practicing this a lot lately—and mostly with her patient tutoring. Thanks to Ari, I can identify just about every tree on our property. I know which ones are likely to serve as homes for barred owls and which ones were planted by our neighbors. I also know which ones burn best on a cold day or make the best whittling project for a juvenile dog with some time on her hands. Ari has taught me all of this over the past twelve months. And then some.

Our yearlong experiment is finally coming to an end. But am I ready for my final exam? I can think of no better time to find out than this month, when Greg and I are about to pack our bags and head to the Midwest for a visit with my family.

It seems strange to test our new sense of local kinship by leaving home—and half of its inhabitants—behind. But that, we decide, is the best solution for everyone. I need to reconnect with my biological family, and there's just no way we can bring our adopted one with us. We arrange with Reilly's older sister, Kelsey, to look in on the cats and promise Reilly she can share in the responsibilities—as long as it's okay with her older sister. Ari, meanwhile, gets a reservation at Green Acres. As much as I hate to leave her, I know that she'll be safe—and much loved—there. Next to our house and the woods, school is her very favorite place to be. And her friends there don't seem to mind that her occasional wild-dog tendencies can make her feel like a lot of work sometimes.

The week before our trip is busy. The holiday recess is almost over, so Greg and I return to our lives at school and plans for the new semester. In between, we try to begin packing for the trip and making sure Ari has extra time to play outside. Two nights before our scheduled departure, Greg and I attend the much-anticipated town meeting regarding the tower application. We're apprehensive. But we're also prepared.

The night becomes a long one. Our neighborhood group convenes at the planning board meeting, armed with documents and personal testimonials. We're not alone. In fact, so many residents have turned out that the meeting must relocate from the tiny conference room at our town office to the old Grange Hall down the street. There we assemble below yellowed portraits of the town's agricultural patriarchs dating back to a time not long after the Civil War. Underneath their staid likenesses, we debate the future of communication in rural communities like ours. Can we hold out for satellite phone capability? Do we compromise human safety in order to preserve landscape? The arguments for both sides are restrained yet impassioned. This is a subject no one takes lightly.

The members of the planning board listen to both sides with heavy concentration. Their expressions say they feel real sympathy for each speaker—and his or her concerns. They are conflicted. The weight of decision has been placed on them, and the townspeople cannot arrive at consensus. Their solution? A one-year moratorium on all permits and construction. The town will build nothing until it understands the real economy of any decision.

In a sign of solidarity, my neighborhood group sits together on a bench near the back of the Grange Hall. The approval of the moratorium is a victory of sorts for us. There will be no tower constructed—at least, not for a while. As the meeting wraps up, we pat one another on the back, taking deep breaths and feeling relieved. We have the gift of time, if nothing else. We can revisit the issue next year, reinforced and prepared for anything.

It's late when Greg and I return home. We want to go to sleep, but we still need to begin packing for the flight two days from now. We walk inside the door, making strategies about laundry and suitcases, then brace for Ari's usual enthusiastic greeting. It is my favorite part of any day and nothing short of pure pageantry. As soon as she hears my car, Ari usually launches from the bed and races downstairs. She stands on her long back legs, looking more faun than dog. By stretching high and placing her front paws on the pane, she can see out the windows that grace the top half of our front door. The effect from outside is a bizarre soft-shoe routine: a crazed, blue-eyed face doing a mad foxtrot from one side of the window to the other and then back again.

Once I'm inside, our reunion ritual is scripted even further by this very clever animal. There is much kissing (on her part) and petting (on mine). Then she takes my hand in her mouth and escorts me from room to room so that we might tour the results of her day's projects: *Look here. I moved the couch pillows into the dining room. They're so much better here, don't you think? And see? My favorite bone. I put it on your side of the bed so you would be sure to notice. Here are the cats. They've been no help at all. Here is Greg. He seems to have returned, too. Now we're all together. Here. Isn't it just perfect?*

This greeting has become my favorite moment of any given day. It's nice to be this loved. So when only Mouse greets us at the door on this particular night, I'm torn between worry and suspicion. The latter soon wins out as I call Ari's name and look up the stairs. There, the caninaturalist lies draped across the top step, wearing her longest hangdog expression. We both know what this means: She's been bad. But how?

Together, we check out the spots where she's most likely to have an accident while Greg and I are away. Nothing. I search for additional clues in each room. As I do, Ari follows me from room to room, answering my inquiries with her own canine version of Twenty Questions. *Did you pee on the living room rug? No? But am I getting warmer? How about the basement floor? Colder?* The blue eyes give away nothing. We check my office and the bedroom, still no clues. But Ari is still doing her meek-dog thing, so I keep looking. Greg's office is next. It seems to be her favorite spot for eviscerating toy animals and shredding manila envelopes. Sure enough, the carpet is speckled with the remains of some kind of disemboweling. The scraps on the carpet are tawny brown—the same color as her favorite stuffed deer and bunny. No worries. Among other things, this dog has a preternatural ability to understand when we're about to leave. She likes to express that understanding with little acts of doggy protest. If shredding one of her stuffed animals is the best way for her to do so, then I can get behind that impulse. I stroke her back and tell her everything's fine, but her ears stay pressed down and her tail is still wedged between her hind legs.

"Everything's *fine,*" I assure her once again. She looks a little comforted and retreats to her bed.

Still later that night, I again climb the stairs, this time to start laundry for our holiday trip. I begin by making three piles: lights, darks, and the few pieces that Greg will need to take to the dry cleaner the next day. It occurs to me at some point in the process that the lid to my wicker hamper was already ajar when I arrived. This alone does not concern me, nor does it cause me to reconsider the scraps in Greg's office: I've already forgotten about them. I don't even really make sense of everything until I try to locate the cashmere sweater I distinctly remember placing in my hamper, if only because getting any laundry into this receptacle is a major accomplishment for me. I turn out its contents, but can find no sweater. I look under the bed, but to no avail. And then the pieces of the puzzle begin to arrange themselves: the guilty dog, the particular shade of brown lying on Greg's office floor, the missing sweater in the same shade.

I look over at my dog, who now pretends to be snoring in her dog nest. Said nest is lined with a suspiciously familiar shade of brown wool. As if following my game of sleuth in her own head, Ari rises and quickly slinks out of the room. In her absence, I reach down and collect her nest lining, noticing with dread that it seems to be missing half of one of its sleeves. I want to weep. My most extravagant piece of clothing, it was a gift from my mother for Christmas last year. This sweater alone is the reason Greg needed to stop by the dry cleaner's: There is an unspoken expectation that holiday gifts are worn on subsequent visits with my family.

If I were a dog, my tail would be between my legs right now. Since I don't have one, I compensate with the rock in the pit of my stomach. It's the same dull feeling of regret I experienced growing up when I accidentally flushed a pair of socks down the toilet (don't ask) or ruined the kitchen table with nail polish remover that under no circumstances was I allowed to use anywhere but the bathroom: *Oh, no.*

I spend the rest of the night scouring the Internet for a site that carries this particular sweater. When I find it, I'm aghast—both at my mother's generosity in purchasing the gift, and the cost of my dog's chew toy. I order an exact replica, double-checking size and shade, and click on the fifty-dollar express-mail icon that will ensure the new sweater makes the trip with us. Greg looks over my shoulder, fretting audibly about the cost. "Do you know what we could do with that much money?" he asks. Of course I do. But this is a small price to pay for family harmony. And I'm sick over the idea that my mother's thoughtfulness will simply be swallowed up by our vacuum cleaner.

Ari checks in a few hours later, standing in the doorway of my office with a tentative expression on her face. I assure her I'm not mad. To prove it, I leave my desk and sit cross-legged on the floor, half averting my eyes to say, in dog language, that I am not confrontational. She comes inside and drapes herself across my lap, burying her muzzle in my hand as if to say: *I don't know what came over me. I just had to do it.* I tell her I understand. She didn't know the sweater was expensive, or that in some strange way it symbolized the success of familial relations to me. It was just a gloriously soft piece of fabric that probably came with an alluring aroma of half-me, half-goat. Besides, I'm the one who left it somewhere that she could grab it. It's my job to know better, not hers.

I stroke the fur on the side of her face and tell her I understand. This is just one of those interspecies compromises we will always have to make. I remind her that she is softer than any wool, no matter the price. Now is no time for me to hold a grudge.

The next day, the new sweater arrives and is promptly packed. We review last-minute cat instructions with Kelsey and then deliver Ari to Green Acres. As always, the pup springs from the car and urges us inside. There, she is greeted by name. She has a lot of friends here—both human and canine. I hand over her fleece bed, her favorite stuffed rabbit (which, unlike the first sweater, is perfectly intact), a chew-toy filled with biscuits and peanut butter. Each is carefully cataloged by Rachel, the kennel's manager. I tell her I hate the idea of leaving Ari, and my voice cracks as I do.

"She's going to be fine," says Rachel. "She'll have lots of playtime outside, and everyone loves her."

I know. But it's still so hard to leave her.

Rachel comes from behind the counter to collect dog and creature comforts. As she does, the caninaturalist gives me the briefest of looks: *Okay! See you later. Gotta go. Bye!* She bounds eagerly alongside Rachel as they head back to the kennel area. At least she's happy to be here.

Back home, Greg and I lug the suitcase into the car and double-check the house one last time. We drive to the airport and check in and do all of the things expected of travelers—and then some. We peer into pet carriers, and chat up the security agent with his drug-detecting dog, then make a game of counting sparrows on the tarmac. Canine naturalism never grows old, and once you get started, it's impossible to stop looking at the world that way.

Even when that world is inside your home.

During the flight I have plenty of time to reflect further on the nature of relationships and kin. Last month was an important one in our project, and I'm bringing it with me now. It's been over a year since I've been home, and six months since my mom visited. I want this trip to go well. I know that that is ultimately up to me.

I suspect that I was a difficult child to raise: brash and vocal; quick to react and reluctant to forgive. The height of my adolescent temperamentalness corresponded with our family's move from a progressive town in Iowa to a far more conservative one in rural Illinois. It took me a very long time to become adjusted. Along the way, I withdrew and became obstructionist. I was morose. One year, I chose to sleep through Christmas. In hindsight, I think this was my way of saying *I don't know how to be here*. I think I was depressed. I don't know exactly how that felt to my family, but I suspect they were concerned and probably a little helpless. As for me, once I was old enough to drive, I found excuses to visit Chicago and St. Louis, thinking city life was the panacea. I spent all the money from my part-time job on theater and museum tickets, along with the gasoline to get me there. As best I can remember, I didn't bother to check in and find out how my parents were feeling about this manifestation of me. When they objected, I grew scornful and peevish.

A dog—caninaturalist or otherwise—would never behave that way. Although they don't necessarily maintain familial bonds after weaning, they do create relationships. And what we know about these relationships suggests that dogs exhibit a fidelity to kin and a willingness to embrace the brilliance of any given moment—which, of course, is why we so love having them in our lives. This is not to say, of course, that dogs are always selfless or even blindly devoted to humans around them: Run enough of an emotional or behavioral debt, and any animal will grow leery of being around you. The thing about dogs, though, is that they seem to be particularly generous in their sense of emotional currency. If I'm running late and forget to call Greg, he might be miffed when I return. Ari will just be ecstatic to see me. The accumulated strength of our relationship can shoulder the weight of a small misstep or oversight. That same impetus has allowed Ari to befriend countless other animals over the past year. And she's a terrific friend—the kind anyone would want to have or be.

Ever since she was a puppy, Ari has been quick to forgive and loath to assign blame. Over the past year, she's had plenty of cause to hold grudges: I've accidentally stepped on her tail; I've dragged her away from forest booty; I've brought the stress and distraction of work or human life home and expected her to make it part of her own existence, too. In every instance, though, she's shrugged it off as an understandable part of living together. The same is true with her interactions in nature. Outside, she never once blames a blue jay for trying to steal a tuft of her fur or a groundhog from hissing at her to *back off!* As for our new habit of walking the same trail in the orchard, that's just fine with her too. And why not? As far as she has always been concerned, it's just great to be outside.

"To walk with a dog," writes Jeffrey Moussaieff Masson, "is to enter the world of the immediate." This assertion, I think, is about recognizing the gladness of now—the novelty of the present. I see this in Ari every time we leave the house: *Hey, look at us! We're walking. Isn't that fabulous?* It's there when we return: *Look! Back at the house with a woodstove and dinner. Fantastic!* The aggregate of these impulses was the first thing that attracted me to Ari, and it is undoubtedly what got us through those early—and somewhat—trying weeks. In the past year, it is what I have grown to respect and admire most about her. Our lived ecology is no longer new to her, but the intensity of her appreciation has yet to wane.

During our experiment, I have learned, at least in part, to make these feelings my own: to jettison a day's plans in order to admire a baby woodpecker, to get down on my hands and knees so that I might smell a feral lily of the valley, to stick my hands in the guts of a deer and learn their contours. None of this is necessarily natural for me, nor is it anything I am predisposed to do. I have had to learn and sometimes struggle to see the wisdom in Ari's approach to the natural world. Can I now bring those impulses home? And not just home to the cabin where we all live, but to my ancestral home—the place where I grew up, the house where my parents and memories of my former self still reside?

If I can, I certainly won't be the first. After spending a year at California Moorpark Community College's Exotic Animal Training and Management Program, the wonderful writer Amy Sutherland found all sorts of applications for positive reinforcement in her own life—and, most notably, in her relationship with her husband. Her essay on this experiment became one of the most popular pieces appearing in the *New York Times* that year, and shortly thereafter became an entire book. The legendary animal trainer Karen Pryor has made this approach famous. She authored the seminal text on positive reinforcement: although titled *Don't Shoot the Dog,* it has been used everywhere from corporate boardrooms to marriage counseling. What both writers understand is this: Just like any mammal, humans respond to all kind of environmental reinforcement. The trick is figuring out the right cue for any given situation, whether it's persuading a dog not to eat a neighbor's chicken or a spouse to stop leaving coffee cups all over the house or yourself to be more positive in your own relationships. Once you do, everybody gets to reap the benefits of praise and productive behavior.

I think they're on to something. What's more, I'm pretty sure Ari is, too. But can I remember how to do it without her? I hope so.

My parents are waiting to greet us at the airport. Mom stands close to the glass, just on the other side of security. She begins waving as soon as we make our way past the gate doors inside the terminal. There are tears in her eyes—and in mine, too. It's good to be back. Dad gives us both a hug and helps us with our bags. Once in the car, my mom fills us in on the trivia of friends and neighbors. I listen with newfound interest, finally understanding that such stories create the kind of local connection I usually forget to value.

We arrive at their house and get settled. It feels strange not wondering what mischief a juvenile dog is causing, or leaping up every few hours to make sure she remembers to pee *outside.* Still, even in her absence the pup is very, very present. During the week, I make a game of asking *What would Ari do?* I stop short of stealing trash or sniffing derrieres, but the rest I try hard to internalize. *Great to see you,* I tell my dad when he returns from work. *Go for a run? I'd love to!* I say to my brother. *Dinner out? Sounds perfect!* I tell my mom. *Oh, no, you choose: I'm just glad to be here. Hey, did you see that crow out there? Isn't it fabulous?*

I mean every last word. I always have—I've just never thought to say as much before. And it works. I am in the moment and full of caninaturalist gladness. It is completely infectious. Without me questioning her restaurant choice, there's no reason for my mom to feel defensive. Since my nose isn't buried in a book, there's opportunity for my sister-in-law to start a conversation. We talk about her family's farm and her father's recent decision to switch over to organic soybeans. My brother tells me about a pheasant-hunting expedition there and seems surprised when I ask if we can try one of the birds now resting in their freezer. Greg looks relieved not to be playing referee. We both are, really. I am listening and watching, not planning and evaluating. And it's working.

On the last day of the trip, the six of us go to brunch on our way to the airport. I am wearing the new sweater, and my mom notices instantly. She compliments both of us. "That was a good choice," she says. "It looks perfect with your skin and hair."

"Yes," I say. "I love it. It's one of my most valued things." I save her from the full reason why. It's enough to know that she was thoughtful and generous in giving it.

We drink mimosas and toast our family: to her upcoming retirement, to my brother and his wife's move southward, to the importance of reconnecting. We are fully in this moment in a way that would make Ari proud.

Do I sound trite and convenient if I tell you it is the best trip home in memory? Probably. But believe me when I tell you it is true—and when I insist that I owe it to an irrepressible dog a thousand miles away. This past year has taught me lessons both large and small. Most significant, I think, are the ways in which this developing puppy showed me what it is to be human—and what it is to be humane. We are a wonderful, powerful, intelligent species. We can splice haddock genes into a strawberry or tell you how warm it was a million years ago by looking at a fossilized tree. We can find oil under thousands of feet of rock and stars well beyond our solar system. Not only that, but in the English language alone we have half a million words to explain these findings. But ours is not the only way of sensing or being. It's certainly not a superior way—at least, not always. Or even often.

I know this because a canine naturalist told me. Honest.

Back home in Maine, Greg and I are greeted by the two sister cats. While he begins to unpack, I race to Green Acres to collect my brilliant dog. The first snowfall of the season is on its way later tonight, and I want to make sure Ari and I get to experience it together from start to finish. And though she may never understand why, I want to thank her for the gifts she has unknowingly given. I owe her so much.

At the kennel, I pay for her boarding time and wait impatiently for her to appear. When she does, it is with her usual fanfare. Towing Rachel behind, Ari bounds from the kennels and into the storefront where I am waiting. I open my arms wide and she returns the hug, putting her paws on my shoulder and licking my nose. Dog spit doesn't bother me—at least not anymore. I give her my hand, which she takes gently in her mouth and walks me around the store. Apparently, while I was gone she figured out how to unlock her kennel door—as well as the door of the boarder next to her.

"She's a wild one," Rachel says, laughing.

"Every single day," I say in return.

"And a pretty smart one," she adds. Rachel says she found the two escapees both out here, doing a little personal shopping. We both agree Ari wants to show me what she picked out for herself. But Ari doesn't seem all that interested in purchasing anything today. Instead, she completes our loop and pushes at the shop's glass door with her nose, giving an assertive *woo-woo* noise as she does. *Time to get home,* she seems to say. I agree.

Back at the cabin, the snow begins to fall in the early afternoon, wafting down out of low, pewter clouds. Ari and I decide to take a quick run to celebrate. By the time we complete our trek, the snow has stepped up its efforts, filling the sky with enormous flakes that cling to tree branches and trail edges and the tail of my yearling pup. With these flakes comes the fragrant stillness of a winter day. Just the inch or so is enough to mute the ambient noise of a leafless forest, pushing everything closer to the earth. This type of snow—wet, gradual, persistent—quickly democratizes the landscape, turning it a single hue. And then there is that telltale scent.

I've tried unsuccessfully for years to match mere words to this phenomenon, sometimes going so far as to ask that my students write essays describing the smell of snow. I've said it has the aroma of warm pewter; it's what the color cornflower blue would smell like, if colors could smell. It's the disembodiment of earth; the metallic sheen of water pulled from the deepest and darkest of wells. Or maybe it would be more accurate to say it smells like the color of the highest, bluest sky—that place where our world meets the infinite. These descriptions are equally awful, I know. And yet I can't for the life of me figure out how to improve on them.

The caninaturalist knows better than to try. Instead, she contents herself by first thrusting her snout deep into the accumulating ground cover, then lifting her nose toward the sky, sucking in this phenomenon we can only experience and not describe. It's been nearly a year since she experienced snow, and she's undergone profound developmental changes since then. None of that matters, though. She hasn't forgotten how to enjoy it. Seeing her do so once again reminds me how to do that, too.

Ari and I will never have completely identical values when it comes to experiencing the natural world. There will no doubt be many days ahead when we once again live out our own episode of *The Odd Couple* as we disagree over the merits of bringing home a squashed snake or whether we should be eating cat vomit. But I also know there will always be days like today, when the stars align and our preferences become symphonic: when we stand on top of a mountain we've just climbed or find a bramble of ripe raspberries warmed by the afternoon sun and just waiting to be eaten.

Or when we walk in the woods amid new snow, breathing deeply. This is where our experiment began. And this, I think, is where we will always return.

By the next morning, our house is adrift in a sea of whiteness. Greg, Ari, and I leap into the car—no fear of car sickness for this confident dog—and return to the town forest. We park under the same pine tree that sheltered us on our first walk in the woods and attach Ari to the same retractable leash we used that day a year ago. Then we walk. Together.

Thanks to the thick snow, the light is particularly brilliant today. The glow banishes shadow and blind spot and exposes every nuance of a snow-covered landscape along with boughs made heavy with the accumulated weight of white. We are not the first to step outside on this snowy morning. Greg and I count innumerable deer hoofprints. The snaky tail trail of a vole. Snowshoe hare and even a bobcat track or two. With fresh snow on the ground, we see for the first time that this path is a superhighway for woodland animals—more so than we ever realized. And there's so much to see. We stop alongside Ari at each set of tracks, witnessing for the first time what she has always sensed. *Now do you get it?* she asks, smiling wide. *Do you see what's really out here?*

At long last, I think we do.

Bibliography

March

Coren, Stanley. *How Dogs Think*. New York: Free Press, 2005.

Hyungwon Kang. "Not Your Average Lap Dog." *L.A. Times,* January 2, 1994.

Lorenz, Konrad. "Autobiography." Stockholm, Sweden: The Nobel Foundation, 1973.

______. *Foundations of Ethology*. New York: Springer, 1982.

Louv, Richard. *Last Child in the Woods*. Chapel Hill, NC: Algonquin Books, 2006.

Masson, Jeffrey Moussaieff. *Dogs Never Lie About Love*. New York: Crown Publishers, 1997.

McConnell, Patricia. *The Other Side of the Leash*. New York: Ballantine Books, 2003.

Vaughan, T. A. *Mammalogy*. Third edition. New York: Harcourt Brace Jovanovich, 1986.

April

Coppinger, Ramond, and Lorna Coppinger. *Dogs: A New Understanding of Canine Origin, Behavior, and Evolution*. Chicago: University of Chicago Press, 2001.

Darwin, Charles. "The Origin of the Species by Means of Natural Selection." In *The Portable Darwin*, edited by Duncan M. Porter and Peter W. Graham. New York: Penguin, 1993, 126.

Kerasote, Ted. *Merle's Door: Lessons from a Freethinking Dog*. New York: Harcourt, 2007.

Livingston, John A. *Rogue Primate: An Exploration of Human Domestication*. Toronto: Key Porter Books, 1994.

Pryor, Karen. *Don't Shoot the Dog*. New York: Bantam, 1999.

Wayne, Robert K. "Molecular Evolution of the Dog Family." *Theoretical and Applied Genetics* 9:6 (June 1993).

May

Coppinger, Ramond, and Lorna Coppinger. *Dogs: A New Understanding of Canine Origin, Behavior, and Evolution.* Chicago: University of Chicago Press, 2001.

Coren, Stanley. *The Intelligence of Dogs.* New York: Bantam Books, 1994, 48.

Grandin, Temple. *Animals in Translation.* New York: Harvest, 2005.

Hawthorne, Nathaniel. "The Canal Boat." *New England Magazine* (December 1835).

Laskin, David. *Braving the Elements: The Stormy History of American Weather.* New York: Doubleday, 1996.

Masson, Jeffrey Moussaieff. *Dogs Never Lie About Love.* New York: Crown Publishers, 1997.

Montgomery, David R. *Dirt: The Erosion of Civilization.* Berkeley, CA: University of California Press, 2007.

Thurston, Mary E. *The Lost History of the Canine Race: Our 15,000 Year Love Affair with Dogs.* Kansas City, MO: Andrews and McMeel, 1996.

Tillyard, E. M. *The Elizabethan World Picture.* New York: Vintage, 1959.

June

Beck, Alan. *The Ecology of Stray Dogs: A Study of Free-Ranging Urban Animals.* Baltimore: York Press, 1973.

Coren, Stanley. *How Dogs Think.* New York: Free Press, 2004, 129.

Gompper, Matthew E. *The Ecology of Northeast Coyotes: Current Knowledge and Priorities for Future Research.* WCS Working Paper No. 17, July 2002.

Himmelman, John. *Discovering Amphibians: Frogs and Salamanders of the Northeast.* Camden, ME: Down East Books, 2006.

Kilham, Lawrence. *Woodpeckers of Eastern North America.* New York: Dover, 1983.

McConnell, Patricia. *The Other Side of the Leash.* New York: Ballantine, 2002, 108.

Short, Lester L. *The Lives of Birds.* New York: Henry Holt, 1993.

Skutch, Alexander. *Life of the Woodpecker.* Santa Monica, CA: Ibis, 1985.

______. *The Minds of Birds.* College Station, TX: Texas A&M University Press, 1996.

July

Andelt, William F., and Brian R. Mahan. "Behavior of an Urban Coyote." *American Midland Naturalist* 103:2 (1980): 399-400.

Beck, Alan. *The Ecology of Stray Dogs: A Study of Free-Ranging Urban Animals.* Baltimore: York Press, 1973.

Butler, J. R. A., et al. "Free-Ranging Domestic Dogs (*Canis familiaris*) as Predators and Prey in Rural Zimbabwe: Threats of Competition and Disease to Large Wild Carnivores." *Biological Conservation* 115:3 (2004): 369-379.

Densmore, Patricia, and Kristine French. "Effects of Recreation Areas on Avian Communities in Coastal New South Wales' Parks." *Ecological Management and Restoration* 6:3 (2005): 182–189.

George, Shalene L., and Kevin R. Crooks. "Recreation and Large Mammal Activity in an Urban Nature Reserve." *Biological Conservation* 133 (2006): 107–117.

Hammitt, William E. "Policy Decision Factors Concerning Recreational Resource Impacts." *Policy Studies Review* 7:2 (Winter 1987): 359–369.

Miller, Scott G. et al. "Wildlife Responses to Pedestrians and Dogs." *Wildlife Society Bulletin* 29:1 (2001): 124–132.

Roberts, Rachel. "A Walk in the Park." *Parks and Recreation* (January 2007): 50–53.

August

Hauser, Marc D. *Wild Minds: What Animals Really Think*. New York: Henry Holt, 2000, 224–227.

Kerasote, Ted. "A Killing at Dawn." *Best American Science and Nature Writing 2001*. New York: Houghton Mifflin, 2001.

Masson, Jeffrey Moussaieff, with Susan McCarthy. *When Elephants Weep: The Emotional Lives of Animals*. New York: Bantam (Delta Trade Paperbacks), 1996.

McConnell, Patricia. *The Other End of the Leash*. New York: Ballantine, 2003.

Roach, Mary. *Stiff: The Curious Life of Human Cadavers*. New York: W. W. Norton, 2004.

September

Dillard, Annie. *Teaching a Stone to Talk: Expeditions and Encounters*. New York: Harper and Row, 1982.

Hollander, Lewis E., Jr. "Unexplained Weight Gain Transients at the Moment of Death." *Journal of Scientific Exploration* 15:4 (2001): 495–500.

Masson, Jeffrey Moussaieff, with Susan McCarthy. *When Elephants Weep: The Emotional Lives of Animals*. New York: Bantam (Delta Trade Paperbacks), 1996.

Nakaya, Shannon Fujimoto. *Kindred Spirit, Kindred Care*. Novato, CA: New World Library, 2005.

Payne, Katy. *Silent Thunder: In the Presence of Elephants*. New York: Simon and Schuster, 1998.

Roach, Mary. *Spook: Science Tackles the Afterlife*. New York: W. W. Norton, 2006.

October

Beck, Alan. *The Ecology of Stray Dogs: A Study of Free-Ranging Urban Animals*. Baltimore: York Press, 1973.

Berkeley, Ellen Perry. *Maverick Cats*. Shelburne, VT: New England Press, 1987.

Malso, Lucien. *Les Enfants Sauvages*, translated as *Wolf Children*. London: NLB, 1972.

McKibben, Bill. *Deep Economy: The Wealth of Our Communities*. New York: Times Books (Henry Holt), 2007.

Middleton, Rusty. "Texotics." *Texas Parks and Wildlife* (April 2007).

Newton, Michael. *Savage Girls and Wild Boys: A History of Feral Children*. New York: Picador, 2004.

Steeves, H. Peter. *The Things Themselves: Phenomenology and the Return to the Everyday*. Albany, NY: SUNY Press, 2006.

Turner, Dennis C., and Patrick Bateson. *The Domestic Cat: The Biology of Its Behaviour*. New York: Cambridge University Press, 1988.

November

Coren, Stanley. *How Dogs Think*. New York: Free Press, 2004.

Fogle, Bruce. *The Dog's Mind*. New York: Howell Book House, 1990.

Giffin, James, and Lisa Carlson. *Dog Owner's Home Veterinary Handbook*. Hoboken, NJ: Howell Book House (a division of Wiley), 1999.

Lopez, Barry. *Wolves and Men*. New York: Charles Scribner's Sons, 1978.

Quammen, David. *Monsters of God: The Man-Eating Predator in the Jungles of History and the Mind*. New York: W. W. Norton, 2003.

Pollan, Michael. *The Omnivore's Dilemma*. New York: Penguin, 2007.

Salvador, R. J. "What Do Mexicans Celebrate on the Day of the Dead?" In *Death and Bereavement in the Americas*. Death, Vale and Meaning, volume 2, edited by J. D. Morgan and P. Laungani. Amityville, NY: Baywood Publishing, 2003, 75–76.

Zimmerman, Francis. "The History of Melancholy." *Journal of the International Institute* 2:2 (1995).

December

Beck, Alan. *The Ecology of Stray Dogs: A Study of Free-Ranging Urban Animals*. Baltimore: York Press, 1973.

Lord, Linda K., et al. "Search and Identification Methods That Owners Use to Find a Lost Dog." *Journal of the American Veterinary Medicine Association*. 230:2 (January 2007): 211–216.

Nelson, Richard. *Heart and Blood: Living with Deer in America*. New York: Knopf, 1997.

Orlean, Susan. "Lost Dog." *New Yorker* 81:1 (February 14, 2005).
Phipps, Frances. "Social Status in the Colonies." *New York Times,* (December 6, 1981).
Rue, Leonard Lee. *The Deer of North America.* New York: Lyons & Burford, 1997.

JANUARY

Bousé, Derek. *Wildlife Films.* Philadelphia: University of Pennsylvania Press, 2000.
McKibbon, Bill. *The End of Nature.* New York: Random House, 2006.
Nelson, Barney. *The Wild and the Domestic: Animal Representation, Ecocriticism, and Western American Literature.* Reno: University of Nevada Press, 2000.
Revkin, Andrew. "A Team of Two." *New York Times,* June 5, 2007.
"Sniffing Out Polar Bears." *Natural History* 116:5 (June 2007).

FEBRUARY

Darwin, Charles. *The Expression of the Emotions in Man and Animals.* London: John Murray, 1872.
Masson, Jeffrey Moussaieff. *Dogs Never Lie About Love.* New York: Crown Publishers, 1997.
Pryor, Karen. *Don't Shoot the Dog.* New York: Bantam, 1999.
Sutherland, Amy. *What Shamu Taught Me About Life, Love, and Marriage: Lessons for People from Animals and Their Trainers.* New York: Random House, 2008.